Modern Political Thinkers and Ideas

Modern Political Thinkers and Ideas: an historical introduction is a stimulating new text that provides students with an accessible introduction to the key areas of modern political thought. Distinctively combining historical and philosophical approaches to the subject, it examines the ideas and writings of some of the most influential thinkers of the modern era, placing them in their historical contexts.

Modern Political Thinkers and Ideas features:

- Key concepts of modern political theory such as: State Sovereignty; Political Obligation and Civil Disobedience; Liberty; Rights; Equality and Social Justice.
- The ideas of key political thinkers such as: Machiavelli; Hobbes; Locke; Rousseau; Burke; Paine; Wollstonecraft; J.S. Mill; T.H. Green; and Marx.
- A clear and coherent framework for each chapter which provides students with an understanding of: (a) the historical development and significance of each concept in modern political thought; (b) how major political thinkers interpreted each concept; and (c) the nature of current debate surrounding each key concept, as explored by contemporary political thinkers.
- Boxed biographies, charting the lives, ideas and theories of the major political thinkers.

Dr Tudor Jones is a Senior Lecturer in Politics at Coventry University.

Modern Political Thinkers and Ideas

■ An historical introduction

Tudor Jones

London and New York

First published 2002 by Routledge
11 New Fetter Lane, London EC4P 4EE

Simultaneously published in the USA and
Canada
by Routledge
29 West 35th Street, New York, NY 10001

*Routledge is an imprint of the Taylor & Francis
Group*

© 2002 Tudor Jones

Typeset in Century Old Style by Wearset Ltd,
Boldon, Tyne and Wear
Printed and bound in Great Britain by
T.J. International Ltd, Padstow, Cornwall

British Library Cataloguing in Publication Data
A catalogue record for this book is available
from the British Library

*Library of Congress Cataloging in Publication
Data*
Jones, Tudor
    Modern political thinkers and ideas : an
    historical introduction / Tudor Jones.
    p. cm.
    Includes bibliographical references and
    index.
    1. Political science–History.
    I. Title.
    JA83 .J65 2001
    320'.092'2–dc21   2001031766

ISBN 0–415–17476–7 (hbk)
ISBN 0–415–17477–5 (pbk)

To the memory of my father

Contents

CONTENTS

Boxed biographies

Acknowledgements

I would like to acknowledge my gratitude to Mark Kavanagh, former commissioning editor at Routledge, for his invaluable advice and patient understanding during the preparation and completion of this book. I would also like to thank his predecessor at Routledge, Patrick Proctor, for originally encouraging me to embark on this project and for preparing the ground.

My thanks are extended, too, to my friend, Emma Hunter, who word-processed the manuscript of the book with great efficiency and patience, and with whom I spent several enjoyable lunches at 'Ma Belle' in Oxford, discussing not only the text but also life in general.

Over the many years I have taught the history of political thought, a number of my university students have kindly suggested that I should one day write a book of this kind. I am grateful for their encouragement and for their many contributions to discussions and debates. More specifically, throughout the period of the book's preparation and eventual completion, my friend and colleague at Coventry University, Alex Kazamias, was a constant source of informed, good-natured and humorous encouragement. So, too, were my dear friend, Frances Burrage, and my beloved late father, Brynmor, who died in February 2000. To his cherished memory I dedicate this book.

Introduction

This book is intended as an introduction to the history of modern political thought (covering, that is, the period from approximately 1500 onwards) organized around five key political concepts. It explores the ways in which those concepts – abstract and general ideas about politics – have been interpreted by highly influential Western political thinkers during that period. It also considers the ways in which political questions, problems and issues have been raised and examined by those thinkers in the five selected areas of conceptual thinking.

Throughout this undertaking I have tried to identify certain theoretical concerns of enduring importance. This task presupposes the existence of major patterns of intellectual development that have stretched since 1500 across the history of modern political thought. Such patterns have, to a large extent, formed around fundamental political concepts which, although interpreted in very different ways in particular historical periods, have provided much of the theoretical basis of modern political thinking. In this book five of those concepts – namely, sovereignty, political obligation, liberty, rights and equality – will constitute the framework within which will be developed descriptive and interpretive accounts of particular theories and arguments advanced by major political thinkers. In this manner I hope to indicate both the changes and the continuities in the ways in which the key concepts that I have highlighted have been formulated and interpreted by political thinkers in the course of their refining their own distinctive insights and visions.

Some comments on methodology

Throughout the book I shall broadly pursue a 'contextualist' approach to the history of political thought, which holds that the great works of political philosophy or theory should be viewed within the contexts of their particular societies and cultures, with their particular political problems, issues and language. Such an approach has been one of those advanced in the methodological debate concerning the history of political thought ongoing in academia since the late 1960s.

The alternative approach, which has been more widely followed since 1945, has been a 'textualist' one, which holds that the classic texts of political thought can be studied without paying close attention to their particular historical contexts. Such an approach, perhaps best exemplified by the writings of John Plamenatz and Andrew Hacker,[1] in turn reflects the fact that political theory has, since 1945, been conceived as a subcategory of philosophy. Its central concerns have thus been regarded as, first, the clarification of concepts used in political discourse and debate and, second, the critical examination and evaluation of political beliefs and principles.[2]

Political theory, therefore, has been widely viewed as a body of philosophical knowledge involving the critical and analytical study of ideas, values and doctrines employed in political thought. Norman Barry has thus offered a definition of political theory as 'a broadly philosophical subject ... analytical in style and concerned with methodology, the clarification of concepts and ... the logic of political appraisal.'[3]

Indeed, it is certainly the case that the methodological practices of philosophy have pervaded much of the interpretive literature on political theory. Many contemporary political theorists have tended, therefore, to be concerned with analysing the concepts, and the logical relationships between them, that are developed in the classic texts of political philosophy. In addition, those theorists have sought to evaluate the arguments deployed in the texts, or even to derive from them certain universally valid or timeless principles.

Moreover, even when these 'textualist' students of political thought have conceded that an understanding of the historical context surrounding one of the classic texts might contribute something to a knowledge of such a work, this has been only a qualified concession. Plamenatz, for example, thus wrote:

> we can learn more about their [political thinkers'] arguments by weighing them over and over again than by extending our knowledge of the circumstances in which they wrote.[4]

In short, according to the textualist view, historical investigation of a past work of political theory, while in some cases yielding some interesting insights, does not play a central role in the interpretation of the major works of Western political thought. For it is above all philosophical analysis that most effectively performs that intellectual task.

In opposition to this point of view, a number of eminent historians of political thought – notably Quentin Skinner, John Pocock, John Dunn and others – have argued that the classic texts, and the political ideas embodied in them, must be examined and appreciated within the historical contexts in which they were produced.[5] This 'contextualist' argument has been advanced since the late 1960s on two main levels. First, the meaning and significance of the text itself should be understood, it is argued, within the context of the political, religious, economic and social factors prevailing in the period during which that text was composed.

Understanding that surrounding context will help, therefore, to elucidate the meaning of the text.

This emphasis on the primary importance of historical context has some important implications for the way in which, as modern students and readers, we approach the classic texts of political theory. In the first place, Skinner and others have argued that we should treat with scepticism the textualists' claim that there are certain universal and timeless questions and problems raised in the great political works of the past. Even less credible, Skinner and others maintain, is the related claim that those writings can somehow supply answers to the fundamental political questions raised in contemporary society. For the great works of political theory, and their underlying moral and political assumptions and beliefs, are historically-specific creations. The questions they raise, and the answers they furnish, should therefore be viewed as relative to the particular societies and cultures from which they emerged.

Another important implication of this contextualist approach is that it underlines the interrelation between political theory and practice, and between political ideas and behaviour, that is inherent in the formulation of theoretical statements about politics. For whether these are produced at the most abstract level of philosophical reflection (usually by professional political philosophers), or at the less intellectually sophisticated and more practical level of, for instance, party policy documents or manifestos, such theoretical statements have at least one thing in common. They are composed in response to particular events, crises, controversies or debates. In short, contextualists argue, as R.N. Berki has observed, 'that political thought issues out of practical experience and not the other way round'.[6] For example, the early French socialist thinkers' vision of a future society based on cooperation and fellowship was conceived in critical reaction to the conditions of industrial capitalism in the first half of the nineteenth century. Their vision did not emerge in an historical vacuum.

In addition to this focus on the need to locate a past work of political theory within its historical context – political, intellectual and socio-economic – a second area of contextual significance has been stressed. For Skinner and other historians of political thought have also pointed out that the political writings of the past were intended communications by particular authors addressed to particular audiences. They have, therefore, stressed the need to appreciate or 'recover' the author's intention and, for that purpose, to comprehend the particular conventions of language and political vocabulary that prevailed at the time of the composition of the text. Only in such a way, it has been argued, can the meaning of a text be grasped. Simply reading it time and time again would not be a sufficiently rewarding exercise.

According, then, to the contextualist approach, the classic texts of political philosophy and theory should be viewed not only within their particular historical settings, but also in terms of particular political discourses – discreet, shared languages – peculiar to those specific periods. In view of both those considerations, it would therefore be unsatisfactory, in Berki's words, 'to approach texts in the "biblical" fashion, as though their meaning could be ascertained simply by reading them, and "reflecting" on their "universal" message'.[7]

The alternative, more realistic concern with the historically-specific nature both of the classic texts of political theory and of the language they contain confers a number of additional benefits besides a deeper historical understanding of their content and purpose. Such an approach has, for instance, broadened the scope and subject matter of political thought. It has emphasized the historical significance of many theoretical statements about politics that do not attain the sophisticated level of the philosophical treatise. Also considered worthy of serious attention, therefore, have been such expressions of political thought as pamphlets, newspaper and journal articles, speeches, sermons, policy statements and manifestos. In addition, the contextualist approach to the history of political thought invites treatment of the work of a wider range of political thinkers than has conventionally been covered in more traditional, textualist studies of the canon of classic works.

For all these reasons, therefore, an historically-grounded approach to political theory seems to me to be the most appropriate and valuable one. However, there are at least three qualifications that I would add to this general endorsement of the contextualist method. First, while recognizing the importance of securely locating an author and his text within their historical context, we must beware of the danger of submerging them beneath it. For, as Iain Hampsher-Monk has observed, that would stifle their capacity 'to formulate statements with any referent beyond the historically parochial', thereby denying them any political significance for the present age. Moreover, an 'exclusive preoccupation' with the conceptual language employed in a classic text might well neutralize any understanding of its historical meaning by distracting attention from the fact that such language is actually being used to make a political statement. As a consequence, there is a strong possibility that 'writer and text can actually fragment and disappear into context'.[8]

Second, it should be stressed that an historical understanding of the context in which a work of political theory was composed is necessary not only for a better appreciation of its meaning, but also for a critical examination of the philosophical arguments that it contains. A contextualist approach to that text might therefore usefully be pursued in order to discover which of those arguments are historically-specific and which, if any, have a validity or substance that cuts across time or place. In this way close attention to the context surrounding the text might give rise both to historical understanding of past political attitudes and beliefs, and to philosophical insight into problems of the present as well as of the past.

Finally, we should also recognize, along with the importance of particular historical contexts, the existence of a broad Western political tradition to which diverse political thinkers, with their varied circumstances and concerns, have all belonged and contributed. The subject-matter of the history of modern political thought, in spite of these wider variations, is thus, as Berki has noted:

> one broadly defined, yet coherent tradition of political discourse. We are not faced with a chaotic whirl of disembodied ideas and texts, but with a concrete world of interlacing and interweaving visions.[9]

There has thus been a virtually unbroken continuity of reflection on, or speculation about, the problems or concerns relating both to the state and to the relationship between the individual and the state. There have also been certain cherished and enduring human ideals – about liberty, equality, rights and so on – which have been interpreted and developed, albeit in very different ways and within different historical contexts, by political thinkers writing within this broad tradition. While it is possible to trace the earliest roots of such a tradition to the Sophists of ancient Greece in the fifth century BC, for the purpose of this book we shall be considering its development throughout the early modern period (from approximately 1500 to 1800) and in the modern period (since 1800).

Moreover, the major political thinkers have usually been aware of this continuing tradition, developing their own ideas by reference to, or in reaction against, the work of their predecessors. As Jeremy Waldron observed in his critical commentary on changing interpretations of the doctrine of the 'rights of man', the political thinkers of the past – including, within the terms of his own study, Burke, Bentham and Marx – were 'aware of the transhistorical character of political writing', drawing 'deeply and sometimes explicitly on traditional texts'.[10] In this way, such thinkers have, in John Morrow's words, 'tended to treat the past as a treasure trove from which they can draw for their own purposes'.[11]

This has also been the case with contemporary political philosophers. John Rawls, for example, in the course of reviving the social contract tradition, has also drawn on the work of Kant, while Robert Nozick has built upon natural-rights theory in advancing his ideal of the minimal state. These philosophers' awareness of the ongoing tradition of Western political thought has thus enabled them to illuminate contemporary problems concerning the nature of, say, distributive justice or the proper role of the state by referring to past ideas and theories considered by them relevant for that analytical purpose. They have thereby, as Richard Tuck has pointed out, 'continued the ancient practice of pillaging the classics in search of ideas and styles to be revived for their own time'.[12]

The approach, layout and content of the book

With these qualifications in mind, then, I shall follow an historically-grounded approach to political theory in the following pages. Indeed, I write them not as a political philosopher or political theorist, but rather as an historian of political thought. My main concern, therefore, is to provide an introduction to the history of modern political thought that pays proper attention to political and intellectual contexts, but which also, through its organizational framework – built around key concepts – draws attention both to issues of enduring concern and to the need for some degree of philosophical analysis or evaluation.

The primary focus will nonetheless be historical in two respects. First, I shall attempt to produce a broad sketch of the development over time of particular political concepts. Second, I shall also, more extensively, seek to provide descriptive and interpretive accounts of the ways in which particular political thinkers, in response to particular political, economic, social and intellectual forces, have interpreted those concepts over time. In doing so, I shall concentrate, perhaps rather conventionally, on a limited number of political thinkers in the early modern and modern periods. This may seem surprising in view of the fact, already noted above, that a contextualist approach to the history of political thought permits treatment both of a wide variety of primary sources and of a wide range of political thinkers. However, I believe that in an introductory work of this kind, it is more helpful to provide accounts of the core ideas of a few really influential political thinkers, approached in some cases here from several distinct, but related, conceptual directions, than to offer more limited sketches of a greater number of arbitrarily selected, and less prominent, political thinkers.

With regard to specific content, Chapters 1 and 2 will describe the historical development of the two foundational concepts of early modern political thought – sovereignty and political obligation. The different theoretical accounts of sovereignty – concerning the nature, source and location of the political authority and power of the emerging secular, territorial states in Europe – will be examined in Chapter 1 in the political thought of Hobbes, Locke and Rousseau. This will follow a discussion of how such concerns were broadly anticipated by Machiavelli in the early sixteenth century.

The problem of political obligation – concerning the proper relationship between the individual and the modern state, and hence the basis, purpose and limits of the state's authority – will then be examined in Chapter 2. Particular attention in this area will be focused on the ideas of the major social contract theorists of the seventeenth and eighteenth centuries – Hobbes, Locke and Rousseau.

Chapters 3, 4 and 5 will shift the focus of discussion on to the ideal ends of politics, the values which, it has often been argued, the state should seek to promote or defend, or, at any rate, which it ought to allow individual citizens to pursue or realize. I have concentrated here on three such values or ideals – liberty or freedom, rights and equality. I have attempted to trace the broad historical development of such ideals since the late seventeenth and eighteenth centuries, examining some of the diverse ways in which they have been conceived and interpreted by political thinkers.

In relation to liberty, I shall explore in Chapter 3 the theoretical reflections of Locke, Rousseau, John Stuart Mill and Thomas Hill Green. In Chapter 4 I shall discuss the theoretical accounts of rights – formulated in terms of 'natural' rights, the 'rights of man', and 'prescriptive' rights – that were developed in the political thought of Locke, Paine and Burke. Finally, in Chapter 5, I shall explore contrasting interpretations of three distinct concepts of equality that were advanced in the political thought of Rousseau, Wollstonecraft, John Stuart Mill and Marx.

In view of the approach and layout of this book, there will inevitably be some overlap of material when a particular political thinker is considered on more than one occasion during the text. I have tried, however, to ensure that each section dealing with a thinker's contribution to theoretical reflection in a particular conceptual area can be read, if desired, as a self-standing introductory discussion. The first reference in the text to each major political thinker discussed in Section B of each chapter will be accompanied by a box containing a summary of the salient facts of his or her life and works.

As for the layout of the book, this will be as follows. Each of the five chapters will be composed of three sections. Section A will explain the ways in which the particular concept under scrutiny has developed historically. The conditions and historical context within which that concept became a critical issue and was interpreted within theoretical discourse will be explored. The changes and continuities in the way in which that concept was employed, including the language in which it was expressed, will also be noted. Moreover, without engaging in conceptual analysis at a sophisticated level, an attempt will be made to disentangle the various uses and meanings of that concept in political debate as it has evolved over time.

Section B of each chapter will provide the bulk of its subject-matter. It will consist of concise introductions to influential political thinkers' interpretations of the key concept under consideration. The central aim will be to describe and explain not only how such thinkers, within very different historical circumstances, developed their theoretical accounts of, for example, sovereignty or liberty, but also how their distinctive contributions in such areas relate to their political thought as a whole.

Finally, Section C will provide a brief introduction to the nature and scope of current debates surrounding each key concept, as explored by contemporary political thinkers. The aim here is not to offer an extended treatment of twentieth-century theoretical writing on each topic. Rather, a broad outline will be presented of how certain influential contemporary political thinkers (e.g. Rawls, Nozick, Hayek *et al.*) have carried on theoretical discussion around a key concept and how they have thereby helped to illuminate contemporary issues and debates. Section C will also include a brief bibliographical guide to post-1945 philosophical and theoretical literature in each conceptual area.

Notes

1   See J. Plamenatz, *Man and Society*, Vols 1–3, rev. edn, London, Longman, 1992 (originally published in 2 volumes, 1963). (This revised edition does, however, restore some of the historical material that had to be omitted from the original, compressed two-volume edition of Plamenatz's most famous work.) See also, A. Hacker, *Political Theory: Philosophy, Ideology, Science*, New York, Macmillan, 1961.

2   See D.D. Raphael, *Problems of Political Philosophy*, 2nd edn, London, Macmillan, 1990, Ch. 1; A. Heywood, *Political Theory: An Introduction*, 2nd edn, London, Macmillan, 1999, Ch. 1.

3   N. Barry, *An Introduction to Modern Political Theory*, 4th edn, London, Macmillan, 2000, p. 2.

4   Plamenatz, op. cit. Vol. 1 (1963 edn), pp. ix–x.

5   For expressions of this contextualist approach, see J. Dunn, 'The Identity of the History of Ideas' (1969) in Dunn, *Political Obligation in its Historical Context*, Cambridge, Cambridge University Press, 1980, pp. 12–28; J.G.A. Pocock, 'The History of Political Thought: A Methodological Enquiry', in P. Laslett and W.G. Runciman (eds), *Philosophy, Politics and Society*, Series II, Oxford, Blackwell, 1962, pp. 183–202; J.G.A. Pocock, *Politics, Language and Time*, London, Methuen, 1971; Q.R.D. Skinner, 'Meaning and Understanding in the History of Ideas', *History and Theory*, 8, 1969, pp. 199–215; J. Tully (ed.), *Meaning and Context: Quentin Skinner and his Critics*, Cambridge, Cambridge University Press, 1990.

6   R.N. Berki, *The History of Political Thought: A Short Introduction*, London, Dent, 1977, p. 32.

7   ibid. p. 31.

8   I. Hampsher-Monk, *A History of Modern Political Thought*, Oxford, Blackwell, 1992, pp. x–xi.

9   Berki, op. cit. pp. 36–7.
10 J. Waldron (ed.), *'Nonsense upon Stilts': Bentham, Burke and Paine on the Rights of Man*, London, Methuen, 1987, p. 5.
11 J. Morrow, *History of Political Thought: A Thematic Introduction*, London, Macmillan, 1998, p. 5.
12 R. Tuck, 'The Contribution of History', in R.E. Goodin and P. Pettit (eds), *A Companion to Contemporary Political Philosophy*, Oxford, Blackwell, 1993, p. 72.

Sovereignty

Sovereignty is a major defining feature of the modern state. For over 350 years it has been a central characteristic of both national and international politics and a key concept in the historical development of modern political thought. In the twentieth century, it has also been a guiding principle in the conduct of international relations as well as an issue of enduring, sometimes bitter, debate and controversy.

SECTION A

Historical development of the concept

The essential meaning of sovereignty is commonly defined as the right and/or ability of a particular body or ruler to exercise ultimate and supreme authority or command within certain defined territorial boundaries. Historically it developed as a key concept in political theory, and became a critical issue in practical politics, as a result of the gradual emergence in Europe of modern states in the sixteenth and seventeenth centuries. This process took place in the wake of the breakdown both of the medieval, feudal social order and of the organized structure of the medieval Catholic Church. Their replacement by centralized absolutist monarchies – notably in England, France, Spain and Portugal – led to the formation of new secular structures of political organization and authority which gradually became dominant, externally, over the Holy Catholic Church and Holy Roman Empire and, domestically, over the landowning feudal lordships – the three main centres of power in the Middle Ages.

The Treaties and Peace of Westphalia (1648) are widely regarded by historians as the crucial development that formalized this gradual transition. Following in the wake of a succession of bloody civil and religious wars that had disfigured Europe in the sixteenth and seventeenth centuries, including in particular the Thirty Years War, the Westphalia settlement heralded a new international order based on independent sovereign states and hence on the institution of secular, monarchical rule exercised within and over them.

The legal and political authority of these newly-emergent states – their right, that is, to make laws and policies – was soon held to be superior to the authority of any other body or institution either within or outside the states' territorial boundaries. In the past, by contrast, during a long conflict that raged from the eleventh to the fifteenth centuries, the authority of kings throughout Europe had been regarded as coordinate with, or even subordinate to, that of the Catholic Church within the framework of the medieval church-state.[1]

The new, dominant political structures of centralized rule throughout Europe gradually developed, through a process of political and economic organization, into nation-states. For the emerging states were typically rooted in the idea of a nation – a community which shared certain vital characteristics, including a common territorial space, language, culture and history.

In the light of these developments, European political thought in the sixteenth and seventeenth centuries became suffused with the modern conception of the state as a supreme, all-powerful, all-embracing authority, as a centralized power structure, usually headed by an absolute monarch and operating within defined national territorial limits. This dominant idea and reality in turn generated the concept of sovereignty, implying that the new secular political structures commanded absolute legal and political authority. During the sixteenth and seventeenth centuries this concept of state sovereignty became the foundation stone of European political thought. It was embryonic in the political ideas of Niccolò Machiavelli (1469–1527) who formulated a view of the state as a secular, independent and morally-neutral entity. He was the first major political thinker to break with the assumptions of medieval catholic thought, rejecting, in particular, the idea of the limited authority of the state, which had implied its subordinate status in relation to the Catholic Church. Machiavelli's conception of the modern state was most clearly apparent in his theory of the powerful ruler – developed in his most famous work, *The Prince* (1532) – who was needed either to found a new state as its ultimate legislator or to reform a corrupt state as its benevolent dictator.

The concept of sovereignty was explicitly developed later in the sixteenth century by Jean Bodin (1530–96) and in the seventeenth century by Thomas Hobbes (1588–1679), the first systematic modern political thinker. Both of them, influenced by their experience of civil and religious wars and civil disorder, regarded sovereignty – understood, in Bodin's words, as the 'most high and perpetual power' – as the essential condition of an orderly and stable political regime, in Hobbes's case, as the only viable alternative to a condition of widespread anarchy. In sharp contrast to earlier acceptance of the much more diffuse and polycentric medieval political order, Bodin and Hobbes thus emphasized the need for the concentration of political authority – of the right to make laws and issue commands – in the hands of a single person or body and within the formal framework of either a monarchy or a republic. Hobbes, in particular, powerfully reinforced this idea with the aid of a sophisticated political theory, developed in his masterwork *Leviathan* (1651), that invested the sovereign ruler with absolute power as the necessary means both of ensuring the security of person and property of the individual and of preventing the ever-present possibility of a descent into chaos and anarchy in human society.

Later in the seventeenth century, John Locke (1632–1704) developed a different perspective on the question of the sovereignty of the modern state. In his *Second Treatise of Government* (1689), Locke argued that sovereignty resided ultimately with the people, who had loaned their power to the English Parliament as their representative assembly, and not with the monarch. He presented this argument as a justification for the English 'Glorious Revolution' of 1688 and hence as a theoretical defence of both a constitutional monarchy and limited government, innovations that had been created by that uprising.

By the second half of the eighteenth century the French political thinker Jean-Jacques Rousseau (1712–78) formulated the first coherent case in early modern political thought (the body of ideas roughly spanning the period from 1500 to the French Revolution of 1789) for *popular* sovereignty. In his most famous work of political theory, *The Social Contract* (1762), Rousseau promoted the ideal of a sovereign community and state, rooted in a form of participatory, direct democracy, that would serve as the embodiment of what he referred to as the general will, a kind of pervasive patriotic spirit engendered by a concern for the common good. In the second part of this chapter we shall examine in more detail the contributions which Machiavelli, Hobbes, Locke and Rousseau made to theoretical accounts and discussions of sovereignty.

Essential aspects of sovereignty: meanings and usages

In employing and defining the concept of sovereignty, modern political thinkers have commonly observed two important distinctions: first, between legal and political sovereignty, and second, between internal and external sovereignty.

Legal sovereignty

Legal sovereignty involves the idea of supreme or ultimate legal authority within a political community – in other words, the right or entitlement of a person, office or body to make, interpret and enforce the laws which govern that community. This right entails an obligation on the part of subjects or citizens within that political community to comply with those laws. Legal sovereignty has often been referred to as *de jure* sovereignty – that is, a claim to exercise supreme legal authority that rests on legal right rather than on force. Such a claim thus presupposes the supremacy of law – of authoritative legal rules binding on all members of society.

A further implication of the notion of legal sovereignty is that the person or body exercising supreme legal authority is not subject to any higher power with regard to the making or enforcement of laws. In view of the fact that the concept of sovereignty has been intimately connected since the sixteenth and seventeenth centuries with the emergence of the modern state, this has also meant that the state's rules override those of any other association within the state's territorial boundaries.

Moreover, legal sovereignty has a political as well as a purely legal dimension since it refers to the supreme authority of legislatures or assemblies as well as that of the courts. This dual aspect has been particularly evident since the nineteenth century in the British political system with regard to the legislative supremacy of the UK Parliament – more precisely, of the Queen in Parliament. In practice, however, Parliamentary sovereignty since 1945 has been increasingly challenged or eroded both by an ever-expanding executive and by the increased powers of the European Community/Union.

For these reasons the meaning of legal sovereignty when applied to the British state has become less clear over time. It has been even more contested in federal political systems such as those of the USA and Germany where discussion of the meaning of sovereignty has become bound up with the question of its location. In the American context, for instance, sovereignty is usually held to be vested in the US constitution rather than in specific institutions such as the Presidency, Congress or the Supreme Court.

Nonetheless, in spite of the practical difficulties raised by its application to particular political systems, legal sovereignty in essence amounts to a definition of the state's supremacy in terms of its ultimate legal authority rather than its supreme coercive power.

Political sovereignty

The notion of political sovereignty defines the state's supremacy in terms of its actual exercise of coercive power rather than its legal authority. It thus refers to the assertion of unlimited political power; to the capacity of a person or institution within the state to command obedience to laws or policy decisions by virtue of coercive force effectively exerted by that person or institution. This process has often been referred to as one of *de facto* (concerning fact or action) rather than *de jure* (concerning right) sovereignty.

A definition based on the notion of political sovereignty has often been regarded, especially by those who consider the idea of legal sovereignty to be too restrictive, as having two concrete advantages. First, it refers to the actual, rather than formal, exercise of power within a political system, the actual process whereby a person or institution controls the apparatus of the state. For example, in the United Kingdom, although legal sovereignty is vested in Parliament, all major political decisions are in fact taken by the government of the UK, specifically by the Prime Minister and his/her Cabinet, with the backing and approval of Parliament.

Second, political sovereignty also refers to the practical reality that the state's claim to ultimate legal authority needs to be guaranteed by its exercise of coercive power. It thus underlines the need for political rulers or institutions to have the effective capacity to exercise formal legal supremacy.

D.D. Raphael has observed that many contemporary political theorists and political scientists have tended to define the sovereignty of the state in these apparently realistic political terms since they have often equated sovereignty with 'supremacy of coercive power rather than of legal authority'.[2] However, stressing the limits of this interpretation, Raphael points out that the state's coercive power is not always a necessary condition for substantiating its claim to supreme legal authority. This is particularly the case in the field of international relations where small sovereign states (e.g. Liechtenstein, San Marino, Ghana) are legally recognized in spite of their political weakness.

In addition, Raphael argues that a state's coercive power is not a sufficient condition for substantiating its claim to sovereignty. Power alone is simply not enough. It must be accompanied, as Hobbes stressed in *Leviathan*,[3] by the people's acknowledgement of the state's legal and political authority; of its right, that is, to make laws and political decisions.

Viewed from this perspective, the sovereignty of the state largely rests, as the eminent German social theorist Max Weber (1864–1920) contended, on the extent to which its exercise of coercive power is widely held to be legitimate. This requires popular acceptance of the need to comply with the state's laws and constitution, which is indeed the objective basis of its authority. According to this view, the essence of the concept of sovereignty may thus be identified as right or entitlement, and hence authority, rather than force or power.

But as Barbara Goodwin has pointed out,[4] another problem with what Raphael calls the power theory of sovereignty is that its ostensibly hard-headed, *de facto* approach to the entire issue makes it impossible to establish the state's *right* to coercive power, and hence to the people's obedience, even if it does make sovereignty easier to identify or locate empirically.[5]

A fundamental point, related to these objections, has also been forcefully made by Noel Malcolm, who observes that the distinction between power and authority is really 'the basis of all legal understanding: if you do not have the concept of authority as something differing from mere power, then you cannot have the concept of law as anything other than the mere application of force'.[6]

Philosophically, these amount to penetrating criticisms of the notion of political sovereignty in spite of the apparent realism of emphasizing the actual exercise of power within the state. They are also criticisms that raise important questions about the nature of the sovereignty of nation-states in relation to international organizations and supranational bodies such as the European Union – a point that will be elaborated later in this discussion.

Ultimately, however, the debate concerning the relative merits of an emphasis on the legal sovereignty of the state, defined in terms of its supreme legal authority, or of a concern with its political sovereignty, defined in terms of its supreme coercive power, is clarified by an awareness of the fact that political authority and political power, though distinct concepts, are in practice intertwined. They are, in Goodwin's phrase, 'Siamese twins'. For as we have seen, the state's claim to ultimate legal authority, in order to be made effective, needs to be reinforced by its coercive power. In turn, that power, in order to be perceived as legitimate, must be backed by a popular recognition of the state's authority, of its right to make laws and political decisions.

Internal sovereignty

The notion of internal sovereignty refers to the source and location of supreme legal and political authority, as well as of supreme coercive power, within the state's territorial boundaries. It thus raises the question of which person, body or institution is entitled to make decisions binding on all individuals and groups within the state's jurisdiction.

For Hobbes, writing against the background of the English Civil War (1642–9), this had been more than just a theoretical question. Rather, it was viewed by him as an issue of pressing concern, as the key to ensuring political stability and civil order in the face of the turbulence and conflict produced by the struggle for sovereignty in England between King and Parliament.

Compared with such acute political tensions, the problems associated with locating sovereignty within contemporary unitary states, such as Britain and France, at first glance appear somewhat less daunting. For unitary states by definition are characterized by one dominant tier of government and hence by one source of supreme political authority.

But even here the real situation is more complicated. The British Parliament, for instance, has long been regarded as the main source or seat of legal and political authority within the United Kingdom. Indeed, the principle of parliamentary sovereignty has traditionally provided the distinctive internal aspect of the British conception of sovereignty. But as has been noted, this principle has, in practice, been significantly weakened by the rise of the executive in British government during the twentieth century, and especially since 1945, as well as by the reality of British membership of the European Community since 1973, which has meant that in certain areas European Community/Union legislation takes precedence over domestic law in the event of any clash between them.

In federal states, by contrast, such as the USA, Canada or Germany, in which legislative authority is diffused across at least two levels or tiers of government, internal sovereignty becomes even more difficult to locate or identify. Federalism entails an apparent sharing of sovereignty between these tiers of government – between the federal government, on the one hand, and provincial or state governments on the other, operating within the boundaries of the same nation-state. Furthermore, within such federal states, sovereignty is usually seen as rooted in a federal constitution (as in the USA), which assigns powers and functions to each tier of government. This is itself a problematic issue since federal constitutions can be amended and by themselves lack coercive power to substantiate their authority unless they can be enforced by some other body (for instance, in the USA by the Supreme Court).

It should be stressed, too, that in federal states the constituent members of the federal union (in the USA, individual states such as Arkansas or California) are in practice subordinate in many policy areas to the supreme authority of the federal government. American states, for instance, like Canadian provinces or German länder, cannot issue their own currencies, or enact commercial tariffs for foreign trade, or enter into international treaties, or formulate national security and defence policy. These responsibilities all lie within the competence and authority of the federal government.

Within these limitations, a defining feature of federal states is, nonetheless, a polycentric concept of sovereignty, implying, at least in principle, a dispersal of sovereignty across different tiers of government. This is in sharp contrast to the monolithic notion of sovereignty, denoting a single source of unchallengeable, ultimate legal authority, that characterizes unitary political systems. However, even in federal states, in spite of a high degree of decentralization or delegation of powers, there is but one supreme political and legal authority which takes decisions over both internal and external affairs.

Such complications or ambiguities come to the fore when attempting to locate the source of ultimate authority within the modern state. Yet those problems have really been inherent in the very notion of internal sovereignty ever since it was developed by Hobbes in his attempt in *Leviathan* to identify and legitimize the centre of supreme power and authority within seventeenth-century England.

External sovereignty

The related idea of external sovereignty refers to the state's recognized existence as an independent political entity in relation both to other states and to other bodies or organizations within the international order. It is thus an attribute which the state possesses in the field of international relations.

Historically, this external aspect of sovereignty – embracing and justifying notions of the autonomy, equal status and interrelationship of sovereign states within the international order – was a comparatively late development in Western political practice and thought. By the nineteenth and early twentieth centuries it had nonetheless become established as a fundamental principle of international politics.

External sovereignty is a political idea that has raised at least three issues. These concern, first, a state's claim to full self-government; second, the international recognition of such a claim; and third, a state's capacity for acting internationally as an independent, self-governing entity.

From the nineteenth century onwards, such issues were often bound up with the struggles for national independence and self-government conducted against imperial or colonial powers. This fusion of ideas eventually helped to shape the modern concept of national sovereignty – the right and capacity of a nation to act in an independent and self-governing manner, a condition recognized by the international community.

In spite, then, of the pre-democratic, or even in some cases undemocratic, nature and application of the original sixteenth- and seventeenth-century concept of state sovereignty, the idea of external or national sovereignty, with its emphasis on the quest for self-government, has often carried within itself clear democratic implications. The extent to which this has been the case has, in turn, depended on the character of the particular nation-state – and hence on its internal organization and political institutions – that has claimed recognition of its sovereignty.

The interdependent world of the modern global era has demonstrably placed limits on this exercise of national independence. Among the most important of these have been the constraints imposed since 1945, first, by international organizations and treaties, and even supranational institutions, above the nation-state (e.g. the United Nations (UN), North Atlantic Treaty Organization (NATO), the European Union (EU) or the International Monetary Fund (IMF)), and second, by the growth in such a climate of bodies of international law (e.g. the European Convention on Human Rights (1950) and the European Court of Human Rights). In addition, the globalization of economic activity, and hence of production, trade and finance, leading, among other things, to the growth of transnational companies; and the emergence, too, of global, notably environmental, issues that clearly transcend national frontiers, have further limited the scope for independent action by individual nation-states.

If external or national sovereignty is understood essentially in terms of political sovereignty – in terms, that is, of the exercise of supreme coercive power – then such constraints have certainly eroded the sovereignty of the nation-state, even calling into question in some accounts its future credibility in the early part of the twenty-first century.[7] There are, however, as we have seen, clear problems inherent in this power theory of sovereignty. It may be noted here, too, that there is an important difference between recognizing, on the one hand, that a nation-state's freedom of action or manoeuvre is limited by the force of material circumstances, and, on the other, maintaining, more contentiously, that the very idea of its sovereign status has been rendered obsolete, or even meaningless, by those circumstances.

Moreover, as Raphael has argued,[8] if external or national sovereignty is equated chiefly with political sovereignty, then in the post-1945 era only the 'Superpowers' – the USA and the Soviet Union – have been truly sovereign states, since they alone (and since the collapse of the Soviet Union in the early 1990s, arguably the USA alone) have possessed the political, economic and military power capable of ensuring their true independence.

Taken to an extreme, such a view might even lead to the kind of disdain for small nation-states expressed by Hitler in 1938, who, following Germany's annexation of Austria, asked:

> What can words like 'independence' or 'sovereignty' mean for a state of only six million?[9]

The limitations of the power theory of sovereignty, when applied to the international order, may be further underlined by observing that during the twentieth century the notion of external sovereignty has also been bound up with the vexed question of national self-determination. This has been expressed both in the quest for national independence, for instance, preceding and following the collapse of the Soviet Union, and in response to the many violations of the internal affairs and sovereign status of one nation-state by another, including, for instance, the invasion of Afghanistan by the Soviet Union in 1979 and of Kuwait by Iraq in 1990.

In such a context, external or national sovereignty may be viewed as an important guiding principle in twentieth-century global politics, with clear implications in international law. It entails the recognition of a nation-state within the international order as an entity that has rights of jurisdiction – based on legal authority rather than mere force – over its own people and territory. It consequently implies the constitutional independence of a particular nation-state – its exercise of supreme legal authority in a manner that is not subject to some higher constitutional authority.

For, as the analyst of international relations, Alan James, has written:

> A sovereign state may have all sorts of links with other such states and with international bodies, but the one sort of link which, by definition, it cannot have is a constitutional one.[10]

Conclusion

It is, then, these concrete features – a state's possession of defined territorial space and boundaries, its exercise of authority over a particular settled people through law and government, and, above all, its constitutional independence – that comprise what another writer on international relations, Georg Sørenson, has called the 'constitutive core'[11] not just of external sovereignty but of the principle and institution of sovereignty in general.

James has maintained that, in view of the centrality of constitutional independence to any meaningful definition of sovereignty, the distinction between its internal and external aspects is misleading since these are really different sides of the same coin. 'A sovereign state,' James writes, 'is all of a piece'; for its condition as a constitutionally independent, or sovereign, entity means that it has both an external and an internal role, and 'that no other entity is customarily in the position of being formally able to take decisions regarding either the internal or the external affairs of the territory in question'.[12]

By 1999, about 190 states in the world enjoyed this status, recognized in international law, of constitutional independence, thereby forming 'the still-Westphalian international society'.[13] Understood in this fundamental sense of the word, sovereignty has remained the stable and dominant principle of political organization – on both national and international levels – since the seventeenth century; since the Peace of Westphalia and the upheavals that prompted the writings of Hobbes and Locke.

It has been, however, the twentieth century, and particularly the period since 1945, that has witnessed major changes in the operation of the principle of sovereignty in practice. For the growth of the forces of international interdependence has restricted or eroded the autonomy of sovereign states in numerous ways, affecting their ability, and even in some cases their perceived right, to make laws and formulate policies for themselves.

Notes

1 For a useful discussion of this conflict, see G. Sabine and T. Thorson, *A History of Political Theory,* 4th edn, Himsdale, Illinois, Dryden Press, 1973, Part II.
2 D.D. Raphael, *Problems of Political Philosophy*, rev. edn, London, Macmillan, 1990, p. 158.
3 See T. Hobbes, *Leviathan* (1651) (ed. R. Tuck), Cambridge, Cambridge University Press, 1996, Part 2, Chs 20, 31.
4 B. Goodwin, *Using Political Ideas*, 4th edn, Chichester, Wiley, 1997, p. 270.
5 ibid. p. 265.
6 N. Malcolm, 'Sense on Sovereignty', in M. Holmes (ed.), *The Eurosceptical Reader*, London, Macmillan, 1996, p. 347.
7 See, for instance, J. Camilleri and P. Falk, *The End of Sovereignty? The Politics of a Shrinking and Fragmenting World*, Aldershot, Edward Elgar, 1992. See also section C below.
8 See Raphael, op. cit. pp. 158–9.
9 Quoted in A. James, *Sovereign Statehood: The Basis of International Society*, London, Allen and Unwin, 1986, p. 2.
10 ibid. p. 24.
11 G. Sørenson, 'Sovereignty: Change and Continuity in a Fundamental Institution', *Political Studies*, XLVII, 1999, p. 594.
12 A. James, 'The Practice of Sovereign Statehood in Contemporary International Society', *Political Studies*, XLVII, 1999, p. 464.
13 ibid. p. 460.

SECTION B

Machiavelli on the Prince's power

In his two major works of political theory, *The Prince* (1513) and *The Discourses on Livy* (1513–19), Machiavelli did not explicitly formulate the concept of sovereignty. He did, however, form a conception of the modern state as an all-embracing, closely-knit and centralized authority and structure. This view

---

Niccolò Machiavelli (1469–1527)

Italian political thinker and diplomat. Machiavelli lived through a turbulent era of uninterrupted European war and widespread territorial conquest by expansionist political rulers. Born in Florence, one of five city-states in a then disunited Italy, in 1498, at the age of 29, he became secretary to the foreign relations committee of the recently created Florentine republican government. He served for fourteen years on various diplomatic missions abroad, including in France, Germany and Italy, and was also involved in the organization of a national defence militia for Florence.

By courtesy of Hulton Archive

When the Florentine republic fell in 1512, the powerful Medici family returned to power. After being imprisoned and tortured by the new regime, Machiavelli was released and, retiring to his farm in Tuscany, in 1513 wrote his most famous work of political theory, *The Prince* (eventually published in 1532), which reflected his first-hand experiences of government service. His other major political work, *The Discourses on Livy*, was probably written between 1515 and 1519 and was based on his intensive study of ancient history.

Both these works of political theory are concerned with the achievement of order, stability and peace by means of political rule exercised through either republics or principalities. In the case of *The Prince*, Machiavelli's focus is on political leadership within principalities or monarchies. It raises the question of how to acquire, retain and increase political power, and examines the character of the ruler who is capable of attaining those goals. *The Discourses on Livy*, on the other hand, uses the ancient historian Livy's account of Roman history as the basis for exploring the institutional character of effective republican government.

With their preoccupation with the pursuit of political power within the newly emerging secular European states of the early sixteenth century, Machiavelli's political analyses and observations, trenchantly expressed in both of his major works, constitute in many ways the starting-point of the historical development of modern political thought.

---

eventually gave rise, in the political thought of Jean Bodin (1529–96) and Thomas Hobbes (1588–1679), to the concept of sovereignty.

Machiavelli's view of the state marks the great divide between medieval and early modern political thought. It implied, first, an acceptance of the state as an all-powerful political association imbued, within its territorial limits, with supreme political authority and thereby claiming the right to command the undisputed loyalty of all its citizens. Second, it entailed a corresponding rejection of medieval ideas about the superior authority of the Church.

This distinctive view of the modern state as an autonomous central authority superior to all other associations within a defined territorial area thus pointed the way towards theories of state sovereignty later formulated by Bodin and, in the seventeenth century, by Hobbes. However, the emergence of the modern concept of sovereignty required the development of political conditions that were absent during Machiavelli's lifetime – in particular, the gradual establishment of the secular and centralized territorial state, evident in Europe from the mid-sixteenth to the mid-seventeenth century. By contrast, the political climate that influenced Machiavelli's writings – one of fragmentation and decentralization – prevented him from articulating or emphasizing a concept which he had at least anticipated. In this respect Machiavelli has often been regarded as a transitional figure in the history of political thought, straddling its medieval and early modern periods and marking the transition from the medieval feudal system to the modern territorial state.

Machiavelli's political thought should be viewed both within its political context of late fifteenth/early sixteenth-century Italy and within its intellectual context of his reaction against the political influence of Christianity and his emphasis on classical and Renaissance philosophy. Politically, Italy during his life-time was disunited and fragmented into five city states – Naples, Milan, Venice, Florence and the Papal State. Intellectually, Italy was then under the sway of the Renaissance, that broad cultural movement embracing the arts and sciences, with its underlying humanistic emphasis on individual self-fulfilment and its mate-rialistic concern with worldly success and achievement. Such a cultural climate engendered, too, a revived interest in the aesthetic ideals of classical Greece and Rome.

Writing against this background, Machiavelli's main concern in both his major works of political theory is with the achievement of order, stability and peace in Italian society by means of political rule exercised through either republics or principalities. Moreover, in each of those works he is concerned both with the causes of the rise and decline of states and with the methods by which political rulers can make states endure. In *The Discourses on Livy*, based on his study of the ancient historian Livy's *History of the Roman Republic*, his main focus is on republican government. Here Machiavelli asks how states are founded and governments organized, how states are enlarged by conquest and other means, and how the decline of a particular state can be arrested for as long as possible.

By contrast, in *The Prince*, Machiavelli's most famous work of political theory, he is concerned with principalities or monarchies – and hence, with absolute government. Here he asks, first, what kinds of qualities or methods are required to produce a strong, lasting absolute monarchy or principality; and second, what kind of individual political leader is entitled to wield absolute power within such regimes.

Addressing those questions, Machiavelli stresses the need for a solitary and hard-headed political leader who, in his role either as founder of a new state or as reformer of a corrupt state, will employ, if necessary, not only force but also characteristics of deception, cunning and ruthlessness in order to achieve the desired goals of order, stability, peace and unity within the state.

Deeply affected by his fourteen years' experience as a senior diplomat in the service of the Florentine Republic from 1498 to 1512, and hence by his first-hand observations of European power politics, Machiavelli formed a clear view of the political methods that were needed in the climate of corruption, lawlessness, dominant vested interests and internal conflicts that characterized the Italian city-states of that period. In the light of those conditions, Machiavelli argued in *The Prince* that a form of dictatorship – specifically, an absolutist monarchy – would be required to unify the Florentine state into a coherent national entity and ultimately to achieve the goal of the unification of Italy. For those purposes Machiavelli attached special importance to political power as the major characteristic of political activity. For in his view, since politics is essentially about the foundation and maintenance of states, it is therefore also about the acquisition and exercise of power in pursuit of that end.

In this area, Machiavelli also underlined the need for the prince to demonstrate what he called 'virtù', a term which denotes a set of manly qualities such as strength, courage, resoluteness, self-reliance and practical wisdom. Influenced here by classical Greek and Roman ideas, Machiavelli maintained that such qualities were needed to promote peace, order and stability within the state. Their practical importance was all the greater, too, he stressed, in view of the permanent threat of political instability posed not only by human weakness and corruptibility, so evident in contemporary Italy (Machiavelli held a consistently pessimistic view of human nature, regarding human beings as innately self-interested and self-regarding); but also by fortune or fate, the unforeseen or unpredictable element in life which is 'the mistress of half our actions'.[1]

The political leader's ability to dominate the state thus springs, in Machiavelli's view, from his own qualities and skills, including his mastery of the ground rules of power politics. Among the latter, which Machiavelli presents in *The Prince* almost as maxims for budding dictators,[2] he underlines as priorities the need for a political leader to be careful to use power ruthlessly, employing a combination of force and fraud; to use persuasion skilfully, applying a range of propaganda techniques; and to act decisively, removing any degree of self-destructive hesitation.

It is all these qualities and skills, then, not the forces of tradition or custom, which enable the prince to exercise political power, thereby controlling his subjects and making laws and political decisions affecting them. Furthermore, Machiavelli argues in *The Prince* that an outstanding political leader, who as supreme lawgiver is depicted as standing outside conventional morality, should be prepared to use methods widely considered unacceptable by normal standards of private morality. Such methods might include violence, deceit, dishonesty or treachery, all of which should be placed at the disposal of a despotic ruler if he wishes to enlarge the powers of the state in order to attain the ultimate goal of peace and order. For when the political stakes are so high, a ruler cannot afford to be bound by conventional moral standards.

This is the source of Machiavelli's notorious and established reputation in the history of political thought as the arch-proponent of the doctrine that the end justifies the means. As he himself observed in Chapter 18 of *The Prince*: 'As to the actions of all men and especially those of princes, against whom charges cannot be brought in court, everybody looks at their result.'[3] Explaining further the reasoning behind this emphasis on suitable methods for particular purposes, he pointed out that:

> Since, then, a prince is necessitated to play the animal well, he chooses among the beasts the fox and the lion, because the lion does not protect himself from traps; the fox does not protect himself from the wolves. The prince must be a fox, therefore, to recognise the traps and a lion to frighten the wolves.[4]

In spite, however, of Machiavelli's preoccupation with political power, he does acknowledge, too, the value of political authority, which a political leader acquires whenever the power he exercises is perceived by the people as morally justifiable. For without that recognized authority a leader would be over-reliant on sheer power or naked force. His position would then be unsatisfactory for several reasons. In the first place, unlimited political power is frequently a crudely ineffective means of controlling an entire population since it entails the deployment of massive and costly forces of suppression. Second, excessive use of coercive power tends to generate strong public resistance, thereby breeding a lurking political instability which may eventually undermine a despotic leader's rule. Third, coercive political power is a transient phenomenon, effective only so long as the prince is able to sustain his dominance.

By contrast, legal and political authority, the recognized right to make laws and political decisions, has a value that transcends the life and capacities of an individual ruler. As Machiavelli observes in *The Discourses on Livy*:

> The welfare ... of a republic or a kingdom does not consist in having a prince who governs it wisely during his lifetime, but in having one who will give it such laws that it will maintain itself even after his death.[5]

Machiavelli's elevated view of the supreme ruler thus clearly anticipates later theories of sovereignty since his vision of a well-ordered state focuses on the peace and stability produced not just by its exercise of supreme political power but also by a widespread recognition of its legal and political authority in the minds of a law-abiding people. As we have seen, the gradual spread of territorial nation-states throughout Europe during the sixteenth century and the beginning of the seventeenth century provided the political backdrop against which theories of sovereignty could be developed – most notably by Thomas Hobbes in his masterwork of political philosophy, *Leviathan* (1651).

Notes

1   N. Machiavelli, *The Prince*, Ch. 25, in *The Prince, Selections from The Discourses and Other Writings* (ed. J. Plamenatz), London, Fontana, 1972, p. 129.

2   ibid. pp. 107–9 (*The Prince*, Ch. 18).

3   ibid. p. 109 (*The Prince*, Ch. 18).

4   ibid. p. 107 (*The Prince*, Ch. 18).

5   N. Machiavelli, *The Discourses on Livy*, in *The Prince and Discourses* (intro by M. Lerner), New York, Random House, 1950, p. 148.

Hobbes: the sovereignty of the *Leviathan* state

Historical context: political and intellectual

The political and intellectual changes which Machiavelli had anticipated – the emergence in the sixteenth and seventeenth centuries of the territorial nation-state, and with it the concept of sovereignty – were clearly and dramatically reflected in the political thought of Thomas Hobbes. Like Jean Bodin before him, Hobbes stressed the need for a strong central power that could fuse the old, diverse feudal forces into a cohesive political entity. He thus put forward an elaborate theoretical case for a supreme and absolutely powerful ruler – a sovereign.

For Hobbes such a ruler would be at the head of the new form of political association in the Europe of his day. This consisted of the new secular governing authorities operating within distinct territorial areas, each claiming independence from the Church and Holy Roman Empire externally and asserting superiority over all feudal lordships internally.

From this standpoint Hobbes developed a powerful theoretical justification for a sovereign state in which supreme political power and authority would be concentrated in the hands of one ruler – in practice, either a monarch or an assembly. The great work of political philosophy in which he presents this case for absolute government, *Leviathan* (1651), was produced against the historical background of the English Civil War which had raged from 1642 to 1649. That conflict had itself been concerned with the struggle for internal sovereignty, involving disputed political authority, between the English King, Charles I, and the English Parliament.

The political context in which Hobbes elaborated his theory of absolute government (which he had actually developed in 1640) was thus a turbulent one that included the abolition of the monarchy and execution of Charles I in 1649; the formation of the English republic (the Commonwealth) presided over by Oliver Cromwell as Lord Protector; and the eventual restoration in 1660 of the monarchy in the person of Charles II. It was a period of social, religious and political conflict, violence and dislocation. Indeed, at the end of *Leviathan*, Hobbes points out that that work was 'occasioned by the disorders of the present time'.[1] The danger of a descent into civil war and dissension, the threat of imminent social and political disorder and chaos, and hence the need to maintain a stable political and social order, consequently emerged as pervasive and persistent themes in Hobbes's political thought.

Thomas Hobbes (1588–1679)

English philosopher and political thinker. Born in Wiltshire, England, Hobbes was educated at the University of Oxford and spent the rest of his long life in the aristocratic households of the Cavendishes, Earls of Devonshire, as tutor and secretary.

A writer of philosophical works since the late 1630s, Hobbes published in 1651 his masterwork of political philosophy, *Leviathan*. This appeared shortly after the end of the Thirty Years War in 1648, which had engulfed central and northern Europe in prolonged religious conflicts. Following the resolution of those events, England was then embroiled in a bitter civil war

By courtesy of the National Portrait Gallery, London

which ended with the execution of King Charles I and the establishment of a republic under Oliver Cromwell's leadership in 1649.

During the course of the English Civil War, in which Hobbes was identified with the Royalist cause, he became tutor in mathematics to the young Charles, Prince of Wales (later Charles II) when he was exiled in France in the late 1640s. However, Hobbes returned to England in 1652, where he lived apparently reconciled to, and undisturbed by, Cromwell's Commonwealth and Protectorate until the restoration of the Stuart monarchy under Charles II in 1660.

Hobbes's major work of political philosophy, *Leviathan*, reflected these turbulent events in its central concern with the quest for political order and stability in a dangerous world. Deeply influenced in its methodology by the new scientific learning in Europe, Hobbes advanced in *Leviathan* a rationalist and scientifically-based defence of strong, absolutist government as the only viable alternative to anarchy, civil disorder and war. Viewed with suspicion at the time by many Royalists because of its apparent political neutrality, *Leviathan* has been regarded ever since as one of the greatest English contributions to the history of political philosophy.

The case for absolute government

The Civil War had led to a disruption of the centralized English monarchy, headed by, first, the Tudors and later the Stuarts, which had become the main source of internal sovereignty within the territorial nation-state emerging in England after 1500. Royal sovereignty had traditionally been justified in terms of the doctrine of the divine right of kings, which attempted to derive their authority from God-given powers and ultimately from their ancestors, the first Patriarchs, sons of Noah. In *Leviathan*, Hobbes sought to provide a new and unorthodox theoretical justification for the political authority of the early modern state. By thereby establishing a legitimate basis for political authority, he could then proceed to define the rights and powers of the sovereign, as well as the limits to the sovereign's right to rule. These were to be the central concerns of Hobbes's theory of absolute sovereignty.

In developing that theory, Hobbes was strongly influenced by Galileo's geometric method, which involved breaking down complex matter into its constituent elements. Applying this method, derived from the natural sciences, to political philosophy, Hobbes sought to deduce his case for absolute government from certain underlying assumptions about human nature. His priority was thus to clarify certain laws of human behaviour – 'laws of nature', as he termed them – which provided the conditions under which a stable society and secure state might be possible.

On the basis of this methodology, Hobbes aimed in *Leviathan* to demonstrate that all political authority should be concentrated in the hands of one sovereign body – whether a monarch or an assembly – rather than divided or separated between one or more bodies. Reinforced by the experience of the Civil War, his concern was with the problem of internal sovereignty – with the controversial issue of where the sovereign authority of the state should be located.

From this standpoint Hobbes poses in *Leviathan* two fundamental questions about government. First, he asks what is its essential function. The answer he gives is: to provide maximum security and safety for the individual in an uncertain and dangerous world. Second, he asks what kind of government can achieve that aim most effectively for the individual. He replies that it can only be a government in which supreme authority is concentrated in the hands of a sovereign ruler.

Hobbes explores these vital concerns in Part 1 of *Leviathan*, subtitled 'Of Man' and dealing with human nature and man's natural condition (which he terms the 'state of nature') and in its Part 2, subtitled 'Of Commonwealth' and dealing with the contractual origins of the state and with the characteristics of the sovereign.

In tracing the origins and legitimate basis of the sovereign state, Hobbes argues that these lie in a contract or 'covenant' between the people. Whether instituted by a formal contract or agreement or acquired by conquest, legitimate political rule thus rests, in his view, on the voluntary agreement of the ruled. Specifically, that entails a willingness on the part of the people to give up their right of governing themselves to a sovereign authorized in his actions by every individual who has helped to form the original contract. Indeed, the sovereign's very existence is the result of the people's interaction in making that 'covenant', the purpose of which is to establish peace and security.[2]

In the first stage, then, of Hobbes's argument for absolute sovereignty, he stressed the need for a social contract or 'covenant' formed among individuals as the necessary means of achieving peace and security. Hobbes then proceeded to demonstrate the need, too, for a sovereign ruler who would enforce that social contract since:

> The only way to erect such a Common Power . . . is [for all men] to conferre all their power and strength upon one Man, or upon one Assembly of men, that may reduce all their Wills, by plurality of voices, unto one Will.[3]

The individual subjects, therefore, should be prepared, Hobbes argues, to give their obedience to the sovereign in return for his establishing a secure and ordered society. The sovereign's existence is necessary because egoistic and self-seeking individuals cannot be trusted to stick to any agreement without fear of punishment by a stronger power. The sovereign is thus, in Dante Germino's words, 'a kind of umpire who presides over the social game and sees that its rules and agreements are not broken'.[4]

Ultimately, then, the political authority of Hobbes's sovereign, of his Leviathan state, stems from the people's own authorization – from a broad, popular agreement rather than from the traditional doctrine of the divine right of kings. For the sovereign has been authorized by his subjects to act on their behalf just as a lawyer acts for his clients.

The sovereign state is thus for Hobbes an artificially created entity, in the form of either an individual monarch or an assembly, which acts 'in those things which concern the Common Peace and Safetie'.[5] This, indeed, is the essential function of an absolute sovereign, of 'that great Leviathan, or rather … of that Mortalle God, to which we owe under the Immortal God, our peace and defence'.[6]

Moreover, Hobbes maintains that a form of government based on the principle of absolute sovereignty is the only effective way of achieving the peace, order and security desired by individual subjects for their self-preservation. Absolute government is also, in Hobbes's view, the only sure guarantee against a return to the anarchic horrors of the 'state of nature'.

Hobbes's argument at this point rests on his assumption that unless supreme political authority and power are concentrated and undivided, there can be no generally accepted arbiter in all cases, including in disputes about the limits of that authority. Hobbes therefore maintains that absolute authority and power should be vested in the hands of one individual or body rather than divided or diffused across two or more institutions.

The power and authority of the sovereign

The secular state thus emerges in Hobbes's political thought as the dominant organizational form in society, controlling all other associations including the Church, which in the Middle Ages had claimed final political authority. To this sovereign secular state he accordingly attributes absolute powers: in making, executing and enforcing laws; in making and preserving peace and declaring war; in appointing ministers and magistrates. Although Hobbes does suggest that many areas of the individual's life – economic activity and interests, for instance – should nevertheless remain free from state interference, he also bestows upon the sovereign extensive powers of censorship within society, as well as the ability to determine the allocation of property rights.

Hobbes's theory of sovereignty does not, however, rest on the assertion of political power alone. It also embraces the notion of the sovereign's political authority, his recognized right to rule. Indeed, as D.D. Raphael has observed,[7] Hobbes makes clear, in Part 2, Chapters 20 and 31 of *Leviathan*, that power alone is insufficient to substantiate political authority or to constitute what he calls 'dominion'. Hobbes insists instead that both power and acknowledged authority are the necessary bulwarks of the sovereign's rule or 'dominion'. For in Hobbes's account of sovereignty, the individual subject acknowledges that the state, as a result of the people's 'covenant', has the right, not just the power, to issue commands and consequently that the subject is thereby morally obliged, and not just compelled, to obey the sovereign.

The sovereignty of the state is thus, in Hobbes's view, partly based on the subject's voluntary obedience, which stems from an acknowledgement of the state's authority. This process may well, admittedly, be assisted by the state's effective exercise of coercive power. But by itself, state power is insufficient or even in some cases self-defeating since, if it is exercised in a brutal or repressive manner, it may generate resistance rather than obedience on the part of the state's subjects.

The sovereign's rights and powers thus ultimately depend on the agreement and support of the people. For those distinctive rights and powers were acquired through the social contract or 'covenant' that authorized the sovereign in the first place. The state's authority endures, therefore, only as long as it is perceived to be performing the essential function for which it was instituted through the social contract – 'namely the procuration of the safety of the people'.[8] If the state fails, however, to achieve that essential goal, its authority is seriously eroded.

The sovereign's formidable powers are thus limited by this overriding obligation which he must fulfil on behalf of his subjects. By the same token, the subject's duty to obey the sovereign is conditional upon the preservation of peace and security within civil society. Furthermore, the individual's right to self-protection remains, Hobbes stresses, inviolable and may even, in extreme circumstances, be asserted individually against the power of the sovereign state.

As a consequence, clear limits are imposed on the exercise of sovereign authority, for the individual has the right to withdraw allegiance, first, if the sovereign fails to establish peace, order and security (the ultimate justification for sovereignty), or second, if he endangers the individual subject's life. As Hobbes states:

> The end of Obedience is Protection; ... the Obligation of Subjects to the Sovereign, is understood to last as long, and no longer than the power lasteth, by which he is able to protect them.[9]

While, then, the power of the sovereign in certain well-defined areas is absolute, his authority is ultimately dependent, in these two vital respects, upon the agreement of his subjects. In broader terms, however, Hobbes offered no middle way between the need, as he perceived it, for absolute government, on the one hand, and the latent danger of anarchy, on the other. He remained preoccupied with the fear of social and political disorder, not with the dangers of dictatorship or despotism. After the Restoration of the English monarchy in 1660, liberal political thinkers such as John Locke were concerned with avoiding both of those pitfalls. Hobbes, by contrast, tended to assume that rebellious subjects can hardly ever have a better case for rebellion than the ruler has for asserting his sovereign power and authority. For without the sovereign's dominant presence, there was always, he stressed, the risk of a rapid descent into the 'state of nature', with all its chaos, uncertainty and violence.

Notes

1   T. Hobbes, *Leviathan* (1651) (ed. R. Tuck), Cambridge, Cambridge University Press, 1996, p. 491.
2   See Chapter 2B for a more detailed account of Hobbes's theory of political obligation.
3   Hobbes, op. cit. p. 120 (Part 2, Ch. 17).
4   D. Germino, *Machiavelli to Marx*, Chicago, University of Chicago Press, 1972, p. 102.
5   Hobbes, op. cit. p. 120 (Part 2, Ch. 17).
6   ibid.
7   D.D. Raphael, *Problems of Political Philosophy*, rev. edn, London, Macmillan, 1990, pp. 160–2.
8   Hobbes, op. cit. p. 231 (Part 2, Ch. 30).
9   ibid. p. 153 (Part 2, Ch. 21).

Locke on sovereignty as trusteeship

Historical context: political and intellectual

John Locke's account of sovereignty may be viewed in important respects as a reaction against Hobbes's theory. Forged by different political concerns – essentially by a fear of dictatorship rather than of anarchy – his own theoretical views formed part of a second wave of political reflection on sovereignty during the late seventeenth and eighteenth centuries. Such thinking was itself an intellectual response to the succession of religious and civil wars of the sixteenth and seventeenth centuries throughout Europe. Whereas Hobbes's theory of absolute sovereignty had been shaped by his concern with the division of political authority and ultimately with the breakdown of sovereignty during the English Civil War, Locke's own preoccupation was with the extent and limits of sovereignty. He thus examined the question of whether, and on what grounds, it was ever legitimate to resist a sovereign ruler. In exploring this highly charged political issue, Locke thereby provided a theoretical justification for the struggles of particular individuals and groups to secure their rights and liberties in the face of the actions of often oppressive and authoritarian governments and states during that period.[1]

Locke's views on sovereignty, a term which he seldom used, are expressed in his major work of political theory, the *Second Treatise of Government*, written in the early 1680s but not published until 1689 following the overthrow of King James II from the thrones of England, Scotland and Ireland. Locke emerged from his authorship of the *Second Treatise* as the principal theoretician of the Whig cause in England, one which sought to defend existing political and civil institutions, notably, a Protestant Parliament and propertied interests, against an increasingly autocratic Catholic Stuart monarchy.

Underlying theoretical assumptions

Locke's theory of sovereignty differs most obviously from Hobbes's in so far as its main focus is on placing formal checks and limits on the authority and power of

John Locke (1632–1704)

English philosopher and political thinker. Born in Somerset, England, and raised in a Puritan family, Locke studied the medieval scholastic curriculum at the University of Oxford before turning to the study of medicine. In 1667 he became the personal physician, close companion and leading adviser of Lord Ashley, the future Earl of Shaftesbury. For the rest of his life, Locke's intellectual interests focused on the study of philosophy, including political theory, and theology.

By courtesy of the National Portrait Gallery, London

Locke's political concerns, however, were by no means predominantly theoretical, for during the 1670s and 1680s he became directly involved in a political movement under the Whig leadership of the Earl of Shaftesbury. That movement, of which Locke emerged as its leading theoretician, was one of principled opposition to the absolutist tendencies of the English Stuart monarchy represented, first, by Charles II, and subsequently by his Catholic brother James (later James II). Locke's connections with the Earl of Shaftesbury, who was charged with treason in 1681, led him to follow his friend and patron into political exile in the Netherlands. Locke returned to England six years later following the Glorious Revolution of 1688 and the consequent accession to the English throne of William of Orange and Mary.

Locke's two major works of political theory, his *Two Treatises of Government* and his *Letter on Toleration*, together with his major work of philosophy, the *Essay Concerning Human Understanding*, were all published in 1689, the year of his return. The *Two Treatises of Government*, written during the early 1680s, was revised and published by Locke as a theoretical justification for the ejection of James II from the English throne following the Glorious Revolution of 1688, which for the first time established a constitutional monarchy in England. The *Second Treatise*, in particular, with its emphasis on the individual's natural rights, on government by consent, and on limited, constitutional government, has firmly established Locke's reputation as a key figure in the early development of Western liberalism.

the state and its political rulers. It thus seeks to retain for the people, through their representatives in Parliament, the supreme authority and power which Hobbes had transferred to an all-powerful, centralized, unitary state. Specifically, Locke delegates that authority and power to the legislature, the branch of government entrusted with making and defining the laws of the state, and in a more limited sense, to the executive, the body entrusted with executing those laws.

For Locke, however, ultimate sovereignty always lies not with the state or the king but with the people, who have merely loaned their powers to Parliament and the government of the day. The legislature, the supreme institution of the state, could therefore, in his view, be dissolved by the people at any time. Moreover, the more limited authority and power of the executive endured only so long as it operated within the framework of law established by the people's legislature. According to Locke, then, state sovereignty is, above all, a form of trusteeship, for the power of the institutions of the state – their capacity to make and enforce laws – is held on trust, it rests on the consent of the people.

Here we begin to encounter certain key assumptions underlying Locke's political philosophy. Like Hobbes, he develops his account of sovereignty on the basis of an attempt to justify the authority of the increasingly centralized English state. Indeed, that task is in many ways, as John Plamenatz observed, Locke's central concern.[2] Like Hobbes, too, Locke asks fundamental questions about the legitimacy of state authority, though both political philosophers were well aware of the dangers of a situation in which political authority was absent. But whereas, for Hobbes, such a situation involved all the anarchic horrors of the state of nature, in Locke's view it would mean, more than anything else, the loss of liberty, a condition in which the individual would be 'subject to the inconstant, uncertain, unknown, Arbitrary Will of another Man'.[3]

Locke did, nonetheless, like Hobbes, base his account of sovereignty on the notion of a pre-social and pre-political 'state of nature'. But Locke held a more favourable view of this 'state of nature', reflecting in turn his less pessimistic view of human nature. For to him the phrase simply described the condition in which human beings as creatures of God enjoyed certain fundamental natural rights and fulfilled certain corresponding natural obligations prior to the formation of the civil societies in which they were to live. Furthermore, this natural state, Locke maintains, is governed by the law of nature, that is, reason, which 'teaches all Mankind . . . that being all equal and independent, no one ought to harm another in his Life, Health, Liberty and Possessions'.[4]

However, the 'state of nature', Locke stresses, also presents an acute dilemma. For where there is no recognized common authority to enforce the law of nature, individuals will, he maintains, work out their own personal interpretations of that code. Becoming, indeed, judges in their own cases, they will thereby interpret and enforce the law of nature in a highly subjective and biased manner. This will lead to a situation in which peace, order and individual freedom all become precarious. At its worst the 'state of nature' might then degenerate into a 'state of war' in which arbitrary force is exercised by one person over another.

The 'proper remedy' for such confusion and insecurity, in Locke's view, is civil government – that is, government in accordance with the principles of reason, with the 'law of nature'. In order to be legitimate, however, civil government must rest on the consent of the governed; otherwise it remains arbitrary rule. Indeed, consent is the only way in which legitimate political societies may be founded since:

> Men being . . . by Nature all free, equal and independent, no one can be put out of this Estate, and subjected to the Political Power of another, without his own Consent.[5]

For Locke, then, the basis of political society is a contract whereby individuals consent to be bound by the laws of a common authority known as civil government. Moreover, the central purpose of this social contract, and hence of political society, which Locke calls 'the commonwealth', is the protection of the individual's natural rights – to life, liberty and property – which are inviolable and held and enjoyed in the state of nature prior to the formation of all social and political arrangements.[6]

Legitimate political power thus amounts, Locke argues, to a form of trust, a contract between members of society that both rests on their own consent and seeks to preserve their lives, liberties and possessions. This trust or social contract therefore not only renders government legitimate; it also clearly defines the functions of government as concerned, above all, with the protection of the rights of the governed.

Distinctive features of Locke's theory

These theoretical assumptions – about the law of nature, the individual's natural rights and a social contract based on consent – firmly underpin Locke's conception of civil government and hence his account of state sovereignty as a form of trusteeship. Furthermore, in that account the people are depicted as the latent sovereign so long as the legislature, the supreme branch of government, exercises supreme power delegated by the people. But once the legislature has been dissolved by the people, for whatever reason, the people regain their active sovereignty. In this way, they retain ultimate control over the legislative power, which was originally granted by them in trust – in Locke's phrase it is a 'fiduciary power' – and which can be recalled by the people whenever the legislators break that trust.

The most distinctive features of Locke's theory of sovereignty are consequently its preoccupation with, first, the formal checks and limits that can be placed upon the exercise of state authority and power, and second, the conditions under which the governed are entitled to resist or even remove their rulers.

With regard to the question of checks and limits, Locke's theory focuses, above all, on the notion of the separation of the powers of government. This approach to formal practical arrangements, designed to ensure that the institutions of government respect and promote the rights of the governed, for Locke rests on his belief that political authority should be divided between the branches of the legislature, which is imbued with full delegated authority, and the executive, which has partial authority. As we have seen, the legislature has the sole right, granted by the people in trust, to make the laws; the executive, constrained to act within the framework of law, has the power to execute the laws, but is ultimately responsible to the legislature. Locke argues that these two functions of government are distinct and should preferably be held in separate hands, and vested in separate branches of government, in order to prevent an accumulation of powers in any one body, with all the subsequent abuses which that might generate.

With regard to Locke's second major concern – the conditions under which the individual might be entitled to resist the authority and power of the state – his attitude is unequivocal. Any government or ruler, he insists, that fails to respect and protect the individual's natural rights – to life, liberty and property – thereby forfeits its claim to the individual's obedience and may even be overthrown by the people. Locke thereby provided both a theoretical justification for popular resistance to political oppression and a criterion for judging the extent to which any particular government protected the individual's natural rights.

Locke sets out the terms of this justification in Chapter 19 of the *Second Treatise*, entitled 'Of the Dissolution of Government'. Without referring explicitly to the individual's 'right to rebellion', he specifies the ways in which the people may exercise their ultimate control over both the legislative and executive branches of government once their trust has been broken. He does this after identifying a number of areas in which the powers of either the legislative or the executive might be abused, thereby leading to a 'dissolution of government'. Such abuses, 'dissolving actions' as he calls them, essentially involve situations in which government betrays the people's trust either by acting in an arbitrary, unconstitutional manner or by violating the individual's natural rights to life, liberty and property.

Active popular resistance, based on a collective judgement of the majority, in such situations, Locke maintains, becomes the only feasible way of expressing disapproval of the government's actions and the only practicable alternative to the people's consent. Moreover, because of the people's latent, supreme power, their resistance of a tyrannical government really amounts to an assertion of their legitimate rights. Indeed, it is the government, Locke stresses, rather than the people that has rebelled in such cases since, by consistently acting in a tyrannical way, it has ceased to be legitimate and has placed itself in a state of war with the people.

Locke also makes it clear that popular resistance to a tyrannical or unjust ruler may be either defensive or radical in its implications. It may thus be concerned either with restoring existing political structures and constitutional rules or with establishing new structures or even a new system of government. Either way the overriding purpose is to oppose the illegitimate use of political power and authority by unjust rulers, particularly by tyrants who exercise their power 'beyond Right'.[7]

Locke thus demonstrates that the people have actively reasserted their sovereignty – their ultimate political authority and power – which they provisionally delegated to the legislature and executive on the basis of trust and which, in Hobbes's theory, they had transferred almost completely to an almighty, centralized Leviathan state.

Significantly, too, a fundamental principle of Locke's account of sovereignty is that, even when government has been dissolved, civil society – that network of groups and associations that exists outside and beyond government – remains intact. Unlike in Hobbes's theory, then, civil society does not disintegrate once a government has been removed, for in Locke's view the people constitute a power superior to the government. Locke underlined this point in his description of the relationship between the people and its legislature, stressing that: 'There remains still in the People a Supreme Power to remove or alter the Legislative, when they find the Legislative act contrary to the Trust reposed in them.'[8]

This central notion of the endurance of civil society in the face of the abuse of state power, with its underlying emphasis on the need for limited, constitutional government in view of that danger, potential or real, thus provides the core of Locke's theory of sovereignty. It was a seminal idea that was to strongly influence the course of Western politics in the eighteenth century and, specifically, to provide a theoretical justification both for the American Revolution of 1776–83 and for the subsequent adoption of the constitution of the United States of America in 1789 following the Philadelphia Convention of 1787.

Notes

1   See A. Gamble, *An Introduction to Modern Social and Political Thought*, London, Macmillan, 1981, pp. 51–4.
2   See J. Plamenatz, *Man and Society*, Vol. 1 (revised by M.E. Plamenatz and R. Wokler), London, Longman, 1992, Ch. 8.
3   J. Locke, *Two Treatises of Government* (ed. P. Laslett), Cambridge, Cambridge University Press, 1988, p. 284 (*Second Treatise of Government*, Ch. 4, sect. 22).
4   ibid. p. 271 (*Second Treatise*, Ch. 2, sect. 6).
5   ibid. p. 330 (*Second Treatise*, Ch. 8, sect. 95).
6   See Ch. 2 on Locke's theory of political obligation; and Ch. 3 on his conception of natural rights.
7   Locke, op. cit. pp. 397–8 (*Second Treatise*, Ch. 18, sect. 199).
8   Locke, op. cit. p. 367 (*Second Treatise*, Ch. 13, sect. 149).

Rousseau and popular sovereignty

Historical context: political and intellectual

The theory of popular sovereignty formulated by the French political philosopher Jean-Jacques Rousseau (1712–78) was his radical response to the social conflicts, divisions and inequalities that characterized and disfigured European states and societies in the second half of the eighteenth century. Philosophically, his theory may be regarded in some important respects as an attempt to supersede and transcend the earlier theories of Hobbes and Locke. Like them, Rousseau tried, too, to resolve the deep-seated and long-running problem in Western political theory of the tension between, on the one hand, the thirst for individual freedom and, on the other, the need for social order and collective authority. But in Rousseau's case, he sought to achieve that end by developing his own distinctive social contract theory which attempted to reconcile liberty with order by conferring sovereign authority on the community as a whole rather than, as in Hobbes's theory, on the all-powerful state or, as in Locke's theory, on a representative assembly acting as the trustee of the people.

Nevertheless, Rousseau did take from Hobbes the notion that, within the terms of the social contract, the individual should be prepared to submit totally to the supreme authority of a collective entity, which was recast, however, in the form of the community rather than Hobbes's unitary state. Rousseau diverged sharply, too, from Hobbes's theory of sovereignty both by regarding the state as a

Jean-Jacques Rousseau (1712–78)

French political and moral philosopher. Born in Geneva, Rousseau received no formal education and left his native city at the age of 16 to lead a nomadic existence in France, Italy and Switzerland. Moving to Paris in 1742, he met leading Enlightenment thinkers such as Diderot and Voltaire.

By courtesy of Topham/The Antman Archives

Rousseau became well-known as a writer for the first time in 1751 with a prize-winning essay, his *Discourse on the Arts and Sciences,* which challenged prevailing eighteenth-century Enlightenment opinion on the benefits of reason and progress by arguing that civilization was corrupting man's natural goodness and innocence.

Rousseau's *Discourse on the Origin of Inequality,* his first major political work, was published in 1755. It advanced, from a similar moral perspective, a trenchant critique of the institution of private property.

Rousseau's second and most famous work of political theory, *The Social Contract,* was published in 1762. It offered a vision of man's moral and political liberation from the ills of existing civil society. Embedded in that vision was Rousseau's concept of the general will, his most distinctive contribution to Western political thought. With the aid of that notion, and the related ideal of popular sovereignty, Rousseau sought to resolve the historic tension within political theory between individual freedom and collective authority.

After sustained persecution by both French and Swiss authorities on account of his radical views, Rousseau died in France in 1778. Eleven years later, however, his political philosophy, including, in particular, his concepts of popular sovereignty and the general will, became one of the major inspirations behind the French Revolution of 1789. His more long-term intellectual legacy has been both wide-ranging and ambiguous, since he has influenced socialist, anarchist, liberal, democratic and, some have argued, even totalitarian traditions of thought.

political association that is formed through a social contract between interdependent individuals, and by viewing government as merely the non-sovereign executor of decisions taken by the sovereign community.

In formulating his own theory of sovereignty, Rousseau turned away not just from Hobbes's absolutism but also from Locke's liberal–constitutionalist approach, which had rested on notions both of a separation of the powers of the state across different branches of government, and of sovereign authority being vested in a representative assembly. For unlike Hobbes and Locke, Rousseau did not separate civil society from the state as two distinct entities fixed in a particular political relationship. Rather, in his view, was the state to be regarded as the embodiment of the citizen body as a whole, which expressed its sovereignty through the exercise of what Rousseau called the general will, the key concept of his entire political philosophy.

An important influence underlying such ideas had been Rousseau's long-standing admiration for the theory and practice of the ancient Greek city-states and Roman republic, as well as the formative experience of the political organization of his native city of Geneva. By contrast, he felt little affinity with those contemporary eighteenth-century thinkers who advocated moderate reform of existing European states whether in the form of an enlightened monarchy, as in the case of Enlightenment philosophers such as François-Marie Voltaire (1694–1778) or by means of constitutional checks and balances as in the case of Charles-Louis de Secondat Montesquieu (1689–1755). Instead of such political reformism, Rousseau favoured nothing less than a radical transformation of the contemporary social and political order into an ideal polity founded on liberty, equality and popular sovereignty.

The sovereign community

Rousseau developed his own theory of sovereignty in his major work of political philosophy, *The Social Contract* (1762), which on its publication was ordered to be publicly burned in both France and Rousseau's native Geneva, with the French government even ordering his arrest. In its pages he maintains that it is what he calls the 'general will' that is sovereign and that legislative power belongs to the people. This idea of the general will, Rousseau's most distinctive contribution to Western political thought, is central to his conception of a co-operative social and political order which, being based on human interdependence, fosters and promotes the common interests and concerns of the community rather than the selfish or sectional interest of individuals or organized groups. The 'general will' is thus for Rousseau the collective view that society holds about what is for 'the common good', in the shared interests of the community as a whole.

Rousseau's distinctive social contract theory, at the heart of which lies his concept of the general will, provides the intellectual foundation of his account of sovereignty.[1] The essence of his social contract is a process in which each individual surrenders his rights not to the state (as in Hobbes's theory), or to a representative assembly (as in Locke's theory), but rather to the community of which he is a member.

The key points in Rousseau's theory that have a direct bearing on his account of sovereignty are, first, that legislative authority ought, in his view, to belong to the entire community of citizens; second, that each individual citizen is thereby subject to the sovereign authority of the community; and third, that each individual nevertheless has a share in that collective authority and ought, therefore, to play an equal part in the law-making process of the community.

Moreover, each individual, having helped to shape the laws that regulate the affairs of his community, subsequently undertakes to obey those laws. For

Rousseau makes it clear that the purpose of his social contract is to create 'a form of association that will defend and protect the person and goods of each associate with the full common force, and by means of which each, uniting with all, nevertheless obey only himself and remain as free as before'.[2]

This insight provided, Rousseau believed, the key to resolving the tension between the thirst for individual freedom on the one hand, and the need for social order and sovereign authority on the other. It also shaped his ideal of a social and political order that bestowed the benefits of human co-operation and interdependence whilst avoiding relationships of dominance and subordination.

Within Rousseau's social contract, then, the individuals involved have not allowed any appointed person or assembly to exercise sovereign rule over them. Instead, the forging of the contract, 'this act of association', as Rousseau describes it, 'produces a moral and collective body' – in the form of a decision-making popular assembly – which assumes the name of 'Republic or of body politic', and 'which its members call "State" when it is passive, "Sovereign" when active'.[3]

Furthermore, for Rousseau the true source of popular sovereignty is the general will of the 'moral and collective body' created by the agreement of the community. Indeed, sovereignty itself, Rousseau stresses, 'is nothing but the exercise of the general will',[4] and must therefore reside in the community.

This sovereignty of the general will, and hence of the community, cannot, in Rousseau's view, be surrendered or delegated to any one person or group of people. Nor, he argues, may it be exercised on behalf of the community through elected representatives, as in eighteenth-century England. What is more, the sovereign, which amounts not to a determinate person or institution but rather to the entire body of active citizens, once they agree on a general policy for the common good, cannot be bound by law since it is itself the source of law. An act of sovereignty is thus 'not a convention of the superior with the inferior, but a convention of the body with each one of its members. A convention which is legitimate because it is based on the social contract, equitable because it is common to all ...'[5]

Rousseau's theory of popular sovereignty, which was to be a major inspiration behind the French Revolution of 1789, rests, then, on his pivotal concept of the general will, his term for the sovereign power. The underlying assumptions of that theory are as follows. First, Rousseau maintains that when the community as a whole meets in the legislative assembly, it is sovereign only when it makes laws that express the general will of the entire community, directed therefore towards the common good. Second, he points out that when sovereign legislative power is vested in the whole community, its members legislate both for themselves and for the community, thereby ensuring the identification of their self-interest (or 'utility') with the public interest (or 'justice').

Third, he contends that, as a consequence, this situation greatly increases the likelihood of voluntary acceptance by citizens of the states' laws, which they themselves have shaped, thereby reducing the need for public law enforcement. Finally, Rousseau recommends that the laws made by the community at popular assemblies, laws which express the general will, should be applied and enforced by an executive, 'an elective aristocracy' as he calls it, which has only a restricted role and is provisional in nature.

The theory of popular sovereignty that is built around these assumptions is developed by Rousseau in the concluding chapters of Book III and in much of Book IV of *The Social Contract*. It holds, above all, that all citizens, rather than particular persons or institutions, directly exercise sovereign authority through their involvement in legislative assemblies. This authentic form of sovereignty, as Rousseau envisages it, is also depicted by him as a vital safeguard against the domination of the community either by the 'particular will' of an individual or by the 'partial will' of an organized group.

The preconditions of popular sovereignty

In *The Social Contract* Rousseau also stipulates certain preconditions for realizing his ideal of popular sovereignty, for sustaining a sovereign assembly that expresses the general will. First, he argues that the state should be relatively small because that would not only enable the people to participate in law-making assemblies, thereby expressing the general will, but also would allow each individual to possess a reasonable share of sovereign power. A small, compact state would tend to foster, too, a strong sense of community and altruism. To further that end, moreover, Rousseau maintains that there should be 'no partial society in the State',[6] in other words, no divisive, intermediate associations, factions or interest groups undermining the relationship between the individual citizen and the community as a whole. A final and not insignificant advantage of a small state would be that the workload of its legislative assembly would be a limited one, since such a state 'needs very few laws'.[7]

In making all these points, Rousseau was working within the theoretical model of a small agrarian state like his own native city-state of Geneva or like Corsica, for which he wrote a draft constitution in 1763–5. Deeply influenced, too, by the historical precedent of the ancient Greek city-states, in particular by Sparta, he commended these political entities, with their small population sizes (of about 300,000 citizens) and their decentralized structures, as desirable and superior alternatives to hierarchical and increasingly centralized early modern European states such as England and France.

As a second precondition for realizing popular sovereignty, Rousseau argued that his desired state and society should also be characterized by a high degree of equality. By this he did not mean absolute equality of wealth or income, but rather that there should be a broad measure of equality in the distribution of property, especially of land. Every citizen, he believed, should possess a certain amount of property since such a condition would confer greater security and independence. By contrast, gross inequalities would generate political inequalities involving disparities of influence and power and hence give rise to relationships of dominance and subordination that would fatally undermine the exercise of the general will.

In Rousseau's ideal state of interdependent equals, therefore, no citizen ought to be dependent on anyone else economically or politically. In his own words, no citizen should ever be 'so rich that he can buy another, and none so very poor that he is compelled to sell himself'.[8]

Finally, Rousseau maintained that a modern state that embodied and promoted popular sovereignty would be one without a representative assembly such as the English Parliament. For, as he argued in Chapter 15 of Book III of *The Social Contract*, sovereignty cannot be represented since its very essence is the exercise of the general will, which is something that cannot be transferred by the community to any other body or institution. For this reason he considered the English system of parliamentary representation to be illegitimate and incompatible with the voters' political freedom. He made this point in a famous passage in *The Social Contract* in which he maintained that:

> The English people thinks it is free; it is greatly mistaken, it is free only during the election of Members of Parliament.[9]

Indeed, the very idea of representative government, Rousseau claimed, 'comes to us from feudal government, that iniquitous and absurd Government in which the human species is degraded, and the name of man is dishonored'.[10]

Instead, therefore, of creating a representative assembly, the people ought, in his view, to participate directly in popular legislative assemblies, casting their votes until a simple majority was obtained on a particular issue. Whenever such majority voting reflected the common good or public interest of the entire community, then it would become a true expression of the general will.

As the operational principles upon which a participatory political society of this kind could be based, Rousseau recommended, first, that every citizen should be entitled to take part in making sovereign decisions which all are required to obey; second, that the people who make those sovereign decisions should do so as individuals and not as members of organized groups; and third, that citizens should make their own laws themselves and not elect representatives to make them in their place. Finally, he made it clear that the body that made the laws – the sovereign legislative assembly – should not also administer or enforce those laws. That task should instead be entrusted to the executive, a body with a strictly limited role within Rousseau's innovative system of popular government.

In practical terms Rousseau's theory of popular sovereignty exercised a major influence on the democratic revolutions of the late eighteenth century – indirectly in America and more explicitly in France. It thus provided an intellectual inspiration for French revolutionaries such as Robespierre before and after 1789, as well as part of the theoretical foundation both of the French Declaration of the Rights of Man and the Citizen, decreed by the French Constituent Assembly in 1791, and of the new French Constitution of 1793. The 1791 Declaration, for instance, though derived mainly from the ideas of Thomas Paine (1737–1809), revealed Rousseau's clear influence in its Article I, which read: 'Men are born free and remain free and equal in rights,' and in its Article VI, which stated: 'The law is the expression of the general will.'

Less directly, but significant nonetheless, the governments and constitutions of the newly-independent American states appealed to French revolutionaries in the 1780s because they appeared to be based on theoretical principles – notably those of popular sovereignty and of popularly created law – that Rousseau had formulated in *The Social Contract* and which eventually inspired the French Revolution.

Notes

1   See Chapter 2B for a more detailed discussion of Rousseau's social contract theory.
2   J.-J. Rousseau, *The Social Contract and Other Later Political Writings* (ed. and translated by V. Gourevitch), Cambridge, Cambridge University Press, 1997, pp. 49–50 (Book I, Ch. 6 (4)).
3   ibid. pp. 50–1 (Book I, Ch. 6 (10)).
4   ibid. p. 57 (Book II, Ch. 1 (2)).
5   ibid. p. 63 (Book II, Ch. 4 (8)).
6   ibid. p. 60 (Book II, Ch. 3 (4)).
7   ibid. p. 121 (Book IV, Ch. 1 (2)).
8   ibid. p. 78 (Book II, Ch. 11 (2)).
9   ibid. p. 114 (Book III, Ch. 15 (5)).
10 ibid. (Book III, Ch. 15 (6)).

SECTION C

Contemporary debates

Major political and economic changes since 1945, noted here already, have significantly affected the practical, substantial operation of the principle of sovereignty. These have included, as we have seen, the growth of international organizations and treaties, and even supranational institutions above the nation-state; the development, too, of bodies of international law; the globalization of economic activity; and the spread of global, and hence transnational, issues such as environmental pollution and international crime.

These changes have consequently altered traditional conceptions or interpretations of sovereignty. But they have also created a climate in which political interest – both academic and practical – in the concept and institution of sovereignty has continued to flourish. This fact was illustrated by the large conference held in July 1998 in Munster, Germany to mark the 350th anniversary of the Peace and Treaties of Westphalia, commonly regarded by historians as the genesis of the modern system of sovereign states.

Much recent academic debate, among both political theorists and international relations specialists, has focused on different interpretations of sovereignty in the light of the changes in the international scene. Some writers have argued that sovereignty, being an essentially contested concept and an ambiguous term, cannot be clearly defined. They have therefore concentrated on examining the definitions of other scholars.[1]

Other writers have tended to advance an 'end of sovereignty' thesis, maintaining both that sovereignty has become more dispersed internally in modern political systems and that nation-states' external sovereignty has been increasingly eroded by global forces and international pressures. According to this view, the concept of sovereignty has become outmoded, since it no longer describes the internal or external realities of modern global politics.[2]

In Britain, and more widely throughout Western Europe, since the 1980s this thesis has gained currency and apparent credence in some quarters in the light of the accelerating pace of European integration – both political and economic – following important developments within the European Community/ Union such as the Single European Act (1986), and the Treaties of Maastricht (1992) and Amsterdam (1997). For such developments have unquestionably eroded the sovereignty of European member-states in a number of significant ways. Moreover, this process has been widely considered to be of a different kind and degree of seriousness from previous losses of national sovereignty which were perceived at the time as limited, conditional and for specific purposes only.

A more qualified, but also generally unfavourable contemporary interpretation of sovereignty has portrayed it as, in Newman's words, 'an unhelpful doctrine'.[3] This analysis presents the usefulness of the term as largely confined to the sense of 'international recognition'. It suggests, too, that other usages could be more clearly expressed in other ways (e.g. 'popular sovereignty' as 'democracy', or 'divided or shared sovereignty' as 'constitutional/institutional relationships within the state'). In general, Newman argues, the term obscures more than it clarifies.

In contrast to these interpretations, contemporary defenders of the concept of state sovereignty have, in the first place, questioned the extent to which the forces of globalization or international interdependence – including closer European integration – have actually succeeded in undermining nation-states as cohesive entities.[4] Second, such writers have pointed to what they consider to be still relevant usages of the term, such as international recognition and, in particular, constitutional independence, highlighted by Alan James and others as the core aspect and hence as the clearest and most meaningful definition of sovereignty for the contemporary political world.[5]

Finally, James has also defended the concept of state sovereignty in terms of its stabilizing functions within the international order. These are evident, in his view, first, in its role of identifying those territorial entities which have, or have not, the capacity to act internationally, itself derived from their sovereignty, and which are, or are not, thereby subjects of international law.[6]

In addition, James has argued, the concept of sovereignty has contributed to the maintenance of order and stability within, as well as between, states – particularly newly independent states – through its association with the unifying, popular cause of national self-determination. It has also promoted the cause of democracy through its related association with the democratic value of independent self-government.

These have all been, in James's opinion, important benefits of what he calls 'this maligned and much-misunderstood concept'[7] of sovereignty. Whatever view might be taken of such a proposition, it seems likely that both in the future development of political thought and in current and future practical political controversies (European monetary union being an important case in point), the nature, scope and application of sovereignty will remain a central and highly contentious issue in national and international politics.

Notes

1   See, for example, J. Bartelson, *A Genealogy of Sovereignty*, Cambridge, Cambridge University Press, 1995.
2   See, for example, J. Camilleri and P. Falk, *The End of Sovereignty? The Politics of a Shrinking and Fragmenting World*, Aldershot, Edward Elgar, 1992.
3   M. Newman, *Democracy, Sovereignty and the European Union*, London, Hurst and Co., 1996, p. 12.
4   See A. Milward, *The European Rescue of the Nation State*, London, Routledge, 1992; R. Jackson and A. James (eds), *States in a Changing World*, Oxford, Oxford University Press, 1993.
5   See A. James, *Sovereign Statehood: the Basis of International Society*, London, Allen and Unwin, 1986; A. James, 'The Practice of Sovereign Statehood in Contemporary Society', *Political Studies*, XLVII, 1999, pp. 457–73; G. Sørenson, 'Sovereignty: Change and Continuity in a Fundamental Institution', *Political Studies*, XLVII, 1999, pp. 590–604.
6   James, 'The Practice of Sovereign Statehood in Contemporary Society', pp. 471–3.
7   ibid. p. 473.

Further reading

J. Bartelson, *A Genealogy of Sovereignty*, Cambridge, Cambridge University Press, 1995.
J. Camilleri and P. Falk, *The End of Sovereignty? The Politics of a Shrinking and Fragmenting World*, Aldershot, Edward Elgar, 1992.
F.H. Hinsley, *Sovereignty*, 2nd edn, Cambridge, Cambridge University Press, 1986.
A. James, *Sovereign Statehood: the Basis of International Society*, London, Allen and Unwin, 1986.
A. James, 'The Practice of Sovereign Statehood in Contemporary Society', *Political Studies*, XLVII, 1999, pp. 457–73.
G. Lyons and M. Mastandumo (eds), *Beyond Westphalia? Sovereignty and International Intervention*, Baltimore, Johns Hopkins University Press, 1995.
M. Newman, *Democracy, Sovereignty and the European Union*, London, Hurst and Co., 1996.
G. Sørenson, 'Sovereignty: Change and Continuity in a Fundamental Institution', *Political Studies*, XVLII, 1999, pp. 590–604.

Political obligation

The question of political obligation is concerned with the moral obligation or duty of the individual citizen to acknowledge the authority of the state and thereby to obey its laws. Throughout the history of political thought, particularly since the seventeenth century, the debate generated by this question has focused largely on how political obligation may be explained and defended. Historically, the idea of a social contract – a formal agreement either among individuals or between individuals and the state – provided, in seventeenth- and eighteenth-century political thought, the classic explanation of political obligation. This underlying notion was in turn rooted in the belief that there were clear moral grounds for respecting the political and legal authority of the state. Indeed, the concept of political obligation has been consistently intertwined with that of political authority. For the individual's obligation to recognize political authority has implied that some other person or body has the right to require that an individual acts in such a manner.

The problem of political obligation has centred mainly on four related issues. First, what are the source and origins of political authority? In other words, how has it come about that I, as an individual citizen, have an obligation to respect the state's authority and to obey its laws?

Second, what are the extent and limits of political obligation? In what respects, that is, am I duty-bound to obey the state? And at what point, if any, am I as an individual citizen justified in disobeying the state and its laws?

Third, what or who is the main focus of political authority? To what political body, that is, or to which individual ruler do I owe political obligation? Finally, and more broadly, what is the proper relationship between the individual citizen and the wider political community to which he or she belongs?

The various theories of political obligation advanced since the seventeenth century have all asserted the general duty of the citizen to respect the authority of the state and to obey its laws. We have already seen that the concept of state sovereignty – and hence the idea of the supreme authority of the state – implies the recognized right of the state to make laws and policy decisions. The problem of political obligation follows on logically from this notion since it raises the question of why the individual citizen is morally, rather than just legally or prudentially, obliged to obey the state and its laws.

This question of the nature and grounds of political obligation has, in fact, generated one of the oldest and most enduring problems in the history of political thought, stretching back, not just to seventeenth century England but even to ancient Greece – specifically, to Athens in the fourth century BC. For in Plato's dialogue *The Crito*, the philosopher Socrates confronted this critical issue in the most dramatic terms when he was prepared to face death rather than renounce his political obligation to the Athenian state. Much more recently, in Britain in the late 1980s, the problem of political obligation once again became central to public debate when large sections of the population vehemently rejected the notion that they had any moral duty to pay a form of local taxation, known as the Community Charge, or more colloquially, as the poll tax, which was widely considered unjust.

SECTION A

Historical development of the concept

The problem of political obligation, and its underlying question of the relationship between government and the governed, became a major concern of early modern political thought (the body of ideas developed in the period stretching from roughly 1500 to 1789), following and developing its initial emphasis on the concept of state sovereignty. Significantly, arguments about political obligation formed a central feature of political debate during historical periods of political crisis, widespread popular dissent or discontent and social dislocation.[1] Such a climate was particularly prevalent in seventeenth-century England, which was riven by religious conflict and civil war, involving even armed insurrection and the overthrow and execution of King Charles I, and leading eventually to a largely bloodless revolution in 1688 that established a constitutional monarchy. During this period the political philosophy of Thomas Hobbes and John Locke in effect provided an elaborate intellectual attempt to hold together a country that was manifestly on the verge of chaos and disintegration.

Voluntaristic theories

The social contract tradition in early modern political thought that emerged from the writings of Hobbes and Locke evolved during the seventeenth and eighteenth centuries into a mode of thinking about the relationship between the individual and his/her political community. Its central concept of a social contract – a formal agreement either among individuals or between individuals and their states – provided a more conditional basis for recognizing political authority, and hence for political obligation, than had been offered by earlier, more traditional theories.

Before the sixteenth century, political authority had been widely depicted as an inevitable fact of either natural or divine will, and hence as a reality that individuals either inherited or passively accepted. The doctrine of the divine right of kings was a notable example of such thinking. From that perspective, even as late as the seventeenth century, the English political thinker Sir Robert Filmer (1588–1653) defended absolute monarchical power in terms of patriarchal authority, which, being divinely ordained, was in his view to be obeyed unconditionally.

By contrast, social contract theories, notably those developed by Hobbes and Locke, provided coherent expressions of the case for *conditional* political authority. By employing the legal term 'contract' to justify political authority, they were thereby based on the notion that political obligation could be compared to the legal obligation of a party to a contract. Such theories thus provided explanatory accounts of political obligation that were both *voluntaristic,* in so far as they stressed the importance of human will, and *individualistic,* since they involved the acceptance by individuals of political authority over them on agreed terms.

This distinctive mode of thinking, with its inherent notion of the individual as a rational and autonomous actor who voluntarily assumes and acquires political obligation, was a distinctive feature of early modern political thought. It arose from the highly individualistic climate that had been shaped in Europe by the Renaissance, the Reformation and the genesis of a new economic system based on private property ownership. The essential idea embedded in these social contract theories was that individuals agreed to obey the state and its laws in return for certain tangible benefits – the guarantee of security of person and property in the case of Hobbes's account, and the protection of natural (i.e. pre-social) rights to life, liberty and property in the case of Locke's.

The wider implication of that idea, therefore, was that political authority, which had arisen from the will and agreement of individual citizens or subjects, was both conditional and restricted in its scope. It had been established to fulfil certain defined purposes for those individuals. Their political obligations to the state thus depended on its effectiveness in attaining particular desired ends on their behalf.

Teleological theories

Among the main alternatives to these voluntaristic, social contract theories of political obligation the most influential have probably been various teleological theories (derived from the Greek word Τελος, meaning purpose or goal). Such theories hold that the individual citizen's obligation to obey the state and its laws rests on the ends or purposes that the state seeks to promote. Teleological accounts of political obligation have been of broadly two types: first, utilitarian ones, which maintain that the individual should obey the state because it seeks to achieve 'the greatest happiness of the greatest number'; and second, common good theories, which hold that the individual should obey the state whenever it promotes the common good or public interest.

Utilitarian accounts of political obligation are based on the theoretical notion of utility, by which is meant happiness or pleasure, or the satisfaction of desires or preferences, an idea which pervades the political thought of the English philosopher Jeremy Bentham (1748–1832), who actually wrote very little on the question of political obligation. The utilitarian theory which he and his followers propounded holds that the ultimate moral obligation facing individuals in life is the promotion of the general happiness and that, since the state is the necessary means of securing that end, individuals are obliged to obey the state and its laws as the essential condition for fulfilling their highest moral obligation. According to utilitarian theory, the state aims to promote the general happiness, or 'the greatest happiness of the greatest number', in Bentham's famous phrase, first, by passing laws that prevent individuals from acting in ways that undermine that supreme goal, and second, by making laws or policy decisions that actually promote the general happiness (e.g. by delivering essential public services.) Such laws, however, should be passed only if they contribute more to the general happiness than the absence of legislation would do. If they fail to serve that utilitarian function, then they should be repealed or replaced.

In such terms the state's existence as the maker and enforcer of laws, and the individual's corresponding obligation to obey those laws, are thus morally justified by utilitarian thinkers. By contrast, other teleological accounts of political obligation – specifically, those based on common good theories – focus on the qualitative question of whether the political arrangements of a community tend to promote the goal of some shared public good. Derived from Rousseau's concept of the general will, such an account is to be found in the political thought of the nineteenth-century English liberal and idealist philosopher T.H. Green (1836–82). Indeed, Green was probably the first political philosopher or thinker to have explicitly used the term 'political obligation', by which he meant:

> the obligation of the subject towards the sovereign, of the citizen towards the state, and the obligations of individuals to each other as enforced by a political superior.[2]

For Green, the state was to be viewed as 'an institution for the promotion of the common good'.[3] In his view, it also provided the political framework within which the individual could pursue the goal of self-realization, which could itself be attained only through each individual willing the common good.

Other 'duty' theories

In addition to these teleological theories, other accounts of political obligation in the history of modern political thought have included theories which stress the view that the individual's obligation stems from a 'natural' duty to obey the state. Prominent among these have been various conservative theories, clearly embodied, for instance, in the writings of Edmund Burke (1729–97), which conceive of political obligation as a natural duty of members of a particular organic community that has developed and evolved over decades or even centuries, shaped and driven by the force of internal institutions, such as the family, church and government, that transcend the lives of individuals.

Moreover, conservative thinkers from Burke onwards have maintained that the political authority of the state is legitimized by the forces of tradition and custom. The state thus has a right, in their view, to make laws, and the citizen has a duty to obey them, because the state, as the maker and enforcer of laws that regulate civil society, consists of institutions that have stood the test of time, demonstrating their enduring practical worth.

At the opposite end of the ideological spectrum, socialist theories of communal duty have since the nineteenth century interpreted political obligation as an expression of the individual assuming his or her share of collective responsibility for the common welfare. Such theories have often rested on the assumption that the state, as the institutional embodiment of the community, is the means of promoting not only its welfare but also the goal of greater equality of both opportunity and outcome.

Limits to political obligation

Anarchist thinkers, including Proudhon (1809–65), Bakunin (1814–76) and Kropotkin (1842–1921), have, by contrast, been at pains to stress the limits to political obligation, rejecting the state's claims to political authority over the individual. They have argued that the state and its laws have arisen without the consent or request of the individual, that they may well operate without moral authority, and that the state is an essentially coercive agency. In such circumstances, anarchists have maintained that individuals therefore have every right to oppose, disobey or even resist the state. However, critics of anarchism have pointed out that, in doing so, those individuals would be relying on their conflicting, and often unreliable, private judgements.

More broadly, many political thinkers have explored the question of where the limits of political obligation may be drawn. At what point, they have asked, may the individual be justified in disobeying the state and its laws? At what point, too, may individuals even be justified in engaging in active rebellion against established state power? Both the English 'Glorious Revolution' of 1688 and the American Revolution of 1776–83 were thus justified theoretically in terms of the idea of the right of rebellion, a notion derived from a theory of conditional political obligation first developed by John Locke in his *Second Treatise of Government* (1690). That theory explained and defended political authority, as we have seen, in terms of the state's duty to protect the individual's natural rights to life, liberty and property. It was later elaborated and amended by Thomas Jefferson in the American Declaration of Independence (1776).

The right to civil disobedience has been concisely defined by Barbara Goodwin as involving 'a principled, purposeful and public disobedience of the law'.[4] It may be considered 'principled', in her view, since it does not merely lead to activity motivated by the pursuit of selfish gain; 'purposeful' because it is a right asserted in order to change particular laws or policies; and 'public' because those who engage in civil disobedience demonstrably aim to create publicity for their cause.

General justification for political obligation

Contemporary political philosophers and thinkers have attempted a general justification for political obligation in light of the evident flaws of both voluntaristic and teleological accounts or theories. We have seen that political obligation is intimately linked to membership of a particular political community. As a concept it is bound up with acknowledging the authority of government and law within that community. In attempting to justify that authority, voluntaristic theories developed since the seventeenth century within the social contract tradition were bedevilled by the unresolved problem of explaining the political obligation of those individuals who simply refuse to consent to the authority of the state and its laws. Teleological theories, on the other hand, particularly of the utilitarian school, too often appeared to have morally dubious implications or consequences. The state's authority could, for instance, be justified on grounds of promoting the general happiness even if it legitimized activities that entailed miscarriages of justice or even victimization of particular groups or individuals.

Nevertheless, the notion of universal political obligations – of, that is, the general duty of individual citizens who reside within the territorial boundaries of a state to abide by its laws and respect the authority of its government – is still widely invoked in modern societies and states as important and valid, in both theoretical and practical terms. One of the most lucid philosophical attempts to underline this point by providing a plausible account of the grounds of political obligation *in general* has been offered by D.D. Raphael, who writes:

> the general obligation to accept the authority of the State depends on the State's pursuit of the moral objectives of justice and the common good.[5]

The individual consequently has a moral obligation to obey the state and its laws since 'state action is an essential means to the pursuit of those ends'.[6] Meanwhile, the authority of the state, Raphael stresses, in turn depends on the consent of the governed.

The *particular* obligation, on the other hand, to obey a specific law, even in the case of an individual's disagreement with, or disapproval of, that law, depends on the convention, widely endorsed in a democratic society, of accepting majority decisions.[7] It might be added that in such a society the acceptance of that convention as sensible and practicable also rests on the understanding that unpopular or controversial laws may in the future be repealed or reversed by constitutional means – a vital democratic safeguard.

Notes

1   See J. Horton, *Political Obligation*, London, Macmillan, 1992, pp. 3ff.
2   T.H. Green, *Lectures on the Principles of Political Obligation and Other Writings* (1881–8), (ed. P. Harris and J. Morrow), Cambridge, Cambridge University Press, 1986, sect. 1.
3   ibid. sect. 124.
4   B. Goodwin, *Using Political Ideas*, 4th edn, Chichester, Wiley, 1997, p. 363.
5   D.D. Raphael, *Problems of Political Philosophy*, rev. edn, London, Macmillan, 1990, p. 205.
6   ibid. p. 208.
7   ibid. pp. 205–6, 208.

SECTION B

Hobbes's theory of political obligation: social contract and security

Historical context: political and intellectual

In examining Hobbes's political thought, and his theory of political obligation in particular, Iain Hampsher-Monk has observed that:

> Ever since Hobbes wrote, the most contentious issues, both in understanding Hobbes's argument, and in assessing its cogency, have been those concerned with his account of the nature and origin of political obligation.[1]

That controversial theory was itself, as we have seen, intimately connected with Hobbes's account of absolute sovereignty. His approach to the problem of political obligation, although developed theoretically by 1640, was thus also influenced by the conflicts and disruptions that characterized the English Civil War of 1642–9.

In propounding his theory of political obligation, Hobbes was mainly concerned with justifying the sovereign authority and security of the modern secular state in the face of pressures from both the Catholic Church and Puritan radicalism. But his political thinking in this area was developed, too, within a distinctive intellectual context – the scientific revolution of the late sixteenth/early seventeenth century which aimed at understanding the world from a strictly empirical point of view. This movement embraced the new Continental European developments in science, particularly the thinking of Copernicus and the method of scientific investigation associated with Galileo.[2]

In his major work of political philosophy, *Leviathan* (1651), Hobbes sought to apply these methods of natural science – particularly of physics – to the study of human psychology and hence to his analysis of politics and government. Specifically he employed Galileo's 'resolutive-compositive' method which involved breaking down complex matter into its constituent parts. In adopting this methodological approach, Hobbes was influenced by the scientific view, advanced by Newton, Galileo and others, that all material reality could be explained in terms of underlying motions or movements of the bodies, or bundles of matter, out of which all physical phenomena are composed. Applying these empirical and materialist assumptions to the political world, Hobbes thus attempted to reduce government to its underlying, elemental motions – namely, social behaviour and ultimately, individual psychology and behaviour.

Hobbes's views of human nature and the state of nature

Hobbes's entire political philosophy, and specifically his theory of political obligation, as set out in *Leviathan*, was rooted in a distinctive view of human nature, which was conceived by him as part of the observable material world. Human beings, their essential characteristics and motivation, were thus regarded in materialist terms as reducible to body and motion. From this perspective Hobbes depicted individual human beings as essentially emotional creatures driven by their desires and physical appetites. All human emotions or passions, he maintained, spring from two basic kinds of motive: desires or aversions. Desires are potential motions or movements towards an object; aversions are potential motions or movements away from an object.

However, while human actions are primarily determined by emotions springing from these motives, human beings are also, Hobbes stressed, combinations of passions (or emotions) and reason. The role of reason, he maintained, is to offer guidance about how best to satisfy one's desires. Moreover, in this view of human nature Hobbes emphasized two overriding emotions. The first of these is fear of death, especially of violent death, which he considered to be a basic psychological and biological disposition inherent in the human condition.

This feeling amounts to an instinct for self-preservation. The second dominant human emotion is the drive for self-advancement. For as Hobbes insists: 'of the voluntary acts of every man, the object is some Good to himselfe'.[3]

However, both these powerful emotions induce, in an unsafe and dangerous world, a human desire for security, which in turn breeds a desire for power of every kind – involving the pursuit of wealth, status and reputation. As Hobbes writes: 'I put for a generall inclination of all mankind, a perpetuall and restlesse desire of Power after power, that ceaseth only in Death.'[4]

Such a condition inevitably generates competition, conflict and mutual mistrust, particularly in the light of the scarcity of goods and resources in the world. And the causes of all these resulting tensions between individual human beings thus lie in the very nature – both fearful and self-interested – of mankind.

From this materialist and individualistic view of human nature stems Hobbes's famous account of the 'state of nature', a concept commonly employed in seventeenth-century political thought. As elaborated by Hobbes, the 'state of nature' emerges as a vivid and disturbing description of what human life would be like without government or legal rules. For him it is a condition that is always lurking beneath the surface of organized, civil society. It is a state in which there are:

> no Arts; no Letters; no Society; and which is worst of all, continuall feare, and danger of violent death; And the life of man, solitary, poore, nasty, brutish and short.[5]

What is more, without any supreme authority to regulate the individual's conduct, the state of nature amounts to 'a warre ... of every man, against every man'.[6] For in such a condition each individual acts like a solitary being, guided by the two basic human urges of survival and self-advancement, and not by any higher moral law. The state of nature is thus a climate in which the natural relationship between human beings is one of mutual suspicion and hostility, which in itself reflects the essential features of human nature.

Hobbes's 'covenant'

This, then, is Hobbes's imaginative depiction not of the actual historical origin of human society but rather of a pre-political condition that lies beneath the veneer of civilization and which is likely, under certain circumstances, to resurface with violent consequences for all concerned. However, the remedy for this amoral and precarious condition lies within our own nature. For in the state of nature each person, Hobbes stresses, has a natural right to self-preservation, using any acceptable means of self-defence. From this one basic 'right of nature', Hobbes derives what he calls the 'laws of nature'; certain rules of conduct shaped by reason and expediency, which human beings should observe in order to stay alive and save their skins.

Of these rules of self-preservation, or 'dictates of reason', Hobbes enumerates, in Chapters 14 and 15 of Part 1 of *Leviathan*, nineteen, of which three in particular are of crucial importance. Of these, 'the first, and Fundamentall Law of Nature ... is, to seek Peace, and follow it'.[7] But in order to seek peace, a second law of nature needs to be observed – namely, that human beings should be prepared to surrender their unlimited right of self-protection in exchange for peace. Finally, through what Hobbes calls a 'covenant', that is, a social contract, individuals should freely agree among themselves to do just that by transferring their natural right to self-protection to a common power, to a sovereign authority vested either in one person or in an assembly, and empowered to act 'in those things which concern the Common Peace and Safetie'.[8]

The third law of nature is, therefore, as Hobbes puts it, 'that men perform their Covenants made',[9] in order to ensure their security and survival. But because individuals are egoistic, mistrustful and self-seeking, they cannot be relied upon to adhere to their original agreement or 'covenant'. For this reason it is necessary, Hobbes argues, for men to authorize a sovereign ruler, equipped with coercive power, to govern them as the only effective way of attaining peace. For as he famously observed:

> Covenants, without the Sword are but Words, and of no strength to secure a man at all.[10]

Like Hobbes's account of the state of nature, his depiction of the 'covenant' is not to be understood here in terms of some actual historical event or condition. Rather, it is presented by him as a general principle employed both to explain the individual's obligation to obey the state and to justify the state's right to make laws and binding decisions.

For Hobbes, then, 'the covenant' or social contract is the very basis of political obligation and hence of legitimate political authority. But what are the further implications of this all-important, collective agreement? First, in Hobbes's distinctive theory, the state, or 'commonwealth', is established directly following a pact among individuals and not on the basis of a contract between the ruler and the people, as in more familiar theories developed in early modern political thought.

Second, the state's authority is legitimate only if it acts in a manner that corresponds to what individuals have agreed among themselves in their 'covenant'. For individuals have contracted out of the state of nature in order that the state may provide peace and security for them.

Third, the 'covenant' confers wide-ranging powers on the sovereign ruler because the individuals who originally made that contract, being 'prudential egoists',[11] judged that it was in their interests not only that a definite person or body should be imbued with supreme authority and coercive power but also that they as subjects should obey that common authority once it was established. In this sense, Hobbes's theory of political obligation is one based on the assumption of long-term, enlightened self-interest and thereby directed at the goal of peace and individual survival.

Fourth, the sovereign is not a party to Hobbes's social contract and therefore cannot be prosecuted for a breach of its terms. For under the 'covenant' individuals have agreed both to forego their natural right to do anything necessary for their self-preservation and to establish the sovereign as their authorized

representative for the purpose of their own protection. But since the original contractual agreement was made between subjects, and not between subjects and
sovereign, then those subjects cannot demand that the sovereign should relin-
quish his powers on the ground that he has breached a contract to which he was
never a party.

But fifth and finally, the individual subject's political obligation is voluntary
and conditional. Hobbes makes it clear that if the sovereign fails to perform his
main duty – to provide security and peace for the individual – the social contract
lapses for two essential reasons. In the first place, the political authority of the sovereign, which derived from the agreement of his subjects, will be undermined if
the sovereign is unable to exercise his power effectively on his subjects' behalf,
just as the authority of an incompetent lawyer would be steadily eroded in the
eyes of his clients. As Hobbes clearly states:

> The Office of the Sovereign ... consisteth in the end, for which he was
> trusted with the Sovereign Power namely the procuration of the safety of the
> people ...[12]

In addition, the subjects' own obligation to obey the sovereign 'is understood to
last as long and no longer, than the power lasteth, by which he [the sovereign] is
able to protect them'.[13] The 'covenant' does not, therefore, irrevocably bind the
individual, who retains the right to shift his allegiance and loyalty for the sake of
his own survival and safety if the sovereign ruler is no longer able to achieve those
fundamental aims. Following the arrest and execution of King Charles I in 1649,
his subjects, including Hobbes himself, were thus free – according to this line
of reasoning – to transfer their political allegiance to Oliver Cromwell and the
Commonwealth as the new source of sovereign authority in England.

Conclusion

Such, then, were the main conditions of Hobbes's social contract, which formed
the basis of a philosophically coherent and innovative theory of political obligation
in the middle of the seventeenth century. Since then Hobbes's varied critics have
tended to direct their fire at three particular characteristics of that theory. First,
they have focused on its underlying individualistic assumptions, which hold that
both civil society and the state and its authority arise from the voluntary undertaking and agreement of separate, independent individuals. This, Hobbes's critics
have maintained, is an essentially misconceived view of the development of civil
society and government. Second, his detractors have also pointed to what they
regard as the unbalanced nature of Hobbes's social contract which emphasizes
both the powers of the sovereign and the obligations rather than the rights of the
subject. Finally, it has been claimed that Hobbes's theory, like the account of sovereignty to which it leads, by vesting such far-reaching powers in the hands of the
sovereign state, has morally and politically unacceptable implications – including,
in particular, the strong possibility of the sovereign's abuse of those powers and
the narrowing of the scope for individual dissent or disobedience.

Each of these objections has some force and validity. Yet each, too, needs to be considered against the historical background that heavily influenced Hobbes's theory of political obligation – namely, that of a society riven by religious and political conflict and convulsed by civil war. Developed within this political context, Hobbes's concerns were thus, above all, with the promotion of peace and the protection of individual human lives. In view of such priorities, it was hardly surprising, then, that Hobbes was intellectually averse to weakening the protective capacity of the sovereign state by placing significant limits upon its political authority.

Notes

1   I. Hampsher-Monk, *A History of Modern Political Thought*, Oxford, Blackwell, 1942, p. 51.
2   On the broader aspects of these seventeenth-century intellectual and political contexts, see R. Berki, *The History of Political Thought*, London, Dent, 1977, pp. 126–32.
3   T. Hobbes, *Leviathan* (ed. R. Tuck), Cambridge, Cambridge University Press, 1996, p. 93 (Part 1, Ch. 14).
4   ibid. p. 70 (Part 1, Ch. 11).
5   ibid. p. 89 (Part 1, Ch. 13).
6   ibid. p. 88 (Part 1, Ch. 13).
7   ibid. p. 92 (Part 1, Ch. 14).
8   ibid. p. 120 (Part 2, Ch. 17).
9   ibid. p. 100 (Part 1, Ch. 15).
10   ibid. p. 117 (Part 2, Ch. 17).
11   Hampsher-Monk, op. cit. p. 54.
12   Hobbes, op. cit. p. 231 (Part 2, Ch. 30).
13   ibid. p. 153 (Part 2, Ch. 21).

Locke's theory of political obligation: social contract, consent and natural rights

Historical context: political and intellectual

John Locke's theory of political obligation, which revolves around the thorny question of the legitimacy of state authority, was conceived against the background of the struggle for succession to the English throne that was waged in the 1680s against King Charles II's Catholic brother, James II, culminating in the latter's downfall in 1688.

Locke was, from 1667, a close associate and leading adviser of Lord Ashley, later Earl of Shaftesbury, a prominent Whig politician and active proponent of the exclusion of the Catholic James from the English throne. After the failure of the Protestant Plot against Charles II, Locke followed Shaftesbury into exile in the Netherlands in 1683, before eventually returning to England in 1689 following the 'Glorious Revolution' of 1688 which overthrew James and established a constitutional monarchy with the accession of William III and Mary II.

In the political struggles of the 1680s the religious issue raised by the existence of a Catholic king, James II, in a Protestant country, though of great significance, was nonetheless subordinate to the even more pressing constitutional issue (which Hobbes had confronted 30–40 years earlier) of the relative authority of King and Parliament – in other words, the problem of internal sovereignty within the English state.

Locke's theory of political obligation, which, like Hobbes's, rests on the notion of a social contract, and is set out in his major work of political theory, his *Second Treatise of Government* (1689), should be regarded as an anti-absolutist Whig theory, offered by him as a justification for resistance to absolute monarchs, to tyrants, and even under certain circumstances, for armed rebellion against them.

Intellectually, too, Locke's theory of political obligation may be seen, like his account of sovereignty as trusteeship,[1] as in many respects a response to – and attempted refutation of – Hobbes's social contract theory. Locke's theory of political obligation thus uses a similar conceptual scheme to that of Hobbes, employing ideas such as a 'state of nature' and, of course, a 'social contract'. But it also advances the innovative and, in its day, radical notion of placing limits on political authority in order to protect and promote certain inalienable natural rights belonging to the individual.

Originally formulated in about 1680, but not published in the *Second Treatise of Government* until 1689, Locke's theory was also designed to replace Sir Robert Filmer's theoretical defence of absolutist monarchy, set out in his *Patriarcha* (1680) essentially in terms of the doctrine of the divine right of kings – a traditionalist position which Locke challenged and repudiated in his *First Treatise of Government* (1689).

Locke's view of the state of nature

In his methodology as well as in his theory of knowledge, Locke, like Hobbes, was both materialist, explaining reality in material terms, and empirical, using observation and experience as the basis of human knowledge. Like Hobbes, too, Locke rejected, as has been noted, the doctrine of the divine right of kings as a theoretical basis for the individual's obligation to accept state authority. Unlike Hobbes, however, Locke argued against absolute sovereignty, asserting instead the liberal principle that the government's power over the individual should be limited.

In developing this more conditional theory of political obligation, Locke rooted it firmly, as Hobbes had also done, in his conception of a pre-political 'state of nature'. For Locke, however, this was a condition in which human beings as creatures of God enjoyed certain fundamental natural, that is, pre-social and pre-political, rights and fulfilled certain corresponding natural obligations prior to the formation of civil society and government. More specifically, in this state of nature each individual, according to Locke, has a natural right to life, liberty and property, and hence a right to be free from violent death, from arbitrary restrictions on his person and from theft of his property. Furthermore, such rights are inviolable; for since their existence precedes all forms of social and political organization, they may not be removed through the individual's interaction with organized society.

Locke explained this point further by stating that the state of nature was governed by the law of nature, that is, reason, which 'teaches all Mankind . . . that being all equal and independent, no one ought to harm another in his Life, Health, Liberty or Possessions'.[2] For in Locke's view, human beings are rational creatures capable of discovering and obeying certain moral truths about good and bad, right and wrong, and hence of following certain rules of moral conduct in their dealings with one another. As rational creatures individual human beings are thus capable, too, of realizing that in dealing with others, they ought to treat them as free, independent and equal; for all human beings in the state of nature are equally concerned with preserving their lives, liberties and property.

Unfortunately, however, Locke stressed, the state of nature did hold certain dangers. These were not, as in Hobbes's view, the constant risks of anarchy and chaos, but rather those of a condition in which there was no written law with fixed penalties but merely an unwritten code of conduct, and no established and impartial magistrates or judges. In the absence of these structures of authority, individuals would rely on their own private and arbitrary judgements in interpreting and enforcing the law of nature, even exercising their right to impose punishments for that purpose. The ensuing climate of uncertainty would be one, Locke feared, in which peace, order and ultimately individual security and freedom would all be placed in jeopardy.

Locke's two-stage social contract

Such a situation, Locke argued, called out for the assertion of the political authority and power of civil government, which alone could establish that orderly process of making and executing laws and imposing penalties that was absent from the state of nature yet necessary for the protection of the individual's natural rights. In order to bring about this state of affairs individuals should therefore be prepared to give up their right of interpreting and enforcing the law of nature. They should also be willing to obey a civil government, which for Locke meant government in accordance with the principles of reason, and hence with the 'law of nature'. Such a government would be entrusted with the political authority to enforce this law of nature, thereby defending the natural rights of individuals.

In tracing the origins of political obligation in this manner, Locke appears to suggest that this process really requires the establishment of two stages of a social contract. The first stage is formed on the basis of a unanimous decision by all individuals to institute a political society. In making that commitment, those individuals volunteer to surrender some of their own liberty in order to secure order and stability. The second stage of the contract rests on an agreement of trust between civil society and government whereby the individuals who comprise civil society undertake, on the basis of a majority decision, to entrust government with a range of legislative, executive and judicial powers. In effect, this means that individuals transfer to government the right and power to make, interpret and enforce the law of nature.

The overriding purpose of both stages of this social contract is to provide more effective protection of the natural rights to life, liberty and property which the individual citizen enjoyed before the establishment of civil government. The wider implications of Locke's two-stage social contract theory are thus, first and foremost, that the individual's obligation to obey civil government is conditional. For his obedience depends upon the government fulfilling its side of the contract – namely, the protection of the individual's rights. After all, civil government in Locke's view exists for the benefit of the governed. It holds its power in trust from the people to govern them well.

Locke's social contract theory therefore also implies that the authority and power of government are limited by its central underlying purpose – to respect and defend the natural rights of the individual. That primary duty on the part of government is, in turn, complemented by the individual citizen's obligation to respect and obey legitimate laws.

Finally, Locke's theory even implies that if government fails to discharge its responsibilities to its subjects, or abuses those powers in an oppressive or tyrannical manner, or rules without obtaining the consent of the governed, then under all those circumstances the individuals who form civil society may exercise their right of rebellion, removing their rulers without actually dissolving civil society itself.

Locke's notion of consent

At the heart of both these stages of Locke's social contract lies his central notion of consent. For Locke this is both the basis of legitimate political authority and the necessary condition of political obligation since:

> Men being ... by Nature, all free, equal and independent, no one can be put out of this Estate, and subjected to the Political Power of another, without his own Consent.[3]

Locke points out that consent, involving the individual's deliberate free choice or decision, is central to the first stage of the social contract: the undertaking by individuals in the state of nature to establish a political society. Locke thus underlines the fact:

> That all Men are naturally in that State, and remain so, till by their own Consents they make themselves Members of some Politick Society.[4]

The second stage of the social contract, involving the collective agreement to institute civil government, rests on the consent of individuals since it derives from an agreed need for 'an established, settled, known Law, received and allowed by common consent to be the Standard of Right and Wrong'.[5]

In seeking to define this central notion of consent, Locke introduces a rather unclear distinction between what he refers to as tacit and express consent. In his view, tacit consent made an individual subject to the laws of a country as long as he remained within its boundaries. It applied to anyone who inherited his father's property, or who owned land within the territory of the state, or even who travelled freely on the highway. By contrast, express, or explicit, consent conferred on an individual full membership of a society will all the corresponding rights and duties attached to that status. Furthermore, Locke stressed that the individual's express consent was required by the state whenever it sought either to confiscate property or to levy taxes.

Locke's distinction between these two forms of consent has usually been regarded by political theorists and historians of political thought alike as problematic and unconvincing. As John Plamenatz, for example, pointed out, Locke introduced into his argument both 'an impossibly stringent and narrow sense of consent' – express or explicit consent – and 'a uselessly wide one'[6] – tacit consent, an elastic notion that appeared to encompass practically anything that the individual could not do safely or conveniently without the assistance of government. What, however, Locke was probably trying to bring out with the aid of this unhelpful conceptual distinction was the important contrast between, on the one hand, the individual's mere subjection to political authority in return for protection of his natural rights and, on the other, his active membership of a particular political society.[7]

Conclusion

In broader political terms, Locke did not try to link his notion of consent with any theory of parliamentary representation. Nor, for that matter, did he maintain that the existence of an elected representative assembly was a precondition of government by consent. Instead, he simply maintained that it was, above all, the consent of the governed that provided the sole basis of legitimate political authority and power.

The true significance, then, of Locke's notion of consent is that the foundation of his theory of political obligation lay in the way it focused attention on the need to justify a ruler's political authority, his right to govern, making laws and policy decisions. The emphasis on the individual's consent thus led in Locke's political thought to a concern less with the obligation of subjects and more with the duties of the rulers of civil societies. Ultimately such a concern even gave rise to the doctrine of the right of resistance to arbitrary or oppressive rulers. Historically, that was the most important ramification of Locke's theory of political obligation – a social contract theory based on the notion of individual consent – which eventually provided the intellectual justification for the overthrow of the absolute monarchy of James II in the 'Glorious Revolution' of 1688 and subsequently for the establishment in England of a constitutional monarchy.

Notes

1   See Chapter 1A.
2   J. Locke, *Two Treatises of Government* (ed. P. Laslett), Cambridge, Cambridge University Press, 1988, p. 271 (*Second Treatise of Government*, Ch. 2, sect. 6).
3   ibid. p. 330 (*Second Treatise*, Ch. 8, sect. 95).

4   ibid. p. 278 (*Second Treatise*, Ch. 2, sect. 15).
5   ibid. p. 351 (*Second Treatise*, Ch. 4, sect. 124).
6   J. Plamenatz, *Man and Society*, Vol. 1 (revised by M.E. Plamenatz and R. Wokler), London, Longman, 1992, p. 352.
7   For further discussion of this point, see M. Lessnof, *Social Contract*, London, Macmillan, 1986, p. 66.

Rousseau's theory of political obligation: the general will and an ideal social contract

Historical context: political and intellectual

In elaborating his own theory of political obligation, Rousseau – sensitive to the developing tradition of Western political thought – retained the concept of the social contract which had been employed by both Hobbes and Locke in the seventeenth century. But his distinctive version of the social contract lacked any conception of government as a party to such a contract since, for Rousseau, government was merely the agent of the people and possessed no independent power. Moreover, Rousseau's own theory, set out in his major work of political philosophy, *The Social Contract* (1762), was inseparable from his depiction in its pages of an ideal social and political order, radically different from the illiberal and unequal European societies of his time.

In *The Social Contract*, civil society was therefore presented not as an aggregate or loose collection of separate and self-seeking individuals, but rather as a community of interdependent citizens. Rousseau's view of the primary importance of community – which for him represented the highest moral value and therefore a collective good transcending the private interests of its members – was thus in sharp contrast to the individualism of Hobbes and Locke, who viewed societies as entities both derived from the individuals who composed them and designed to protect the interests of those individuals, including, in particular, their security, liberty and property.

In spite of its innovative nature, Rousseau's theory of political obligation may nonetheless be regarded as 'the culmination of one major phase of the social contract tradition'[1] which had spanned the seventeenth and eighteenth centuries in European political thought and had attempted to analyse the origins and legitimacy of political authority in terms of a contract involving those subject to that authority. For Rousseau the conditions of political obligation and hence of legitimate political authority are based on the terms of the social contract set out by him in his masterwork of political philosophy, which sought to challenge the European *ancien régime* of the 1760s. Indeed, that book's very title, *The Social Contract*, indicated his awareness of the tradition of Western political thought within which he was writing and to which he was thereby actively contributing.

Like Hobbes and Locke before him in England, Rousseau was concerned both with the problem of striking a balance between individual freedom and state authority and with the need to establish the grounds of political obligation. However, Rousseau's attempted solution to these problems was rooted in his conviction that there was no necessary conflict between individual freedom and state authority since the individual was to be regarded as a citizen who was thus an active member of the state.

Furthermore, unlike Hobbes in *Leviathan*, Rousseau was not really engaged in explaining why it is clearly in the individual's interests to obey established government. Nor did he attempt, as Locke had done in his *Second Treatise of Government*, to define the limits of political obligation in actual, existing states. Instead, Rousseau's *The Social Contract* described the ideal to be pursued, the kind of hypothetical social and political conditions that would reconcile individual freedom with both social order and state authority.

In *The Social Contract*, Rousseau was therefore preoccupied with the notion of an *ideal*, rather than actual, historical contract; in other words, with how government and political authority *ought* to have been established, rather than with how they actually were established, before the development of civil society with all its social and economic inequalities. Through the lens of this idealized social contract, which stipulated the conditions of legitimate political authority, Rousseau thus offered a vision of a future society that provided both a yardstick for judging existing social and political institutions and a goal to be aimed at in plans for social and political reform.

Rousseau's ideal social contract

In developing his view of an ideal social contract, Rousseau contrasts it sharply with what he regards as the illegitimate social contracts that had originally preceded the development of the corrupt, unequal civil societies of his day. Such contracts, Rousseau argues, had in effect legitimized the gross inequalities of condition that disfigured those societies, thereby institutionalizing the rule of the powerful and rich over the weak and poor. The real basis of early modern societies in Europe had thus not been a contract in any meaningful sense but rather the exercise of force and deception.[2]

For Rousseau, therefore, 'the fundamental problem' of political philosophy, to which he believed his ideal social contract 'provides the solution',[3] was:

> To find a form of association that will defend and protect the person and goods of each associate with the full common force, and by means of which each, uniting with all, nevertheless obey only himself and remain as free as before.[4]

This 'fundamental problem', in Rousseau's view, thus involved the search for a social and political order that would provide all the benefits of human co-operation and community whilst respecting the freedom and autonomy of the individuals who made up such a community. The proposed 'solution' to the problem lay in a radical social contract theory that would seek to reconcile individual freedom with social order by conferring sovereign authority upon the community as a whole.

Rousseau therefore maintained that this desirable 'form of association' could be created only by a process of contract or agreement between free individuals in which they would be prepared to give up their 'natural liberty' – their freedom, that is, which they had enjoyed before the formation of civil society, to satisfy basic and immediate human needs – in exchange for the 'civil freedom' to be secured through their participation as citizens in the life of the community.

This collective agreement, moreover, would require the 'total alienation of each associate with all of his rights to the whole community'.[5] Such a process would depend upon each individual's willingness to be subject to the sovereign authority of the community. But it would also entail each person retaining a legitimate share of that authority as a freely participating citizen, with an equal voice in the legislative process. Only thus, Rousseau argued, would a situation arise in which 'each, uniting with all' would 'nevertheless obey only himself and remain as free as before'.[6]

Rousseau's concept of the general will

The key to understanding the true meaning of this idealized social contract lies in Rousseau's concept of the 'general will', which lies at the heart of his theory and is central to his conception of a co-operative social and political order. Rousseau states that the process of contracting by individuals, the 'act of association' between them, 'produces a moral and collective body'[7] in the form of a popular legislative assembly in which each individual citizen participates. Moreover, this popular assembly acquires a collective or general will (or purpose) of its own, which both embodies and transcends the individual wills (or purposes) of its members. For Rousseau the essential core of his ideal social contract is a condition in which:

> Each of us puts his person and his full power in common under the supreme direction of the general will . . .[8]

Rousseau elaborates this point further by observing that the general will is not simply the will of the majority, since that grouping may well be fallible whereas, in his view, the general will is always infallible. Nor does the general will amount to the will of sectional interests in society, what he calls 'partial wills'. Rather, he insists that the general will is discovered whenever citizens, voting after discussion and debate in the popular assembly, support a policy directed at the common interests of the community as a whole rather than at the special interests of powerful individuals or groups.

For Rousseau, then, the general will is aimed at the common good. It arises when each person within the community thinks and acts not as a self-interested individual but as a public-spirited citizen who takes into account, on the basis of reason, emotion and experience, which policy would produce the most desirable outcome for all concerned.

In order to bring about a situation in which the general will promotes the common good, Rousseau maintains that the general will 'must be so in its object as well as its essence'.[9] By this he means that the general will must give rise to policy decisions and laws that affect all citizens equally rather than just particular individuals or groups. In this way no citizen will have any reason to vote for an unjust or discriminatory or oppressive law since each person will be equally affected by all laws passed by the popular assembly.

Rousseau further contends that the common good is both the proper aim of each individual citizen and the real object of his desires – what, that is, he would truly wish for if he had complete foresight about the likely consequences for the community of various policy decisions. For those reasons Rousseau believed that the self-interest of each individual and the public interest of the community could be reconciled and that, as a result, the historic problem, in political theory and practice, of the conflict between individual freedom and collective authority could at last be resolved.

Rousseau's ideal social contract thus revolved around the concept of the general will, his major contribution to Western political thought. For the process that underlay his proposed contract – the establishment of a sovereign assembly in which each individual citizen participated – was designed to produce laws and policy decisions, binding on all citizens, that reflected the general will of the community. That, in turn, gave rise in his theory to the notion of government as 'an intermediate body established between subjects and Sovereign so that they might conform to one another'.[10] The main duty of government, as a subordinate element in the constitution, was thus, in Rousseau's view, to execute the laws reflecting the general will that had already been passed by majority decision in the sovereign assembly.

Since, therefore, government should be based on the expression of the general will, that provides for Rousseau the sole ground of political obligation, the only justifiable basis for the individual obeying the state and its laws, which should, after all, be concrete reflections of the general will. The individual citizen ought, then, Rousseau stresses, to obey the state and its laws and, indeed, really wishes to do so since it is his real 'will', as long as he thinks and acts in a public-spirited manner, as a citizen who takes into account the common good rather than just private or sectional interests.

The community may therefore even be justified in coercing an individual who refuses to obey the state's laws. For a necessary condition of the social contract is 'that whoever refuses to obey the general will shall be constrained to do so by the entire body; which means nothing other than that he shall be forced to be free'.[11] In this much-quoted and notorious passage, Rousseau was contending that, in forcing a dissident individual to obey the law, the community would really be protecting his real interests. For in disobeying a law that reflects the general will of the community, the individual's actions are determined by his private desires or impulses, by, that is, his selfish or 'particular' will rather than by his 'real' will, which is directed at promoting the common good or public interest. Such an individual has thus become unable, through either selfishness or short-sightedness, to recognize that the general will of the community actually coincides with his 'real' will as a public-spirited citizen and thus embodies his real interests.

Rousseau depicts those interests as involving, too, the attainment of both civil and moral freedom – the great benefits that the individual derives from the social contract.[12] By 'civil freedom' is meant the ability of each individual to play an equal part in the law-making process of the community and subsequently to obey laws which he has helped to make. As Rousseau points out:

What man loses by the social contract is his natural freedom ... what he gains is civil freedom and property in everything he possesses.[13]

The individual also gains 'moral freedom' as a result of the social contract – by which Rousseau means the ability to live according to one's 'higher' social self rather than one's 'lower' private self, in other words, the ability to think and act in terms of the common good rather than being enslaved by narrow personal impulses and desires. According to Rousseau, it is freedom in this moral sense 'which alone makes man truly the master of himself; for the impulsion of mere appetite is slavery, and obedience to the law one has prescribed to oneself is freedom'.[14]

Conclusion

Important objections have been levelled by Rousseau's critics at this aspect of his social contract theory and at what they regard as its authoritarian or even totalitarian[15] implications. Unlike Locke, for example, Rousseau did not appear sensitive to the possibility that the individual could be oppressed by a sovereign assembly exercising its collective authority through majority decisions that might enable the community to compel that individual 'to be free'. Nor did Rousseau seriously consider the equally strong possibility that genuine differences of opinion might well exist about what constitutes the common good.

Equally questionable are other key assumptions that underlie Rousseau's theory – for instance, his absorption of the individual in the organic collective body of the community, and his identification, too, of the general will with the individual's 'real' will and interests, which allowed him to disregard the need for guaranteed rights for the individual in relation to the community.

In making these critical observations, the special conditions stipulated by Rousseau as necessary for fulfilling the general will, and thereby for realizing his ideal of popular sovereignty,[16] need, of course, to be borne clearly in mind. These include, in particular, the existence of a small-scale, decentralized state and the absence within its boundaries both of intermediate associations and of gross economic inequalities.

Ultimately, therefore, Rousseau's theory of political obligation, rooted in his idealized social contract and his concept of the general will, aimed to describe a hypothetical, ideal social and political order clearly distinct from the practice of actual states in the eighteenth century. His ideal society would be one that would reconcile the desire for individual freedom with the need for the collective authority of a unified and cohesive community and its political institutions. In attempting to strike such a balance, Rousseau's theory arguably eroded the individuality of each member of that community in a number of significant ways. But it did at least address in a radical and innovative manner the central problem that had dominated Western political thought since the gradual emergence in Europe of the modern territorial state in the sixteenth and seventeenth centuries.

Notes

1 M. Lessnof, *Social Contract*, London, Macmillan, 1986, p. 2.
2 See J.-J. Rousseau, *Discourse on the Origin of Inequality* (1755), Part II, in Rousseau, *The Discourses and Other Early Political Writings* (ed. and trans. by V. Gourevitch), Cambridge, Cambridge University Press, 1997, p. 173.
3 J.-J. Rousseau, *The Social Contract and Other Later Writings* (ed. and trans. by V. Gourevitch), Cambridge, Cambridge University Press, 1997, p. 50 (Book I, Ch. 6).
4 ibid. pp. 49–50 (Book I, Ch. 6).
5 ibid. p. 50 (Book I, Ch. 6).
6 ibid. pp. 49–50 (Book I, Ch. 6).
7 ibid. p. 50 (Book I, Ch. 6).
8 ibid.
9 ibid. p. 62 (Book II, Ch. 4).
10 ibid. p. 83 (Book III, Ch. 1).
11 ibid. p. 53 (Book I, Ch. 7).
12 See Chapter 3B for further discussion of Rousseau's concept of freedom.
13 Rousseau, *The Social Contract and Other Later Writings*, pp. 53–4 (Book I, Ch. 8).
14 ibid. p. 54 (Book I, Ch. 8).
15 For the classic statement of this critical view of Rousseau's theory, see J.L. Talmon, *The Origins of Totalitarian Democracy*, London, Secker and Warburg, 1952.
16 See Chapter 1B.

SECTION C

Contemporary debates

The historical development of Western political thought after 1918, and particularly after 1945, was marked by a sharply reduced emphasis upon the problem of political obligation and indeed upon other normative questions concerning the purposes of government and the state.

This was largely because both voluntaristic theories of political obligation – based on the idea of a social contract – and teleological theories as well – based mainly on the notions of a general will and a common good – were attacked and rejected during this period by philosophers, and later by political scientists, who largely adhered to the school of logical positivism.

Highly influential since the 1920s and 1930s, and pursued by philosophers such as Bertrand Russell, G.E. Moore and A.J. Ayer, this was a philosophical approach which held that all propositions should be analysed into statements that could be verified by experience and observation. Logical positivism therefore rejected as metaphysical nonsense political questions or statements based on what were judged to be fictitious notions such as 'social contracts' or 'general wills' because they were lacking any empirical basis.

As a consequence, the problem of political obligation, since it invoked such abstract notions, was widely dismissed by positivist philosophers as largely meaningless. Since it focused, too, on the question of why the individual should obey the state *in general*, rather than *particular* regimes or laws, political obligation was also viewed by positivist philosophers and political scientists, especially in the

1950s and early 1960s, as itself an absurdly general problem. Instead they preferred to direct their attention to specific practical problems concerning the obligation to obey or accept particular states or laws or policies. Those problems alone were seen as amenable to empirical investigation and hence as meaningful and fruitful areas of enquiry.

However, as logical positivism, together with its characteristic method of linguistic analysis, concerned with the clarification of concepts, declined in appeal from the late 1960s onwards, so the revival of political philosophy, with its underlying concern with normative questions, in turn led to a resurgence of interest in both the general problem of political obligation and its related, contentious issue of civil disobedience.

John Rawls's major work, *A Theory of Justice* (1971), commonly regarded as having played a major role in sparking the revival of normative political theory, thus employed a novel form of social contract theory. While Rawls's main preoccupation in that work was with the notion of social or distributive justice, and with the role of the state in promoting that ideal, he nonetheless sought to combine his theory of justice with his own account of the nature and extent of the individual's political obligation. In this manner Rawls was thereby both building on a 300-year-old tradition of modern political thought and suggesting possible forms of future reflection on this enduring problem of Western politics.

Further reading

Among the most useful general introductions to the problematic question of political obligation are:

J. Horton, *Political Obligation*, London, Macmillan, 1992 (provides a sound historical account of theories of political obligation expounded by some leading figures in the history of modern political thought).

M. Lessnof, *Social Contract*, London, Macmillan, 1986 (provides extended historical discussion of theories of political obligation developed within the social contract tradition).

A.J. Simmons, *Moral Principles and Political Obligation*, Princeton, Princeton University Press, 1978 (critically examines several theories of political obligation).

See also:

J. Dunn, *Political Obligation in its Historical Context*, Cambridge, Cambridge University Press, 1980.

R. Flathman, *Political Obligation*, New York, Atheneum, 1972.

L. Green, *The Authority of the State*, New York, Wiley, 1979.

M. Menlowe, 'Political Obligation', in R. Bellamy (ed.), *Theories and Concepts of Politics*, Manchester, Manchester University Press, 1993.

J. Plamenatz, *Consent, Freedom and Political Obligation*, 2nd edn, Oxford, Oxford University Press, 1968.

Liberty

Liberty – or freedom, which are usually treated as synonymous in theoretical discourse (they are two words for the same concept in the English language) – has been a central concept and area of debate in modern political thought for over 300 years. As John Gray has pointed out:

> There is a conception of liberty at the heart of every well-developed political theory in the Western tradition.[1]

Liberty, or freedom, has at the same time been an enduring value and ideal in Western political systems and societies.

Liberty is also, however, not just a deep-rooted concept but also a highly ambiguous, emotive and commendatory term widely invoked by both political thinkers and politicians to justify a wide variety of regimes or policies. In both political theory and practice there has consequently been a long-running debate about the nature and precise meaning, or meanings, of liberty or freedom. There has been considerable dispute, too, about the different conceptions, or interpretations, of the concept of liberty, and indeed even about whether there is more than one concept of liberty itself.

For these reasons, it has sometimes been argued that liberty, like sovereignty, is what philosophers refer to as an 'essentially contested' concept, one that is subject to endless and inconclusive debate about its essential core meaning, conducted by the advocates of competing accounts of liberty. Since liberty is a value-laden term, each of those accounts in turn rests on certain prior moral or ideological assumptions, on certain preconceived views either about human values or about how the ideal, or least undesirable, society ought to be ordered. Indeed, as Tim Gray has observed, there has been so much dispute over the meaning of freedom because 'people often seek to define freedom in such a way as to accommodate their differing views on society and human values'.[2]

Throughout the history of modern political thought, different political thinkers have been not only advancing their own preferred theoretical accounts of freedom, developed within distinctive philosophical and ideological traditions, but also critically evaluating other competing accounts or interpretations of freedom. A long-running theme in these accounts of liberty or freedom has been the realization that absolute freedom is both unattainable and undesirable in an ordered society, and that there must be certain agreed limitations on individual freedom. Indeed, without the imposition of such limits, liberty, it has been widely acknowledged, degenerates into license, the abuse of others' liberty that arises from one individual's unlimited freedom of action.

Moreover, there has also been a widespread recognition among political thinkers, since Hobbes and Locke in the seventeenth century, that in an ordered society a conflict between individual freedom and state or collective authority is a constant reality, and that it is therefore impossible for complete freedom and complete authority to coexist. In the case of Hobbes, his deep-seated fear of anarchy led him to advocate the assertion of the supreme power and authority of the centralized, unified state. This would in turn entail, in his view, a severe curtailment of individual freedom in many areas of conduct. By contrast, Locke argued that constitutional checks and limits should be placed on the powers of the state in order both to protect individual freedom and to preclude the danger of dictatorship.

Historical development of the concept: different traditions of interpreting liberty

In the twentieth century the eminent historian of ideas, Isaiah Berlin (1909–98) attempted to distinguish between what he depicted as 'positive' and 'negative' concepts of liberty in the history of political thought. In his celebrated and highly influential essay, 'Two Concepts of Liberty' (1958), he examined past accounts of liberty, outlining the similarities and differences between them. He also sought to analyse and evaluate the two different concepts of liberty as they had been developed by different political thinkers, whilst at the same time advancing his own compelling argument for the superiority of the concept of negative liberty.

Berlin's analysis provides a useful and coherent framework within which different conceptions, or interpretations, of liberty, and different traditions of thinking about liberty, may be examined. Indeed, recognizing the intellectual influence exerted by this conceptual distinction, John Gray has considered that it has provided both 'the dominant theme in recent reflection on liberty' and 'the focal point in post-war discussion [of liberty] in analytical political philosophy and in the history of political ideas'.[3]

Among those different traditions of thinking about liberty that can be incorporated into Berlin's analysis, probably the two most influential over the last 350 years or so have been the liberal and idealist schools of thought. These have amounted to what David Miller has called 'families of ideas', consisting not so much of cut and dried conceptions of freedom, but rather of 'clusters of ideas held together by a family resemblance among their members'.[4]

The liberal tradition of thought about liberty has been developed in the West over the last 300 years since it was first articulated in the political philosophy of John Locke. It has focused on the idea that liberty, or freedom, belongs to individuals and consists in the absence of constraints on, or interference with, their actions imposed either by the state or by other private individuals. The idealist tradition of thinking about liberty, by contrast, has been developed in modern political thought since its articulation in the political theory of Jean-Jacques Rousseau. It has focused on the idea that liberty, or freedom, is bound up with the internal forces that govern the way in which a person acts. According to this view, liberty thus consists, above all, in the individual's rational self-direction – his capacity for acting according to his 'true', rational desires and beliefs rather than his irrational impulses.

On the basis of Berlin's influential, if contentious, distinction between negative and positive liberty, since 1945 both political philosophers and historians of political thought have analysed various significant accounts of liberty developed within these liberal and idealist traditions. Broadly speaking, the liberal tradition or family of ideas has thus usually been associated with the negative sense of liberty, or 'freedom from', in simple terms, whilst the idealist family has been linked to liberty in its positive sense, or in other words, 'freedom for'.

Berlin defines negative liberty as essentially the absence of constraints on the individual, and specifically the absence of constraints that result from deliberate or intended human coercion – by, for example, the state or by other individuals. It amounts to 'an area within which a man can act unobstructed by others'.[5] In other words, this constitutes what D.D. Raphael has called the 'common sense notion of freedom', implying that someone is free, 'in so far as he is not restrained from doing what he wants to do or what he would choose to do if he knew that he could'.[6]

Moreover, underlying this negative sense of liberty have been two important notions or assumptions. First has been the emphasis in the liberal tradition on the need for privacy – for a clear distinction between 'private' and 'public' realms of human existence. This has been accompanied by the belief that the private sphere – in which individuals are free to act, think and express themselves in ways they choose – should be protected and even enlarged, and that any invasion of an individual's privacy by the state or any other body is an infringement of his/her liberty.

A second assumption underlying the negative sense of liberty, and developed throughout the Western liberal tradition, has been that of human rationality, the belief that individuals have the capacity to make rational and informed choices in life, free from coercion or interference. Furthermore, this process of rational decision-making has been viewed by liberal thinkers as the means by which the individual assumes personal responsibility for his or her life and thereby acquires the opportunity for self-development and self-fulfilment.

In sharp contrast, the positive sense of liberty, broadly related to the idealist family of ideas, was defined by Berlin as concerned with, not 'the area within which the subject – a person or group of persons – is or should be left to do or be what he is able to be, without interference by other persons'[7] (the domain of negative liberty), but rather 'the *source* of control or interference that can determine someone to do, or be, this rather than that'.[8] More specifically, too, positive liberty implies the ability to do something positive or worthwhile by pursuing certain goals or ideals or by exercising certain capacities.

In the history of modern political thought, particularly in the political philosophy of Rousseau, this positive sense of liberty has embraced the notion of rational self-direction and self-mastery – the belief that the individual should have the ability to control his 'lower', irrational self, thereby overcoming the internal barriers to 'true' freedom that lie within the hearts and minds of individuals themselves. Since Rousseau, this notion has been expanded into the idea of the widest possible opportunity for the individual to control the conditions of his life – not just on this personal level of self-mastery, but also, in the political sphere, through the achievement of self-government.

Accounts of 'negative' liberty in the history of modern political thought

Since the seventeenth century, two of the most influential accounts of negative liberty, in the sense defined above by Berlin, have been those of John Locke (1632–1704) and John Stuart Mill (1806–73). In very different historical contexts, both these liberal thinkers defended liberty in the form of a realm of private activity within which individuals should be allowed to live their lives free from deliberate coercion by the state, the church, public opinion or other private individuals in society.

In Locke's political philosophy, liberty in its negative sense is intimately connected to the notion of rights held by the individual against either the state or other individuals. In Locke's account of liberty, developed in his *Second Treatise of Government* (1689), firm emphasis is also placed on the need for a legal framework which can define both the individual's natural right to liberty and his natural obligation to respect the same right in others. For, as Locke argued, 'the end of Law is not to abolish or restrain, but to preserve and enlarge Freedom'.[9]

Writing against the historical background of seventeenth-century England, Locke was concerned in particular with the cause of freedom from the tyrannical rule both of the Catholic Church and of an absolutist Stuart monarchy. More generally, he was preoccupied with the cause of freedom from the constraints of arbitrary and authoritarian governments. By contrast, the nineteenth-century English liberal philosopher, John Stuart Mill, in his essay *On Liberty* (1859), a classic expression of liberal thought, focused his attention on the need for freedom from what he depicted as the stifling effects of public opinion, and hence on the need for freedom from social and moral conformism.

Mill presented his own eloquent case for liberty in this negative sense in terms of a broader argument for freedom of self-regarding conduct – of actions, that is, which directly affect only individuals themselves, including especially freedom of expression in its various forms. Society and the state, he maintained, only had the right to interfere with the individual's freedom in order to protect other citizens from direct material harm – in other words, at the point at which the individual's actions directly injured others. However, Mill also gave this case for negative liberty a firmly positive twist by affirming the value of freedom as a means to the self-development – both moral and intellectual – of each individual.

The negative conception of liberty flourished within the nineteenth-century liberal tradition – not just in the political writings of John Stuart Mill but also within English utilitarian thought (by which he was deeply influenced), as well as in the political theory of the anti-statist philosopher Herbert Spencer (1820–1903) and in the ideas of the classical political economists, prominent among whom was David Ricardo (1772–1823).

Throughout the nineteenth century, this liberal tradition of emphasis on negative liberty had clear ideological implications for the role of the state. For, in the view of classical liberal thinkers, liberty in its negative sense usually required for its protection and promotion a restricted, or even in some accounts minimal, role for the state – both within the economy and in society at large.

This emphasis changed as the Western liberal tradition made the transition from its classical phase (roughly spanning the period from the late eighteenth century to the 1860s) to its revised, social-liberal stage from the 1870s onwards. For against the background of the development of both industrialization and mass democracy, the growth of social liberalism produced new theoretical justifications for state intervention of various kinds. These, however, were usually advanced, by, for example, the liberal philosopher T.H. Green (1836–82), on the ground that the state could promote liberty in its *positive* sense – involving, that is, the opportunity or capacity for self-development.

Nevertheless, in the twentieth century, and particularly after 1945, the classical liberal commitment to negative liberty was revived and extended by a wide range of political and economic thinkers, who have usually advocated both a limited state and a market economy.[10] These have included, notably, the Austrian political thinker and economist, Friedrich von Hayek (1899–1992), the American libertarian political philosopher Robert Nozick, the American market-liberal economist Milton Friedman and the liberal historian of ideas, as already indicated, Isaiah Berlin.

Accounts of 'positive' liberty in the history of political thought

By contrast, the tradition of thought about liberty in its positive sense, which Berlin incisively explored in his 1958 essay, can be traced back to the political philosophy of Rousseau (1712–78). In his major work, *The Social Contract* (1762), the French political thinker maintained that true liberty consisted not in satisfying one's selfish desires or impulses, but rather in obeying a moral law amounting to what he called the general will, or collective view of what is in the public interest. Such a law, Rousseau stressed, was something which individual citizens both made and imposed upon themselves within the framework of participative democratic institutions.

Furthermore, Rousseau maintained that if, after participating in such institutions, an individual citizen found himself at odds with the general will, then that person must really be enslaved by his selfish will and lower self, and therefore not truly free. In such circumstances, Rousseau concluded, the community might well be justified, paradoxical as it might seem, in 'forcing' that anti-social individual to be free.

Rousseau's conception of positive liberty thus focused on the notion of the individual's self-mastery, of his rational control over destructive internal forces. It thereby rested, too, on a view of a divided self – one, that is, composed of both higher and rational, and lower and irrational, dimensions. Such a view has been attacked by Berlin and others as replete with dangerous moral and ideological implications.[11]

It was, however, above all, Rousseau's notion of freedom as rational self-direction, and hence as a condition of the self, that was to shape the development of the idealist tradition of thinking about positive liberty. This was evident in the late nineteenth century in the political thought of T.H. Green. From both an intellectual perspective of philosophical idealism and a political standpoint of social (or 'New') liberalism, Green applied the positive conception of liberty to his examination of contemporary social and economic problems, notably in his lecture, 'Liberal Legislation and Freedom of Contract' (1881).

In developing his own definition of liberty, Green did not, any more than Rousseau before him, actually use the phrase 'positive liberty or freedom'. He did, however, employ the term 'positive', explaining that for him liberty or freedom meant a 'positive power or capacity of doing or enjoying something worth doing or enjoying'.[12] He was concerned with 'freedom in the positive sense: in other words, the liberation of the powers of all men equally for contributions to a common good'.[13]

For Green, freedom thus meant more than the mere absence of restraint or interference. Rather, it amounted to the individual's effective power, and hence opportunity, to act – a power that was too often limited, not just by state legislation, but also by restrictive economic and social barriers, including poverty, unemployment, sickness and disease. In general terms, Green therefore identified 'freedom in the positive sense' both with the achievement of individual self-realization in the face of those barriers and with the pursuit of desirable communal goals in civil society at large.

Within the idealist tradition or 'family of ideas', other nineteenth-century political thinkers developed their own distinctive positive conceptions of liberty which bore a broad family resemblance to Green's. Georg Wilhelm Friedrich Hegel (1770–1831), the German idealist philosopher, had thus already advanced, notably in his major work of political theory, *Elements of the Philosophy of Right* (1821), the ideal of the individual's realization of inner freedom through the identification of his will with that of the state. For, in Hegel's political philosophy, the state is depicted as an ethical, because altruistic, entity that represents an external, public expression of the individual's will and seeks to promote certain common goals.

Under the influence of Hegel's philosophy, the German economic historian and revolutionary socialist thinker, Karl Marx (1818–83) viewed the attainment of liberty as part of an historical process in which the individual would identify with the will of the victorious proletariat, the rising class within capitalist society. In more fundamental philosophical terms, expressed notably in his early writings such as *The Economic and Philosophic Manuscripts* (1844) and *The German Ideology* (1846), Marx also equated individual freedom with the industrial worker's rational control over the process of productive activity. That ideal condition, he stressed, was in stark contrast to the servitude and alienation of the wage-labourers of the capitalist system, who, as a result of their lack of ownership of the means of production, were unable to exert any creative influence over the application of their own labour.

Conclusion

In the next section, particularly when considering the political thought of Rousseau, we shall identify some important objections which Berlin and others have levelled at the positive conception of liberty. In the meantime, we may conclude this introductory account of changing views of liberty in the history of modern political thought by making two pertinent observations. First, it is worth bearing in mind that a full understanding and appreciation of the meaning and nature of liberty requires attention to the ideas and insights of both of the main 'families of ideas', in Miller's phrase, or traditions of thought about liberty – both liberal and idealist – that have been outlined above. Indeed, Miller himself has added a third and older family – a 'republican' one – to this twofold contrast. This tradition of thought, stretching back to the ancient Greek philosophers, embraced an overtly political conception of freedom as a condition of someone who is a citizen of a self-governing community, living under social and political conditions which he has helped to shape.[14] This view of liberty clearly influenced Rousseau's political philosophy, as will be seen later in this chapter.

A second, concluding point worth noting, I think, is that the need to draw upon the insights of both the liberal and idealist traditions of thought about liberty suggests, too, a similar flexibility when considering the main conceptual framework – Berlin's distinction between negative and positive liberty – within which those traditions have often been examined. In other words, it might well be possible to combine both negative and positive elements in a meaningful definition of liberty.

This has certainly been the view taken by a number of political philosophers since Berlin's 1958 essay was published. Gerald MacCallum, in particular, attempted in 1967 to formulate a formal, value-free definition of a single concept of liberty in terms of a 'triadic' relationship. According to this view, all questions or statements about a person's freedom can be analysed in terms of the formula:

X (the agent) is free from Y (the obstacle or impediment) to do or become Z (the objective).[15]

MacCallum and his supporters[16] have maintained that this formula provides a neutral definition of the concept of liberty that is broadly acceptable to those with diverse moral, political and ideological views, who therefore advance very different conceptions, or interpretations, of liberty.

Nevertheless, controversy still rages in political philosophy about what precisely is the nature of the 'Y' variable (the obstacle) in MacCallum's formula. Is it, as in the liberal, 'negative' view of Berlin and others, deliberate human coercion? Or does it, as in the idealist, 'positive' view, also encompass economic or social restrictions?

This problem helps to explain why and how people disagree about the meaning and nature of liberty – not just in abstract philosophical terms, but also with regard to practical social, economic and political issues and concerns. For different conceptions of liberty usually hinge on what are considered to be the most serious obstacles that lie in its path.

The kind of analysis provided by MacCallum and others does, however, at least help to clarify the conceptual links common to various accounts of liberty in the history of modern political thought, in spite of their varied political and intellectual contexts. Such analysis helps, too, to underline differences in the ways in which the constraints on individual freedom have been identified and interpreted in the contrasting traditions of thought about liberty. In the next section we shall consider four different conceptions of liberty drawn from the liberal and idealist traditions – those held by Locke and John Stuart Mill, on the one hand, and by Rousseau and T.H. Green, on the other.

Notes

1   J. Gray, introduction to Z. Pelczynski and J. Gray (eds), *Conceptions of Liberty in Political Philosophy*, London, Athlone Press, 1984, p. 1.
2   T. Gray, *Freedom*, London, Macmillan, 1991, p. 83.
3   J. Gray, op. cit. pp. 4, 6.
4   D. Miller, introduction to D. Miller (ed.), *Liberty*, Oxford, Oxford University Press, 1991, p. 2.
5   I. Berlin, 'Two Concepts of Liberty' (1958), reprinted in *Four Essays on Liberty*, Oxford, Oxford University Press, 1969, p. 122.
6   D.D. Raphael, *Problems of Political Philosophy*, rev. edn, London, Macmillan, 1990, pp. 58, 56.
7   Berlin, op. cit. pp. 121–2.
8   ibid. p. 122.
9   J. Locke, *Two Treatises of Government* (1689) (ed. P. Laslett), Cambridge, Cambridge University Press, 1988, p. 306 (*Second Treatise*, Ch. VI, sect. 57).
10 For further development of these points, see Chapter 3C.
11 Berlin, op. cit. pp. 132–4.
12 T.H. Green, *Liberal Legislation and Freedom of Contract* (1881), reprinted in Miller (ed.), op. cit. p. 21.
13 ibid. p. 23. Berlin later pointed out that the term 'positive freedom' was suggested to him by Green's phraseology. See Raphael, op. cit. p. 63, n. 3.
14 See Miller, op. cit. pp. 2–3, 5.
15 G.C. MacCallum, 'Negative and Positive Freedom' (1967), reprinted in Miller (ed.), op. cit. pp. 100–22.
16 See, for example, T. Gray, op. cit.

SECTION B

Locke on liberty as a natural right

Historical context: political and intellectual

John Locke's conception of liberty has widely been regarded as the precursor of a long liberal tradition of thinking about liberty that has developed in the West over the last 300 years. That tradition has focused, above all, on the idea that liberty, or freedom, belongs to individuals and consists in the absence of constraints on, or interference with, their actions that may be imposed either by the state or by other individuals.

Locke's account of liberty is contained largely in his *Second Treatise of Government* (1689), a work designed to provide a theoretical justification for the assertion of the rights of certain individuals and groups – particularly the propertied interests represented by the English Parliament – in the face of the oppressive and authoritarian actions of the Stuart monarchy headed, first by Charles II and later, from 1685, by his Catholic brother, James II. Furthermore, Locke's *Second Treatise of Government* was conceived against the background of the Exclusion Crisis of 1679–81, which involved an abortive attempt to compel Charles II to exclude his Catholic brother James from accession to the English throne. That crisis was the prelude to a succession of events involving the leading Whig politician, the Earl of Shaftesbury, Locke's friend and patron, in a concerted campaign of sedition against Charles II. The Royalist backlash against this insurrection prompted Shaftesbury's flight to the Netherlands in 1682 and the execution of two of his prominent Whig colleagues, Algernon Sidney and Lord William Russell after the exposure of the Rye House Plot in 1683. Locke joined Shaftesbury that year in exile in the Netherlands, where he was to remain for six years, not returning to England until 1689 in the wake of the Glorious Revolution of the previous year.

Under the political leadership of the Earl of Shaftesbury, Locke had been deeply involved in this Whig movement of opposition to Charles II, one that aimed both to exclude James from the English throne, replacing him with the Duke of Monmouth, one of Charles II's illegitimate sons, and thereby to overthrow an absolutist Catholic monarchy. Indeed, Locke's *Two Treatises of Government*, his masterwork of political theory, was, as Richard Ashcraft has noted, 'the political manifesto of this movement'.[1] Shaftesbury's exile in 1682 and the brutal suppression of the Monmouth Rebellion in 1685 appeared, however, to have undermined the Whigs' campaign of resistance and rebellion – at least for the time being.

The religious issue with which Locke and his political associates were concerned in this struggle involved the need to introduce toleration for non-Catholic dissenters, a particularly urgent cause in a Protestant country ruled after 1685 by a Catholic monarch and, before that, by one with evident Catholic sympathies. This religious concern coexisted, however, with the equally pressing constitutional issue of internal sovereignty with the English state. This centred on the relative political authority of the King and Parliament, and hence on the perceived need to shift the balance of such authority away from the King and towards Parliament, the chief representative body of the English people, either by extending the franchise or, if necessary, even by armed rebellion. Moreover, these religious and constitutional issues were widely seen at the time as intertwined since, with the examples of neighbouring France and Spain in mind, there was a widespread conviction in seventeenth-century England that Catholicism and political absolutism were causally linked dangers.[2]

Locke's conception and account of liberty should therefore be viewed within the political context of these turbulent events and overriding concerns, which were reflected both in his own commitment to the Whig cause of constitutional change and in his close association with the leading figure in that struggle, the Earl of Shaftesbury. Locke's account of liberty should also be considered against the background of the theoretical problems and discourse of his day, which were in turn responses to the political circumstances which he helped to influence.

Within this intellectual context, Locke's view of liberty should in large part be regarded as a theoretical reaction to Sir Robert Filmer's rejection of the 400-year-old tradition of thinking about the natural liberty of man that had been expressed in the ideas of the sixteenth-century English philosopher and theologian Richard Hooker (1554–1600), who in turn had traced his concept of natural law back to the philosophical and theological thought of Sir Thomas Aquinas (1224–74).[3] At the same time, Locke was reacting, too, against Filmer's related charge that Locke's own conception of liberty, which drew upon that natural law tradition, had anarchic implications.

Locke had been spurred already, in his *First Treatise of Government*, to respond to Filmer's invocation of the doctrine of the divine right of kings as a theoretical justification for absolute government. He had thus sought to refute Filmer's traditionalist argument, whilst developing his own defence of limited government and advancing his case for parliamentary sovereignty[4] – both major Whig causes in the political movement of which Locke had become principal intellectual spokesman.

Natural and civil liberty: the distinction and connection between them

In developing his account of liberty, in the *Second Treatise of Government*, in response to these political conditions and concerns, as well as to the theoretical problems and issues that they raised, Locke conceived of liberty, as John Plamenatz observed, 'not as Hobbes had done – as absence of obligation in the state of nature or as the right to do what the law does not forbid in civil society – but as a moral right which it is the duty of governments to protect'.[5] At the outset, therefore, Locke distinguished between two types of liberty: first, *natural* liberty, which man enjoys in the state of nature before the formation of political or civil society; and second, *civil* liberty, which man ought to enjoy in political or civil society under the protection of civil government.

Locke explains this conceptual distinction in these terms:

> The Natural Liberty of Man is to be free from any Superior Power on Earth, and not to be under the Will or Legislative Authority of Man, but to have only the Law of Nature for his Rule. The Liberty of Man, in Society, is to be under no other Legislative Power but that established, by consent, in the Common-wealth, nor under the Dominion of any Will, or Restraint of any Law, but what the Legislative shall enact, according to the Trust put in it.[6]

Locke adds combatively that freedom in civil society is therefore 'not what Sir R.F. [Filmer] tells us, . . . A Liberty for every one . . . to live as he pleases, and not to be tyed by any Laws'. For civil liberty is not, Locke stresses, to be equated in this way with license. Rather, it is the case, he argues, that:

> Freedom of Men under Government, is, to have a standing Rule to live by, common to every one of that Society, and made by the Legislative Power erected in it; A Liberty to follow my own Will in all things, where the Rule prescribes not; and not to be subject to the inconstant, uncertain, unknown, Arbitrary Will of another Man.[7]

It is clear from these extended definitions that Locke's conception of liberty, like his conditional theory of political obligation, was firmly rooted in his notion of a pre-social and pre-political 'state of nature'. For him that was a condition in which all human beings, as creatures of God, enjoyed certain fundamental natural rights and fulfilled certain corresponding natural obligations prior to the formation of both civil society and government.

In particular, Locke believed that in this state of nature each individual had an inviolable natural right to life, liberty and property, and hence a right to be free from violent death, from arbitrary restrictions on his person, and from theft of his personal possessions. For the state of nature, in Locke's view, was governed by the law of nature, a set of objective, universally valid and God-given moral principles that indicated how mankind ought to behave. Moreover, that law of nature was discoverable by human reason and 'teaches all Mankind ... that being all equal and independent, no one ought to harm another in his Life, Health, Liberty and Possessions'.[8]

Among, then, the moral truths derived from the law of nature, truths which human beings as rational creatures are capable of discovering, understanding and observing, is the fundamental principle that, in dealing with other people, they ought to treat them as free, independent and equal, since all human beings are equally concerned with preserving their lives, liberties and property. In referring here to property, it should be noted that Locke uses this term in both a narrow and a broad sense. In the former, more restricted usage, he refers to the exclusive personal use of external possessions which can be sold for money. Property in this narrow sense, in Locke's view, is a precondition of, or means to, liberty since it is a safeguard of personal independence. But he also refers to property in a larger and broader sense as 'life, liberty and estate', thereby encompassing the three fundamental natural rights. Every person, Locke maintains, has 'a Property in his own Person which no Body has a Right to but himself'.[9] In this broader sense, Locke is thus clearly equating property with the natural rights to self-preservation and liberty, the right both to survive and to think and act freely.

For Locke, the law of nature defines these natural rights, and their corresponding obligations, from which natural liberty is derived. In the state of nature the individual's natural right to liberty is limited only by the natural obligation to respect that same right in others. Any further limitation of the individual's natural liberty, Locke adds, requires the consent or agreement of that person who possesses and exercises it.

Furthermore, human freedom, Locke argues, is the product of reason, which enables us as human beings to understand the law of nature and to live our lives on the basis not only of freedom of choice and action but also of respect for others having the right to do the same. A rational understanding of the law of nature thus allows human beings to govern themselves according to a kind of natural morality, peculiar to humankind, which provides the framework within which freedom can flourish.

Unfortunately, however, the state of nature, with its essentially moral and social character, does also involve certain 'inconveniences', as Locke calls them, which arise from two harsh realities. First, the law of nature is an unwritten code, or set of moral guidelines, which might be ignored if at times the powerful passions or personal interests of some individuals are engaged. Second, it is regrettably also the case, Locke observes, that without any recognized common authority to enforce the law of nature, certain individuals might interpret that unwritten code in a subjective, biased manner, becoming judges in their own cases.

As a consequence, the natural liberty of others, and even peace and social order, might well, Locke warns, be placed in jeopardy. The state of nature, which ought to be a state of freedom, would then be characterized instead by a loss of liberty, by a condition in which the individual person would be 'subject to the inconstant, uncertain, unknown, Arbitrary Will of another Man'.[10] At its worst, this situation might even degenerate into a state of war in which arbitrary coercion is imposed on one person by another.

Such circumstances required, Locke argued, the eventual establishment of civil government, imbued with its political power and authority, on the basis of a social contract, founded on trust, which aimed to protect the natural rights to life, liberty and property. Locke thus points out that 'the great and chief end ... of Mens uniting into Commonwealths, and putting themselves under Government, is the Preservation of their Property'.[11] For in his view, the formation of civil or political society, and hence subsequently of civil government, has no other purpose than the preservation of the people's 'Lives, Liberties and Estates, which I call by the general Name, Property'.[12] Here again Locke is thus referring to property in the larger sense, equating it with liberty, with the right to act freely, following one's own will.

This freedom, however, that is established and protected under and by civil government – in other words, civil liberty – is freedom under law. It is not absolute freedom, nor is it, as Filmer had alleged, license, but rather it is freedom circumscribed by certain limits set by law. Locke develops this point, in a famous passage from the *Second Treatise*, stressing the fact that:

> The end of Law is not to abolish or restrain, but to preserve and enlarge Freedom. For in all the states of created beings capable of Laws, where there is no Law, there is no Freedom. For Liberty is to be free from restraint and violence from others which cannot be, where there is no Law.[13]

Freedom from arbitrary coercion by others – the core meaning of Locke's right-based conception of liberty – is thus only a possibility in civil society, he maintains, within a framework of legal rules provided by government. Moreover, since it is designed to preserve individual freedom, that legal framework is one 'that ill deserves the Name of Confinement which hedges us in only from Bogs and Precipices'.[14]

For Locke, then, both the forms of liberty which he distinguishes in the *Second Treatise of Government* – natural and civil liberty – are bounded by law. In the state of nature man's natural liberty is constrained by the law of nature, which defines the natural rights and obligations of individual human beings. In civil society, man's civil liberty is limited by positive laws, which are in accordance with the law of nature, enacted and established by the legislative branch of government. Yet that 'Legislative Power' remains, in Locke's account, founded on consent and limited in its legal competence by the central purpose for which it was set up in the first place – namely, the preservation of the individual subject's natural rights to life, liberty and property.

Locke's defence of religious freedom

Closely related to Locke's concept of civil liberty were the ideas that underlay his defence of freedom of religious belief and practice contained in his *A Letter on Toleration* (1689). This work was written in the face of the perceived threat to the religious freedom of the persecuted Protestant communities of France and the Netherlands that was posed by the absolutist Catholic monarchy of Louis XIV of France.

Locke's argument for religious toleration rested on his view that any political regime that sought to limit the freedom of religious belief and practice was seriously at fault on two grounds. First, it was straying from its proper role of protecting strictly secular human goods and interests. Second, that regime was absurdly and improperly intervening in the personal relationship between the individual and his or her God.

Moreover, any attempt by a political ruler or government to impose religious conformity upon a particular individual or society would constitute, Locke argued, a further breach of the people's trust and this would provide another justification for political revolution. In this respect, Locke's defence of religious freedom, like his account of civil liberty, implied the possible formation of a rational, collective judgement on the part of the people – evident, for instance, during the Exclusion Crisis of 1679–81 – about the occasion for such an uprising.

Locke believed, however, that religious freedom should be withheld from Roman Catholics, whose religious commitments were not only politically subversive in a Protestant country such as England but also involved primary allegiance to the Pope. Locke also considered that the right to religious toleration should not be extended to atheists since, lacking either any religious beliefs of their own or any fear of God, they could not be said to have the religious duties that corresponded to such a right. In addition, for those reasons atheists were, in his view, deprived of any rational basis for moral conduct in civil society.

Central to Locke's advocacy of religious toleration, which thus excluded Catholics and atheists, was his conviction that religious and moral questions were quite separate from political issues – something that Catholic regimes such as those of France and Spain declined to acknowledge. It was the role, by contrast, of civil government to protect both civil and religious freedom, not to infringe the individual's freedom of action without his consent, or, more specifically, to impose certain forms of religious belief or practice, thereby abusing the legitimate powers of government. This clear separation by Locke of civil and political from ecclesiastical authority amounted to an unorthodox and radical departure from the practice of most seventeenth-century European states.

Some historians of political thought, such as John Dunn and James Tully, have maintained that this emotive theme of religious freedom and toleration was central to Locke's political thought as a whole. They have pointed out that his rights-based conception of liberty had a firmly theological foundation.[15] For natural law, itself an expression of God's will, and the natural rights that were based on it, ultimately derived, in Locke's thinking, not from the human condition but from man's relationship with God.

Conclusion

Based on an essentially negative conception of freedom – as the absence of arbitrary coercion of, or interference with, the individual, Locke's account of liberty formed a central part of a political philosophy that had been developed in the early 1680s to provide a theoretical justification for organized political opposition towards, and even armed rebellion against, an absolutist Catholic monarchy in England. The eventual publication in 1689 of that philosophical creed in the form of Locke's *Two Treatises of Government* took place at a defining moment in British political history – the immediate aftermath of the Glorious Revolution of 1688, which for the first time established a constitutional monarchy in England.

The even wider historical significance of Locke's account of liberty, in particular, is that it provided the philosophical foundation of the Western liberal tradition of thinking about its core value – liberty itself. That foundation was securely built since it consisted of an unconditional, rights-based espousal of liberty – one that rested on the belief that all human beings had an unqualified right to liberty by virtue of their humanity.

Moreover, that profoundly influential view of liberty was advanced within the broader theoretical context of what John Plamenatz described as 'the most persistent of European political doctrines, especially in the liberal West' – namely, Locke's advocacy of limited government, based on consent and designed to protect the natural rights of the individual, or in other words, his case for 'power held on trust to secure freedom'.[16] With the support of that doctrine, Locke thus developed and bequeathed 'the first of the great political philosophies to make freedom, conceived in a larger sense than the ability to do what the law allows or what God commands, its central theme'.[17]

Notes

1   R. Ashcraft, *Revolutionary Politics and Locke's Two Treatises of Government*, Princeton, Princeton University Press, 1986, p. 9.

2   See I. Hampsher-Monk, *A History of Modern Political Thought*, Oxford, Blackwell, 1992, pp. 69–71, for further discussion of this point.

3   On Locke's response to Filmer, see J. Dunn, *The Political Thought of John Locke*, Cambridge, Cambridge University Press, 1969, pp. 47–76.

4   See also Chapters 1 and 2.

5   J. Plamenatz, *Man and Society*, Vol. 1 (revised by M.E. Plamenatz and R. Wokler), London, Longman, 1992, pp. 358–9.

6   J. Locke, *Two Treatises of Government* (ed. P. Laslett), Cambridge, Cambridge University Press, 1988, p. 283 (*Second Treatise of Government*, Ch. 4, sect. 22).

7   ibid. pp. 283–4 (*Second Treatise*, Ch. 2, sect. 6).

8   ibid. p. 271 (*Second Treatise*, Ch. 2, sect. 6).

9   ibid. p. 287 (*Second Treatise*, Ch. 5, sect. 27).

10   ibid. p. 284 (*Second Treatise*, Ch. 4, sect. 22).
11   ibid. pp. 350–1 (*Second Treatise*, Ch. 9, sect. 123).
12   ibid. p. 350 (*Second Treatise*, Ch. 9, sect. 123).
13   ibid. p. 306 (*Second Treatise*, Ch. 6, sect. 57).
14   ibid. p. 305 (*Second Treatise*, Ch. 6, sect. 57).
15   See, for instance, J. Dunn, *Political Obligation in Historical Context*, Cambridge, Cambridge University Press, 1980, Ch. 3, pp. 31–2; J. Dunn, *The Political Thought of John Locke*, Cambridge, Cambridge University Press, 1969, Ch. 9; J. Tully, 'Locke on Liberty', in Z. Pelczynski and J. Gray (eds), *Conceptions of Liberty in Political Philosophy*, London, Athlone Press, 1984, pp. 77–8.
16   Plamenatz, *Man and Society*, Vol. 1, p. 377.
17   ibid. p. 378.

Rousseau on moral and political freedom

Historical context: political and intellectual

Rousseau's conception of liberty has often been regarded[1] as the earliest expression of the idealist tradition of thinking about liberty in the history of modern political thought. That tradition, or 'family of ideas', has centred on the view that liberty is essentially a condition bound up with the internal forces governing the way in which a person acts. Liberty thus, in the idealist view, consists in the individual's capacity for rational self-direction – his ability, that is, to act according to his 'true' rational beliefs rather than his irrational drives and instincts.

Rousseau has also, however, been portrayed by historians of political thought as an important regenerator of the republican tradition of thinking about liberty. Stretching back to the ancient Greek philosophers, that tradition has centred on an overtly political conception of liberty as a condition of someone who is a citizen of a self-governing community. According to this view, then, liberty or freedom amounts to a condition of self-government.

In the historical evolution of interpretations of liberty in its social and political aspects, Rousseau, by either bequeathing or drawing upon both of these traditions – idealist and republican – undoubtedly exerted a major influence. As Patrick Gardiner has written:

> It is fair to say that no political theorist has pitched the claims of liberty higher than he, or has insisted more eloquently upon its implications for a proper understanding of man's development and potentialities in a social setting.[2]

Certainly Rousseau helped in the eighteenth century to reshape the terms of the political debate about the nature and meaning of the ideal of liberty by exploring the interrelationship between individual freedom, civil society and the modern state. It should be added, however, that, just as Rousseau's political thought in general has been subjected to conflicting interpretations, so, too, has his view of the political implications of liberty. His account has thus been regarded as part of a wider advocacy not only of a radical, participatory democracy, but also of an authoritarian social and political order.

What, at any rate, pervades Rousseau's thought and writings on liberty is his consistent hostility to restrictions of freedom that arise from the subjection of one individual to another's will, and hence to all relationships of domination and subordination or servitude. This central theme resonates throughout his major work of political philosophy, *The Social Contract* (1762), and is also outlined in his early political writings, notably his *Discourse on the Arts and Sciences* (1750) and his *Discourse on the Origin of Inequality* (1755). It is clear from these works that Rousseau's conception of liberty, which comprises, as we shall see, notions of both moral and civil or political freedom, was advanced, like his related theory of popular sovereignty, as part of a theoretical project for radically transforming and superseding existing eighteenth-century European societies, most of which he judged to be corrupt, unequal and unfree.

Furthermore, like his account of political obligation based on the concept of the general will, Rousseau's conception of liberty was also developed as a central part of his attempt to resolve the deep-rooted tension in Western political thought between the desire for individual freedom, on the one hand, and the need for collective authority and social order on the other. His response to this historic problem sprang from his firm conviction that there was no necessary conflict between those two desired goals since, in his view, the individual was to be considered, above all, as a citizen who was an active member of both the community and the state.

In his major work, *The Social Contract* (1762), Rousseau set out, therefore, to describe the kind of hypothetical social and political conditions that would reconcile the freedom of the individual citizen with the collective authority of the community to which he belonged. Indeed, for Rousseau, as we have seen, the 'fundamental problem' of political philosophy, to which he believed his idealized social contract 'provides the solution',[3] was:

> To find a form of association that will defend and protect the person and goods of each associate with the full common force, and by means of which each, uniting with all, nevertheless obey only himself and remain as free as before.[4]

In other words, the long-running search for an ideal social and political order involved, in Rousseau's view, providing the benefits of human cooperation and interdependence whilst at the same time respecting the freedom and autonomy of the individual. Rousseau's proposed 'solution' to this 'fundamental problem' in turn lay in the formation of a radical form of social contract that would bring those often conflicting objectives into harmony by conferring sovereign authority not upon the all-powerful, unitary state, as Hobbes had urged, or upon a representative assembly, as Locke had advocated, but rather upon the community as a whole.

Moreover, this process of collective agreement which would thereby create the desired 'form of association', so different from existing European societies, would in turn, Rousseau argued, produce a qualitative change in the nature of human freedom. For the individuals involved in Rousseau's idealized social contract would be required to surrender their 'natural liberty' – enjoyed before the formation of civil society and involving the ability to satisfy basic and immediate human needs – in exchange for 'civil freedom', to be enjoyed through active participation as citizens in the life of a radically transformed society.

The erosion of natural liberty

As a political thinker Rousseau has often been interpreted in varied and conflicting terms: as an individualist and as a collectivist, as a radical democrat and as a precursor of totalitarianism. But in spite of such variations, and, indeed, inconsistencies, too, within his own political thought, what is far less contentious is the moralistic character and tone of his reflections on human society and on the role of freedom within it. Rousseau was thus essentially concerned with the moral redemption of human beings from the destructive and corrupting effects upon them of their modern social environment. He maintained that both civil society, with its underlying institutions of private property and the family, and the modern state had enslaved the individual by gradually generating gross inequalities between the rich and poor. Civil and political society had therefore, in his view, been established upon the basis of the entrenched and selfish interests of the rich and powerful. In the famous opening sentence of *The Social Contract*, Rousseau thus declared:

> Man is born free, and everywhere he is in chains.[5]

In his earlier *Discourse on the Origin of Inequality*, Rousseau had argued that, before the formation of civil society and government, natural man, animated both by the instinct of self-preservation and by pity or compassion, enjoyed in a primitive, pre-social state a condition of natural liberty. This amounted to the ability to satisfy certain basic, immediate needs and appetites, whilst not being subject to the will of another person. However, civil society, based on the family, private property, laws and institutions, gradually eroded this natural liberty because it gave rise to, and reinforced, deep inequalities of wealth, status and political power. At a personal level, too, this development involved the transformation of man's natural instinct of self-preservation into the egoistic drive for self-advancement in civil society.

Rousseau described this corrupting and degrading process in these vivid terms:

> All ran towards their chains in the belief that they were securing their freedom; for while they had enough reason to sense the advantages of a political establishment, they had not enough experience to foresee its dangers . . .

> Such was, or must have been, the origin of Society and of Laws, which gave the weak new fetters and the rich new forces, irreversibly destroyed natural freedom, forever fixed the Law of property and inequality, transformed a skillful usurpation into an irrevocable right, and for the profit of a few ambitious men henceforth subjugated the whole of Mankind to labor, servitude and misery.[6]

Nevertheless, Rousseau was convinced that human beings were not born into slavery, but rather had been deceived into accepting oppressive social and political conditions. Indeed, throughout human history, he observed, some men had succeeded in creating free societies of citizens rather than being mere subjects – in ancient Sparta or contemporary Geneva, for example. In *The Social Contract* Rousseau therefore set out to demonstrate how that could be achieved, and how natural liberty, destroyed in most contemporary states, could consequently be transformed into civil liberty. He also aimed to address and answer the question already raised in his *Discourse on the Origin of Inequality* – namely, how that newly-established condition of civil or political liberty, involving man's capacity for self-government, could coexist with the workings of a transformed civil society.

The two aspects of 'true' freedom: moral and civil

There are two aspects of what Berlin referred to as Rousseau's 'positive' view of liberty – defined, that is, in terms of the ability to do something positive or worthwhile. These are, first, *moral* freedom – the individual's capacity for rational self-direction, for acting according to his 'higher' social self and hence in line with his 'true', rational beliefs; and second, *civil* or *political* freedom – the individual's condition of acting as a self-governing citizen, capable of living under social and political conditions that he has helped to mould.

Moral freedom

For Rousseau moral freedom involves the individual's liberation from his selfish and irrational drives and impulses, as well as his subsequent identification with the interests and concerns of his community. Rousseau had ascribed man's corrupted and depraved condition in civil society to the ascendancy of the particular, private will to self-advancement over the general will to public service. In his view, therefore, the remedy for this destructive state of affairs was to encourage the spread of the general will, or collective interest, throughout the whole of society. Only then would the individual be released from the chains of society and attain 'true' freedom. Just as Christians claimed that they achieved spiritual freedom by serving God, 'the service of God' being 'perfect freedom', so Rousseau maintained that the individual attained moral freedom by being in harmony with, and of service to, the community.

For Rousseau, moreover, this harmonious relationship was forged by a number of interconnected processes – by the individual's performance of his moral duty to the community; by his rational control of his personal drives and desires; and by realization of his 'higher' social self, whereby he chose a course of action that promoted the common good, as directed by the general will, rather than what satisfied his private interests. The result of all this would be a condition of rational self-direction and self-mastery, through which each individual acted according to principles laid down by his own reason and conscience.

The essence, then, of moral freedom, in Rousseau's view, was a condition 'which alone makes man truly the master of himself; for the impulsion of mere appetite is slavery, and obedience to the law one has prescribed to oneself is freedom'.[7] Yet for Rousseau such a condition was itself intimately bound up with the public sphere of society and the state, and thus closely connected to the second aspect of his conception of liberty – civil or political freedom, which man comes to enjoy in a radically restructured civil society.

Civil freedom

In seeking to define civil and political freedom, Rousseau thus envisaged a form of social and political organization that would no longer be characterized by relationships of domination and subordination. In a properly constituted state, he believed, individuals would instead live under laws which they imposed upon themselves as participants in a sovereign legislative assembly of political equals. Rousseau saw no inherent conflict between individual freedom and obedience to the law since, in such a state, legal rules would embody and express the general will of the community. Moreover, in obeying laws which they had helped to make, citizens would be subordinate to no external or alien power, but rather would be acting as free members of a self-governing community.

In prescribing this state of self-government, Rousseau employs, like Hobbes and Locke before him, the conceptual device of the social contract to explain the process whereby individual human beings agree to curtail their natural liberty – their unrestricted capacity to satisfy their immediate private needs – and to submit to a higher collective authority. The purpose of this agreement, Rousseau explains, is to reap the benefits – namely, human cooperation and interdependence – that civil society ought, but to date has largely failed, to provide.

As a result of this social contract, therefore, the individual surrenders his natural liberty in exchange for civil and political freedom, a condition of self-government absent from most contemporary European societies. However, this newly-experienced state of affairs depends, Rousseau stresses, upon two inter-related preconditions: first, the individual's voluntary submission to the sovereign authority of the community of which he is a member; and second, his retention of a legitimate share of that collective authority which he holds as a freely participating citizen. Only in such a way would 'each, uniting with all . . . nevertheless obey only himself and remain as free as before'.[8]

Rousseau's conception of civil or political freedom as a capacity for self-government was thus indissolubly linked to his theory of popular sovereignty. It was concerned, therefore, largely with the proper source of legitimate legal and political authority rather than, as in Locke's interpretation of the concept, with the extent and limits of such authority. For Rousseau, moreover, that source was located in the collective decisions of the entire citizen body, rather than in some remote political entity – whether it be a unitary state or a representative assembly.

Rousseau believed that political freedom as he thus envisaged it was most attainable in small, egalitarian communities. It was less realizable in large-scale states. For if a private citizen lived in a state of, say 10,000 citizens, then he contributed a corresponding 1/10,000 share of that state's sovereign authority. But as the overall size of the state increased, so the individual contributed a diminishing share of its sovereign authority. Within a larger state he would therefore become more of a passive subject and less of an active legislator. His civil or political freedom would consequently be steadily eroded.

Within, then, the framework of a small state, characterized both by a broad measure of economic equality and by the absence of intermediate groups or associations, Rousseau argued that political liberty would flourish. Consisting in a condition of self-government, it would require, of course, that citizens should only obey laws that, as participating legislators, they had helped to make. It would require, too, that such laws should truly reflect and express the general will, aimed at the common good of the entire community.

'Forcing' someone to be free

However, if any citizen refused to comply with such laws, then, in Rousseau's view, that person was in effect opposing not just his own 'real' interests but also his 'real' wishes or desires. The community of which he was a member would therefore be justified in compelling that dissident individual to conform to its laws. In doing so, it would actually be protecting his real interests and forcing him to be free – in the sense of enabling him to fulfil his proper functions and obligations as a citizen. As Rousseau explained, in a highly controversial passage of *The Social Contract*:

> whoever refuses to obey the general will shall be constrained to do so by the entire body: which means nothing other than that he shall be forced to be free ...[9]

Rousseau's reasoning here is that, by disobeying a law that reflects the general will, that individual's actions are determined by his private desires or impulses, that is, by his 'particular' and selfish will rather than by his 'real' will, which ought to be directed towards promoting the common good or public interest. That anti-social person has therefore become unable, through either selfishness or short-sightedness, to recognize that the general will coincides with his 'real' will as a public-spirited citizen and thus embodies his 'real' interests.

For Rousseau the individual's recognition of this truth is the key to his attainment of both civil and moral freedom – the great benefits which, along with human cooperation, he derives from the social contract. As Rousseau puts it:

> What man loses by the social contract is his natural freedom ... what he gains is civil freedom and property in everything he possesses.[10]

By 'civil freedom' is clearly meant the individual citizen's capacity for self-government, for playing an equal part in the law-making process of the community and subsequently for obeying the laws which he has helped to frame. At the same time, each individual gains moral freedom through this process of collective agreement. For he achieves, too, the condition of rational self-direction, of living according to his 'higher' social self, the source of his rational, long-term goals, rather than according to his 'lower' private self, the source of his irrational, short-term impulses.

In other words, the morally-free individual is one who, in Rousseau's view, possesses the ability to think and act in terms of the common good instead of being enslaved by his narrow personal desires. It is this capacity, Rousseau stresses, 'which alone makes man truly the master of himself; for the impulsion of mere appetite is slavery and obedience to the law one has prescribed to oneself is freedom'.[11]

Rousseau's entire argument relating to these two intertwined aspects of 'true' freedom – civil and moral – rested on his presupposition that the economic, social and political conditions necessary for the fulfilment of the general will were all present in the transformed civil society that he advocated. Such conditions included, as we have seen, approximate equality of property ownership, a small-scale, participatory society and polity, and the absence of intermediate groups or associations. As Norman Barry has observed, Rousseau's case for 'true' liberty thus did 'not depend upon a naïve altruism, but rather upon democratic institutions being so designed that we have an incentive to impose laws upon ourselves that advance common interests'.[12]

The critique of Rousseau's view of liberty

Much of the critique of Rousseau's conception of liberty has focused on his paradoxical notion that, in order to set the individual free, it may be necessary for the community and the state to apply coercion to that person, thereby forcing him to be free. Rousseau's notion has been widely attacked as not only logically unsound but also politically dangerous since it provides the pretext for a virtually limitless coercion of individuals by dictatorial rulers or regimes.

Certainly some of the theoretical assumptions that underlie Rousseau's view of freedom appear highly questionable. In the first place, his equation of moral freedom with a condition of rational self-direction and even self-mastery rests on the presupposition that there is a proper sphere of human activity that revolves around certain rational, long-term goals or purposes towards which the 'higher' social self ought to be directed. Second, Rousseau's belief that there are circumstances in which the individual citizen should be 'forced' to be free presupposes that political coercion by the state or the community may help to encourage that individual along the path of rational enlightenment. Such coercion might well, according to Rousseau, achieve that end by indicating to the recalcitrant individual, even against his will, ways in which his 'higher' social self rather than his 'lower', private self might be realized.

Yet, as Raymond Plant has pointed out, each of those presuppositions underpins a wider 'moralized' view of liberty that has generally characterized subsequent 'positive' conceptions of liberty – whether formulated by Hegel, Green or Marx – of which Rousseau's own account was the forerunner. Such a view of liberty has in turn rested on two general evaluative assumptions: first, about what constitutes the better, more desirable aspect of human nature – the 'higher', rational self; and second, about what constitutes the morally desirable goals, purposes or capacities that the individual ought to pursue or exercise.[13]

It has been noted, too, that that first assumption about human nature itself raises another contentious philosophical issue. For Rousseau's celebration of the 'higher', social self led him to argue that all actions motivated by short-term personal desires, which derive from the 'lower', private self, were essentially unfree. Yet, as D.D. Raphael argued, human motivation by desire is only in certain extreme circumstances – involving, for instance, drug addiction, compulsive gambling or alcoholism – a form of bondage.

In addition, it has often been objected that Rousseau's moralized view of liberty has dangerous, authoritarian implications. For it rested, as we have seen, on his identification of the individual's 'real' will and interests with the general will and collective interest of the community. Yet that linkage has led in practice to the subsequent identification of the citizen's 'higher', rational goals or purposes with those of collective entities such as the sovereign community, in the case of Rousseau, or the nation, race or social class, in the case of later political thinkers.

This process has, in turn, involved transferring responsibility for defining liberty away from the individual himself to the collective judgement of others. The result has all too often been the submission of the individual to the will of the ostensibly enlightened community or even to the will of a single, all-powerful political leader. From Robespierre in the 1790s to Hitler and Stalin in the twentieth century, such a ruler has thus readily assumed the role not only of articulating and promoting the interests and concerns of the community but also of declaring on behalf of the individual citizen what goals and purposes he or she truly wished to pursue.

Down such a road, as Berlin and others have observed and warned, has occurred the destruction of personal independence and hence of liberty in its 'negative', liberal sense of freedom from arbitrary coercion or interference. Yet regardless of the pernicious ways in which the doctrine of 'positive' liberty has been interpreted by his successors, it is fair to say that Rousseau himself often appeared insensitive to the possible dangers posed by popular legislative assemblies exercising their collective authority by means of majority decision making. Certainly he did not acknowledge, unlike Locke before him, the need to safeguard certain guaranteed rights for the individual in the face of the coercive pressures inherent in the theory and practice of popular sovereignty.

Conclusion

Rousseau's positive view of liberty arose both from his account of political obligation and his corresponding belief that sovereign authority should be vested in the community, in the entire citizen body. These theories were in turn rooted in his idealized form of social contract and his concept of the general will, his major contribution to modern Western political thought. This body of ideas aimed to describe and commend a hypothetical ideal social and political order that was clearly distinct from the practice of actual European states in the eighteenth century. For Rousseau's ideal society and political system would be one based on equality, popular sovereignty and what he considered to be 'true' freedom.

In positing such an ideal, Rousseau developed a radical and innovative approach to the problem that had bedevilled Western political thought ever since the gradual emergence of the modern territorial state in the sixteenth and seventeenth centuries – namely, the need to reconcile the desire for individual freedom with the need for the collective authority of an ordered and cohesive society. His proposed solution to this historic problem involved defining the nature and meaning of freedom in ways that both revived an ancient Greek republican tradition of political thought and fathered a distinctively idealist family of ideas.

In the former case, Rousseau's revival of the republican tradition of thinking about liberty led him to equate the ideal with a condition of self-government, with a set of social and political arrangements which the individual citizen had helped to fashion. By initiating, too, an idealist tradition of thinking about liberty he also sought to equate the ideal with a condition of rational self-direction, and hence with a state of being under the guiding influence of the general will.

Rousseau's notions of civil and moral freedom – the interrelated aspects of his conception of liberty – thus either sprang from, or anticipated, those republican and idealist traditions respectively. With the aid of such ideas he was able to contrast his social and political ideal with contemporary forms of absolute government that either denied or suppressed the opportunity for popular self-government or else sought to stifle, in a climate of submissive conformity, the ability of the individual to order his life according to his own reason and conscience.

But the fervent and collectivist tone in which Rousseau expressed his case for popular sovereignty made him at times inattentive to the risks it created both for individual rights and for personal independence. The ways, too, in which he developed and illustrated his central concept of the general will – particularly with regard to the making of laws without unanimous agreement – tended to undermine his interpretation of civil freedom as the exercise of self-government. Ultimately, then, Rousseau's attempt to transcend, from these republican and idealist standpoints, the earlier individualist 'negative' view of liberty, formulated by Locke and others, appears flawed in a vitally important respect. For his radically different perspective on the nature and meaning of liberty led to him to undervalue the most important feature of the Lockean approach – its emphasis on the need to preserve a sphere of private activity, free from arbitrary coercion, and insulated from the constant threat of the abuse of political power.

Notes

1   See, for instance, I. Berlin, 'Two Concepts of Liberty' (1958), reprinted in *Four Essays on Liberty*, Oxford, Oxford University Press, 1969.

2   P. Gardiner, 'Rousseau on Liberty', in Z. Pelczynski and J. Gray (eds), *Conceptions of Liberty in Political Philosophy*, London, Athlone Press, 1984, p. 83.

3   J.-J. Rousseau, *The Social Contract and Other Later Writings* (ed. and trans. by V. Gourevitch), Cambridge, Cambridge University Press, 1997, p. 50 (Book 1, Ch. 6).

4   ibid. pp. 49–50 (Book 1, Ch. 6).

5   ibid. p. 41 (Book 1, Ch. 1).

6   J.-J. Rousseau, *Discourse on the Origin of Inequality*, Part II, sect. 32 and 33, in *The Discourses and Other Early Political Writings* (ed. and trans. by V. Gourevitch), Cambridge, Cambridge University Press, 1997, p. 173.

7   Rousseau, *The Social Contract and Other Later Writings*, p. 54 (Book 1, Ch. 8).

8   ibid. pp. 49–50 (Book 1, Ch. 6).

9   ibid. p. 53 (Book 1, Ch. 7).

10   ibid. pp. 53–4 (Book 1, Ch. 8).

11   ibid. p. 54 (Book 1, Ch. 8).

12   N. Barry, *An Introduction to Modern Political Theory*, 3rd edn, London, Macmillan, 1995, p. 218.

13   See R. Plant, *Modern Political Thought*, Oxford, Blackwell, 1991, Ch. 6, pp. 221ff.

John Stuart Mill's defence of personal liberty

Historical context: political and intellectual

John Stuart Mill's essay *On Liberty* (1859) was described by the historian of political thought, George Sabine, as 'along with Milton's *Areopagitica*, one of the classical defenses of freedom in the English language'.[1] Certainly it provides one of the most eloquent and celebrated statements of the liberal view of personal liberty within the entire Western liberal tradition. It is hardly surprising, therefore, that, since its publication in 1859, Mill's work has been an essential reference point in subsequent debates in the history of political thought about the nature and extent of personal liberty.

The main concern of *On Liberty* is with the threat to personal liberty posed not so much by authoritarian governments and political regimes as by what Mill considered to be the intolerant and oppressive climate of public opinion in mid-Victorian England. Mill's essay was thus, in Sabine's words:

> an appeal not for relief from political oppression or for a change in political organization, but for a public opinion that is genuinely tolerant . . .[2]

These preoccupations, which pervade *On Liberty*, need to be viewed within the context of the intellectual influences that shaped both that essay and Mill's other works. They also need to be considered against the background of the major political concerns of his day.

John Stuart Mill had been subjected as a child to an excessively demanding educational regime by his father, James Mill. This rigorous upbringing, which involved, for instance, John Stuart being required to begin studying ancient Greek at the age of three, had been designed by his father as the necessary training for his son to become in time the intellectual leader not only of the philosophical school of utilitarianism but also of the political movement, later known as Philosophical Radicalism, that was derived from it. Utilitarianism was a school of moral philosophy of which Jeremy Bentham (1748–1832), a friend and associate of James Mill, was the principal advocate. Developed in the late eighteenth and

John Stuart Mill (1806–73)

British philosopher, liberal political thinker, economist and social reformer. Born and raised in London, John Stuart Mill was subjected from an early age to an intensive education by his father, James Mill, friend of the leading utilitarian philosopher, Jeremy Bentham. Following a nervous breakdown at the age of twenty, John Stuart Mill to some extent moved away from the utilitarian principles which he had imbibed, embracing other intellectual influences. These included the works of romantic, sociological and early socialist writers and thinkers.

By courtesy of the National Portrait Gallery, London

Mill's political writings reflected this plurality of influences. His most famous work of political philosophy, his essay *On Liberty* (1859), provided an eloquent defence of personal liberty and individuality in the face of an increasingly conformist industrial society. His *Considerations on Representative Government* (1861) explored the electoral methods that would ensure, he believed, a proper balance between wider popular participation in government, on the one hand, and adequate representation of minorities, on the other. Finally, his essay on *The Subjection of Women* (1869), written partly under the influence of his wife, Harriet Taylor, was a powerful statement of Mill's long-held view that women should enjoy the same legal rights – particularly within marriage – as men, together with equal political liberties, including the right to vote.

Mill's major work on economics, *Principles of Political Economy* (1848), which was published in seven successive editions, combined an endorsement of a market economy with an increasingly sympathetic view of contemporary socialist criticisms of the gross inequalities of wealth generated by early industrialism. This perspective was developed further in Mill's *Chapters on Socialism,* written in 1869 and published after his death.

John Stuart Mill's political thought is central to the development of British, and Western, liberalism since it refined classical liberal beliefs whilst anticipating later, more collectivist forms of liberal thinking in the face of both industrialization and a growing socialist movement.

early nineteenth centuries, most notably in Bentham's *Principles of Morals and Legislation* (1789), utilitarianism as a doctrine held, first, that individuals are rationally self-interested beings who are motivated primarily by their desire both to achieve happiness or pleasure and to avoid unhappiness or pain; and second, that the moral 'rightness' of a human action can be measured by its tendency to promote happiness or pleasure. Furthermore, applied to society at large, the utilitarian doctrine held that individual human beings, out of a social motive of benevolence or sympathy, should also aim to promote the general happiness, or 'the greatest happiness of the greatest number', as Bentham put it. In society and government, therefore, policies, laws and institutions should all be judged, above all, by their tendency to promote that desirable goal.

Founded on this utilitarian philosophical basis, the political group later known as the Philosophic Radicals drew their intellectual inspiration from Bentham and James Mill. They thus believed not only, in accordance with utilitarian principles, that all individuals sought to maximize their own happiness and well-being, but also that the overriding purpose of government was to promote the general happiness. The central concerns, therefore, of Philosophical Radicalism were to oppose aristocratic political regimes and to support instead the cause of radical constitutional change and social and legal reforms. All this would require the establishment of a system of representative democracy based on a wide franchise (and eventually universal suffrage), periodic elections and a secret ballot. Philosophical Radicalism therefore offered a justification for reformist movements of the early nineteenth century that sought to accelerate the transition from traditional aristocratic regimes to modern democratic political systems operating alongside market economies.

By the 1830s, however, John Stuart Mill was becoming increasingly sceptical about both universal suffrage and majority rule as effective means of securing good government. Yet he remained committed to the ideal of representative democracy, leading a small group of politicians and radical journalists in the pursuit of that goal through the use of parliamentary methods.

About the same time in his life, Mill had also experienced a growing tension between his utilitarian educational upbringing and the countervailing influence of different intellectual traditions. This had greatly contributed towards his suffering a nervous breakdown in 1826, at the age of twenty. Following his recovery, and his father's death ten years later, Mill at last began to develop his own distinctive approach to both ethical and political questions. This involved revising central assumptions of utilitarian thought in important respects. First, he came to regard the pursuit of individual happiness as a yardstick rather than the central aim of moral action, viewing it as a consequence or by-product of pursuing some other ideal. He thereby questioned Bentham's utilitarian belief that egoistic pleasure-seeking was either a universal human motive or an adequate explanatory principle of individual or social behaviour. Second, Mill also modified utilitarian thinking by attaching greater importance than Bentham had done not only to altruistic motives but also to ideals other than the immediate maximization of pleasure.

In revising utilitarianism in these ways, Mill thereby developed a broader and more refined conception of human nature and motivation. In doing so, he had been influenced by romantic writers such as Samuel Coleridge (1772–1834), who had challenged the narrow rationalism of much of eighteenth-century Enlightenment thought, affirming instead the ideals of human self-development and self-fulfilment. In addition, Mill had come under the intellectual influence both of the sociological thought of Auguste Comte (1798–1857) and of early English and French socialist thinkers. Nevertheless, he continued to adhere to the individualism of Locke and Bentham, regarding the individual as prior to organized society and consequently believing that the essential function of government was to serve the individual's goals and interests.

On a more intensely personal level, the composition of Mill's *On Liberty*, in particular, and later his essay, *The Subjection of Women* (1869), had to a significant extent been influenced by his relationship with Harriet Taylor, a married woman with whom Mill had fallen in love in 1830 and whom he eventually married twenty-one years later following the death of her husband.

By his early fifties, Mill had established an unrivalled intellectual pre-eminence in English public life – as a moral philosopher, an economist and a political thinker. Before the publication of *On Liberty* in 1859, his works *Systems of Logic* (1843) and *Principles of Political Economy* (1848) had thus become established textbooks in British universities. His essay *Considerations on Representative Government* (1861) was to prove itself a major influence on democratic thought for the next generation, while his short essay *Utilitarianism* (1863) has had an impact on debates in moral philosophy that has endured to the present day.

Mill's main concerns in On Liberty

At the beginning of *On Liberty* Mill observed that throughout the history of political thought the idea of liberty had usually been interpreted as meaning 'protection against the tyranny of political rulers'.[3] Such protection had been associated, too, with two particular devices: either with insistence on the recognition by governments of certain rights or liberties held by individuals that ought not to be infringed, or with constitutional checks placed on governments by the people or their representatives. In *On Liberty*, however, Mill made it clear that his essay's central concern was with the danger of a tyranny of the majority exercised not so much by the institutions of government as by society itself.

Mill was therefore committed in *On Liberty* to the goal of achieving protection for the individual from what he called 'the tyranny of the prevailing opinion and feeling'.[4] In Mill's view, such a form of tyranny, exercised by 'society collectively, over the separate individuals who compose it',[5] was even more oppressive than many kinds of political oppression. For there were no institutional safeguards against the all-pervasive pressures of social convention. 'Social tyranny,' Mill thus declared, '. . . leaves fewer means of escape, penetrating much more deeply into the details of life, and enslaving the soul itself.'[6]

Moreover, this tyranny of public opinion was viewed by Mill as so dangerous as well as pervasive essentially because it suppressed individuality in people, stifling their spontaneity and their capacity for developing their own tastes and potentialities. As a consequence, Mill commented:

> At present individuals are lost in the crowd. In politics it is almost a triviality to say that public opinion now rules the world . . .[7]

Such a force promoted, in his view, both dull conformity and popular prejudice.

In the face of this most grave of dangers, Mill concluded that:

> Protection, therefore, against the tyranny of the magistrate is not enough; there needs protection also against the tyranny of the prevailing opinion and feeling; against the tendency of society to impose, by other means than civil penalties, its own ideas and practices as rules of conduct on those who dissent from them . . .[8]

In mid-Victorian England, during the 1850s and 1860s, Mill considered that the need to protect the nonconformist or dissident individual from such an intolerant and restrictive climate was the most urgent issue of the day. Critical of aristocratic attitudes, Mill was also opposed to the growing body of what he regarded as philistine and semi-educated middle-class opinion, personified by industrialists, clergymen and tenant farmers, which tended both to persecute individuals with unconventional views and tastes and to block the implementation of sensible social reforms.

In order, therefore, to protect unconventional or eccentric individuals from the tyranny of public opinion, Mill sought in *On Liberty* to establish certain universal, rational principles that would demarcate a wide area of private conduct in which individuals should be free to act as they chose without interference by society or the state. Such principles would thereby serve, first, to define the proper boundaries between individual freedom and collective interference and, second, to protect the individual, in certain areas of conduct, from both social pressures and governmental controls.

With these fundamental aims in mind, Mill states in Chapter 1 of *On Liberty* that:

> The object of this essay is to assert one very simple principle . . . that the sole end for which mankind are warranted, individually or collectively, in interfering with the liberty of action of any of their number is self-protection. That the only purpose for which power can be rightfully exercised over any member of a civilised community, against his will, is to prevent harm to others. His own good, either physical or moral, is not a sufficient warrant.[9]

Mill was thus concerned with revising and enlarging the view of liberty that lay at the heart of nineteenth-century classical liberal doctrine. He aimed to do this by extending to society at large the realm of the individual's free choice, thereby moving beyond merely political and economic arrangements that protected the individual either from absolutist and authoritarian regimes or from state interference with private economic activity.

Mill's view of liberty

In developing his own definition of liberty, Mill began with the negative conception of it as the freedom of the individual to do as he or she wished without interference by others or by some other agency. This view of liberty is grounded on the belief that the individual person has a capacity for free choice. He or she is thus an autonomous agent, free to exercise supreme control over his or her life and circumstances.

From this classical liberal starting-point, however, Mill moved towards a more positive notion of freedom as human self-development. For in his view, liberty did not merely consist in the unimpeded ability to do as one wished. Rather, it was viewed by him as the necessary condition of the individual's moral, intellectual and cultural self-development and hence of the realization of individuality.

The eminent historian of ideas, Isaiah Berlin, described this dual view of liberty in these terms:

> Mill believes in liberty, that is, the rigid limitation of the right to coerce, because he is sure that men cannot develop and flourish and become fully human unless they are left free from interference by other men within a certain minimum area of their lives, which he regards as – or wishes to make – inviolable.[10]

Furthermore, in elaborating his defence of individual liberty, Mill did not rely on an underlying Lockean theory of natural rights. Indeed, he rejected the notion of abstract right as something independent of the idea of utility. He thus pointed out, in terms that also underlined his own revision of utilitarian thought:

> I regard utility as the ultimate appeal on all ethical questions; but it must be utility in the largest sense, grounded on the permanent interests of a man as a progressive being.[11]

Mill thus advanced his argument for liberty on broad and revised, rather than narrow and orthodox, utilitarian grounds. It was an ideal whose practical fulfilment, he believed, would have beneficial effects both on the individual and on society at large. For liberty was to be valued, in his view, as something humanly ennobling, as a means to human self-development – morally, intellectually and aesthetically – and self-fulfilment through the making of free choices in life. Liberty was also to be defended and promoted as a means to the progressive advancement of civilized societies. This would result, he maintained, from the promotion of knowledge and truth that freedom of discussion and expression would make possible.

Moreover, Mill's view of liberty as a vital means to both personal development and social and intellectual progress was closely linked to his notion of human character and of the contribution that liberty could make to its refinement. This notion, which was characteristic of much of Victorian liberal thought in the mid-nineteenth century, revolved around such valued ideas as autonomy (the individual's capacity for self-directed choice), diversity, experimentation, independence of thought, and individual and social improvement.[12]

It is, then, from this subtle ethical perspective that Mill proceeds to argue in *On Liberty* that the only justification that society has for interfering with the individual's freedom of action, against his will, is 'to prevent harm to others'[13] – more specifically, to prevent direct material harm being inflicted upon others.

Mill develops this 'harm' principle further in terms of a distinction between self-regarding actions, which affect only the individual and over which that person should therefore have supreme control, and other-regarding actions, which adversely affect other people's interests. Mill explains, however, that both the 'harm' principle and this consequent distinction may only be applied to members of a 'civilised community', to people 'in the maturity of their faculties', who have reached 'the capacity of being guided to their own improvement by conviction and persuasion'.[14] The principle and distinction are thus not applicable, in his view, to children or invalids, whose behaviour needs regulating by others, or to members of backward races.

Mill develops his argument further by identifying three areas of self-regarding conduct, in which the exercise of liberty harms no-one but the individual participant and which should therefore be completely beyond the control of society or the state. These include, first, freedom of thought, discussion and expression in its various forms. In Mill's own words, this area consists of 'the inward domain of consciousness', embracing 'liberty of conscience, in the most comprehensive sense; liberty of thought and feeling; absolute freedom of opinion and sentiment on all subjects, practical or speculative, scientific, moral or theological'.[15]

The second and third areas of self-regarding conduct identified by Mill are 'liberty of tastes and pursuits' – that is, freedom to pursue the kind of lifestyle which we choose; and 'liberty ... of combination' – in other words, freedom of association of individuals who 'unite for any purpose not involving harm to others'.[16] With regard to these three categories of individual action, Mill states unequivocally that:

> No society in which these liberties are not, on the whole, respected is free, whatever may be its form of government; and none is completely free in which they do not exist absolute and unqualified.[17]

In Chapter 2 of *On Liberty* Mill develops a closely reasoned case – covering almost a third of his entire essay – for the first of these three liberties of self-regarding conduct – freedom of thought and discussion. He begins by affirming his belief in absolute freedom of opinion or principle and by denouncing all suppression of freedom of discussion in these eloquent terms:

> If all mankind minus one, were of one opinion, and only one person were of the contrary opinion, mankind would be no more justified in silencing that one person, than he, if he had the power, would be justified in silencing mankind.[18]

Moreover, Mill points out that freedom of thought and 'the liberty of expressing and publishing opinions' are 'practically inseparable'.[19] Defending freedom of private thought and belief therefore involved, too, protecting freedom of expression in its various forms – including freedom of speech and publication. The urgency of that task was, in Mill's view, underlined not just by the historical experience of the persecution and suppression of heretical, subversive and unconventional thought, but also by the contemporary threat posed by 'the tyranny of the prevailing opinion and feeling' in mid-nineteenth-century England.

Mill's defence of freedom of thought and discussion rests on his conviction that those freedoms are essential means to the discovery of truth and the advancement of knowledge and understanding – goals that are both intrinsically valuable and beneficial for society at large. That conviction leads him to deploy three particular arguments against the suppression, and for the toleration, of opinions that may conflict with received or established majority opinion. First, a minority opinion under threat of suppression may well be true, whilst a majority opinion may be false. Every age, Mill observes, has held many opinions which 'subsequent ages have deemed not only false but absurd' – such as, for instance, the belief that the earth was flat.[20] By contrast, many ideas denounced as dangerous or heretical were later warmly embraced by subsequent generations. Socrates and Jesus, for example, were condemned and put to death for promoting allegedly subversive or blasphemous views or doctrines, yet were later revered as great moral teachers. The history of human ideas and discovery thus provides us with a clear warning against making any assumption of infallibility with regard to orthodox views or opinions. Yet 'all silencing of discussion,' Mill declares, 'is an assumption of infallibility'.[21]

The second argument that Mill advances for freedom of thought and discussion as means to the discovery of truth is that while a suppressed minority opinion may well be false, the truth is actually reinforced through the intellectual process of refuting that false opinion. For suppression of that minority view will only deprive those who hold the received, true opinion of the means of understanding the reasons for its truth. Indeed, there is little value, Mill insists, in holding an opinion that happens to be true without such an understanding.

Moreover, the process of examining and discussing, fully and frequently, even a true opinion will also prevent it from degenerating in time into 'a dead dogma, not a living truth'.[22] For in the absence of such a critical climate, Mill observes, 'both teachers and learners go to sleep at their post, as soon as there is no enemy in the field'.[23]

Mill's third and final argument rests on the recognition that an opinion may be predominantly false, yet may still contain an element of truth. It may, in other words, as is often the case, be a mixture of truth and falsehood. The process of critically scrutinizing such an opinion will help therefore to disentangle its true from its false aspect, strengthening the former and eliminating the latter. Only free debate and discussion, Mill contends, will make this possible, thereby correcting existing, partially true or valid views or beliefs.

In spite, however, of the vehemence and eloquence of Mill's advocacy of the cause of freedom of discussion, he did not believe that the advancement of truth would be its inevitable and universal effect. 'The dictum,' he wrote, 'that truth always triumphs over persecution, is one of those pleasant falsehoods which men repeat after one another till they pass into commonplaces, but which all experience refutes.' For 'history,' he observed, 'teems with instances of truth put down by persecution'.[24] He nonetheless argued a passionate case for toleration with regard to novel or unconventional opinions and beliefs and for an attitude of open-minded scepticism towards existing orthodoxies, however widely held and propagated. Only through a constant process of free discussion and debate, he maintained, would 'wrong opinions and practices gradually yield to fact and argument'.[25] Such an outcome, Mill argued from his revised and refined utilitarian standpoint, would be beneficial both for the individual in terms of his moral and intellectual development, and for society as a whole in terms of its intellectual and cultural progress.

Mill on the importance of individuality

The remainder of Chapter 3 of *On Liberty* is concerned with what Mill presents as the vitally important question of freedom of personal tastes and pursuits, or, in short, individuality. For 'the free development of individuality,' he declares, is 'one of the leading essentials of well-being'.[26] This form of freedom really amounts to the freedom of individuals to act upon their opinions and beliefs 'without hindrance, whether physical or moral, from their fellow-men, so long as it is at their own risk and peril'.[27] It thus constitutes the second area of self-regarding conduct that Mill is intent on defending from collective interference.

Like freedom of thought and discussion, Mill regarded freedom of personal tastes and pursuits as beneficial both for each individual and for society as a whole. For a diversity of lifestyles, as well as of opinions and beliefs, created the opportunity of discovering better, more fulfilling ways of life. Mill thus maintains that:

> As it is useful that while mankind are imperfect there should be different opinions, so it is that there should be different experiments of living; that free scope should be given to varieties of character, short of injury to others; and that the worth of different modes of life should be proved practically . . . [This is] quite the chief ingredient of individual and social progress.[28]

Moreover, 'in proportion to the development of his individuality,' Mill argues, 'each person becomes more valuable to himself, and is therefore capable of being more valuable to others'.[29] For by exploring his own tastes and pursuits, the individual is exercising his own capacity for free choice and independent judgement. He is thereby fostering his moral, intellectual and aesthetic self-development.

Yet such individuality was also, Mill stressed, beneficial for the rest of society since the free, developed individual, by offering fresh insights and developing new modes of behaviour, could thereby 'set the example of more enlightened conduct, and better taste and sense in human life'.[30] Furthermore, even undeveloped and unoriginal members of society would benefit indirectly from the presence and activity of a minority of creative and innovative individuals, 'the salt of the earth', without whom society would become a 'stagnant pool'.[31]

Even though Mill's main concern here was with protecting the free development of exceptional individuals of that kind, he made it clear that this was a valuable form of freedom that should be enjoyed by all mature adults. 'Nor is it only persons of decided mental superiority,' he thus wrote, 'who have a just claim to carry on their lives in their own way.'[32] Nevertheless, Mill was convinced that English society of the mid-nineteenth century, permeated as he felt it was by 'the tyranny of the prevailing opinion and feeling', tended to suppress individuality and the qualities that it embraced and expressed – namely, originality, eccentricity, diversity, spontaneity and independence of mind and spirit. In their place, he believed, contemporary society tended to produce mindless conformists devoid of 'human faculties of perception, judgement, discriminative feeling, mental activity and even moral preference'.[33] Such people, he feared, did 'not desire liberty, and would not avail themselves of it'.[34]

Individuality was thus, in Mill's view, a powerful defence against the stifling forces of social conformity and 'collective mediocrity',[35] forces that had created a climate of opinion in which the qualities associated with individuality were either under threat or else viewed with grave suspicion. The reality was, for instance, 'that individual spontaneity is hardly recognised by the common modes of thinking as having any intrinsic worth ... but is rather looked on with jealousy'.[36] The result of these conformist pressures, Mill wrote, was that 'the despotism of custom is everywhere the standing hindrance to human advancement'.[37]

Throughout his discussion of individuality, Mill drew a sharp distinction between the passivity and inertia of these forces of custom and conformity, on the one hand, and the active, energizing effects of innovation and originality, on the other. The individual, he stressed, was a living being, not an inert object moulded by custom or convention. He or she was not formed mechanically but rather developed organically, like a tree, 'according to the tendency of the inward forces which make it a living thing'.[38]

For Mill, then, liberty of personal tastes and pursuits – the individual's capacity for freely choosing how to lead his life – was the necessary, vital condition of his all-round human development – morally, intellectually and aesthetically. It was thus an ideal consistent with Mill's broad, revised utilitarian principle of 'utility in the largest sense, grounded on the permanent interests of man as a progressive being'.[39]

Limits to freedom of expression and action

Mill devoted the rest of *On Liberty* – that is, the remainder of Chapter 3 as well as Chapters 2 and 5 – to exploring the question of the legitimate extent and limits of the individual's liberty of action. In Chapter 1, as we have seen, he had carefully distinguished between, first, self-regarding actions, affecting only the agent himself, which should be free from interference by society or the state, and, second, other-regarding actions, through which some perceptible, direct harm or injury was inflicted on another person or persons. At that point, Mill believed, society or the state had the right to intervene, for 'as soon,' he wrote, 'as any part of a person's conduct affects prejudicially the interests of others, society has jurisdiction over it'.[40]

Whilst he had argued passionately against any collective interference with freedom of thought and discussion, Mill thus cited, at the beginning of Chapter 3, the example of a situation in which the free expression of certain opinions might have certain harmful effects and might therefore be legitimately restricted. He observed that:

> An opinion that corn-dealers are starvers of the poor, or that private property is robbery, ought to be unmolested when simply circulated through the press, but may justly incur punishment when delivered orally to an excited mob assembled before the house of a corn-dealer, or when handed about among the same mob in the form of a placard.[41]

Society is therefore justified, Mill argues, in interfering with an individual's freedom of action in order to protect its other members from behaviour that might damage their interests. For each individual person in society:

> should be bound to observe a certain line of conduct towards the rest. This conduct consists ... in not injuring the interests of one another; or rather certain interests, which either by express legal provision or by tacit understanding, are considered as rights.[42]

Mill was referring here to certain rights-based interests, centred on personal security and safety, that were protected by law or at least recognized by society. Such interests might include, for instance, the right to retain one's private property in the face of another person's attempt to acquire it by force. More generally, they would involve an entitlement to be protected not only from theft or robbery but also from assault and the threat of murder, as well as from fraud and deception.

At this important point in his argument, Mill's position derived both from a rejection of the Lockean notion of natural rights and from a residual adherence to Bentham's more concrete view that

> Right ... the substantive right ... is the child of law ... from real laws come real rights ...[43]

However, the notion of legal rights that Mill was reaffirming rested, as at other stages of his defence of personal liberty, upon a revisionist rather than orthodox utilitarianism, invoking once again the principle of 'utility in the largest sense, grounded on the permanent interests of man as a progressive being'.[44] From that standpoint he therefore argued that such interests were best promoted by defending a private sphere of activity, free from social or political interference, whilst at the same time conceding the possibility of legitimate intervention in a public sphere for purely utilitarian reasons – that is, to prevent direct harm to others.

Mill underlines and summarizes this crucial point in Chapter 5 of *On Liberty* by restating his 'one very simple principle' in the form of 'two maxims which together form the entire doctrine of the Essay'. These, he writes are: 'first, that the individual is not accountable to society for his actions, in so far as they concern the interests of no person but himself ...'; and 'secondly, that for such actions as are prejudicial to the interests of others, the individual is accountable, and may be subjected either to social or to legal punishment, if society is of the opinion that the one or the other is requisite for its protection'.[45]

In exploring this distinction, Mill here cites various examples of those 'moral police' in society who consider themselves entitled to restrict a person's freedom of action on the ground that they find that person's conduct offensive or distasteful. He mentions, in particular, the Moslem majority in certain societies who forbid Christians from eating pork; Puritans who decry public amusements; Sabbatarians who seek to impose on others their objection to working on Sundays; and abstainers who seek to prohibit the sale and consumption of alcoholic drinks.

In none of those instances, Mill argues, does the fact that certain individuals or groups find others' behaviour morally repugnant constitute grounds for the suppression or limitation of those practices. Underlying his argument at this point is the clear contrast he draws between *objective* injury that may be inflicted by other-regarding actions and *subjective* offence, deriving from other people's moral or social attitudes, that may be caused by self-regarding actions. In the latter case the individual agent concerned 'is not accountable to society for his actions', affecting as they do only his own interests, and therefore should not be restricted or coerced by society or the law.

In defending on these grounds his all-important distinction between self-regarding and other-regarding actions, and in thereby reaffirming the 'harm' principle that underlay it, Mill had thus firmly ruled out any collective interference with individual freedom of action on paternalistic grounds – on the basis, that is, of the idea that society or the law should intervene to promote what society or the state considered to be in the individual's best interests, morally or physically. He had also ruled out any collective interference on moralistic grounds – on the basis, that is, of the idea that some acts are intrinsically immoral and ought therefore to be prohibited or punished, irrespective of whether they affect someone else injuriously. Indeed, a prominent contemporary critic of Mill's, Sir James Fitzjames Stephen, concentrated on precisely this shortcoming, as he regarded it, of Mill's entire argument for personal liberty.

Viewing such ethical considerations from a contemporary perspective, it is certainly the case that many laws of modern societies in the late twentieth and early twenty-first centuries would be hard to defend in terms of Mill's distinction and 'harm' principle. For such laws have been enacted and established on the basis of moralistic or even paternalistic arguments. They would include, for instance, laws against euthanasia, incest between siblings, or certain aspects of prostitution, as well as those in favour of some forms of censorship.

Conclusion

Apart from the line of criticism cited above concerning the linkage between law, liberty and morality,[46] much of the subsequent debate generated by Mill's distinction between self-regarding and other-regarding actions has revolved around two other questions: first, whether there are in fact any purely self-regarding actions; and, second, what actually constitutes 'harm' to others. On the first point, it has been objected that, since there are very few actions which fall into the category of purely self-regarding conduct, Mill's 'harm' principle is left with too narrow a range of practical application. Furthermore, it has been objected that what are ostensibly self-regarding actions – those, for instance, involving an individual taking risks with, or even abusing, his physical health by smoking or taking drugs – in practice affect that individual's dependants or close friends, and thus have social effects or implications. In addition, it has been argued, all human actions, even ostensibly self-regarding ones, affect others by example.

With characteristic intellectual honesty Mill acknowledged the fact that his distinction between private conduct and public behaviour would be 'one that many persons will refuse to admit'. He therefore posed the problematic issue at stake in these terms:

> How (it may be asked) can any part of the conduct of a member of society be a matter of indifference to the other members? No person is an entirely isolated being; it is impossible for a person to do anything seriously or permanently hurtful to himself, without mischief reaching at least, to his near connections, and often far beyond them ... Finally, if by his vices or follies a person does no direct harm to others, he is nevertheless ... injurious by his example.[47]

Mill's own defence of his distinction hinged, as we have seen, on his insistence that there is a clear difference between actions which do, and do not, directly damage others' interests, defined in terms of their personal security and safety. The second, related area of controversy – concerning what actually constitutes 'harm' to others – Mill attempted to clarify with a corresponding distinction between objective injury and subjective offence. Arguably, each of these distinctions is contentious or imprecise, yet also philosophically coherent and defensible.[48] For as John Plamenatz observed, if Mill's criterion of direct harm inflicted on others, and with it his principle of freedom of self-regarding conduct, were entirely useless or without validity, then 'it would be impossible ever to have good reason for saying that a man was minding his own business. The distinction between self-regarding and other-regarding actions is one of the commonest we make.'[49]

Besides, the crucial point emerging from these areas of debate, as Stefan Collini has argued, is not that Mill's 'harm' principle 'enables us always to draw a hard and fast line' between different human actions, but rather that it 'puts the burden of proof on those who propose to restrict the liberty of others'. Furthermore, with regard to the equally contentious question of what constitutes 'harm' in any given case, Mill's principle again 'places the onus of producing evidence of "harm" on the proposers of interference, and, even more important, it rules out intervention on any other basis'.[50]

Employing, then, these ideas at the heart of his argument, Mill revised classical liberal theory by extending the advocacy of freedom of choice and action beyond the political and economic spheres to many areas of individual and social conduct, specifically to those areas where the interests of others were not adversely affected. Within the intellectual and political contexts of mid-nineteenth-century Britain, this involved his refining the utilitarian idea of the pursuit of individual happiness by identifying social, as well as political and economic, obstacles that lay in the path of individual freedom and hence human contentment and well-being. In so doing, he bequeathed to the Western liberal tradition one of its most impassioned, intellectually rigorous and influential defences of the enduring value of personal liberty.

Notes

1   G. Sabine and T. Thorson, *A History of Political Theory*, 4th edn, Hinsdale, Illinois, Dryden Press, 1973, p. 641.

2   ibid. p. 642.

3   John Stuart Mill, *On Liberty and Other Writings* (ed. S. Collini), Cambridge, Cambridge University Press, 1989, p. 5.

4   ibid. p. 8.

5   ibid.

6   ibid.

7   ibid. p. 66.

8   ibid. p. 8.

9   ibid. p. 13.

10   I. Berlin, 'J.S. Mill and the Ends of Life', in *Four Essays on Liberty*, Oxford, Oxford University Press, 1969, p. 190.

11   Mill, *On Liberty*, p. 14.

12   On this point, see R. Bellamy, *Liberalism and Modern Society*, Cambridge, Polity Press, 1992, pp. 22–35.

13   Mill, op. cit. p. 13.

14   ibid. pp. 13–14.

15   ibid. p. 15.

16   ibid. p. 16.

17   ibid.

18   ibid. p. 20.

19   ibid. p. 15.

20   ibid. pp. 21–2.

21   ibid. p. 21.

22   ibid. p. 37.

23   ibid. p. 44.

24   ibid. pp. 30–1.

25   ibid. p. 23.

26   ibid. p. 57.

27   ibid. p. 56.

28   ibid. p. 57

29   ibid. p. 63.

30   ibid. p. 64.

31   ibid.

32   ibid. p. 67.

33   ibid. p. 59.

34   ibid. p. 64.

35   ibid. p. 66.

36   ibid. p. 57.

37   ibid. p. 70.

38   ibid. p. 60.

39   ibid. p. 14.

40   ibid. pp. 75–6.

41   ibid. p. 56.

42   ibid. p. 75.
43   J. Bentham, 'A Critical Examination of the Declaration of Rights', in B. Parekh (ed.), *Bentham's Political Thought*, London, Croom Helm, 1973, p. 288.
44   Mill, op. cit. p. 14.
45   ibid. p. 94.
46   See Chapter 3C for a brief discussion of this area of political debate in the post-1945 period.
47   Mill, op. cit. p. 80.
48   For a defence of Mill's position on this point, see, for example, J.C. Rees, *John Stuart Mill's On Liberty*, Oxford, Oxford University Press, 1985.
49   J. Plamenatz, *Man and Society*, Vol. 2 (revised by M.E. Plamenatz and Robert Wokler), London, Longman, 1992, p. 266.
50   S. Collini, Introduction to J.S. Mill, *On Liberty and Other Writings* (ed. S. Collini), p. xvii.

T.H. Green's positive view of liberty

Historical context: political and intellectual

Thomas Hill Green's positive conception of liberty was the most significant part of his influential revision of British liberal thought during the 1870s and early 1880s. Both an academic philosopher at the University of Oxford after 1860 and a leading

---

Thomas Hill Green (1836–82)

British philosopher and liberal political thinker. T.H. Green, who had been a philosopher at the University of Oxford since 1860, played a significant role in the revision of liberal thought – particularly with regard to changing views both of the nature of liberty and of the appropriate role of the state – during the 1870s and early 1880s.

Green advanced the case for a more positive conception of liberty, his most distinctive and important contribution to Western liberal thought. This involved an ethical interpretation of liberty as the individual's opportunity to realize his potentialities. In addition, Green provided a theoretical justification, in terms of this revised view of liberty, for a more interventionist role for the state in the face of the social problems generated by industrialization.

These innovations in liberal thought were developed in Green's *Lectures on the Principles of Political Obligation* (1882), as well as in his highly influential lecture, 'Liberal Legislation and Freedom of Contract', delivered in early 1881. The liberal philosophy expressed in those works was influenced neither by Lockean natural-rights theory nor by Bentham's or J.S. Mill's utilitarianism, but rather by German – particularly Hegelian – idealist philosophy, by evangelical Christianity, and by political ideas, too, that had their roots in classical Greek thought.

Green's revised and idealist version of liberalism was to exert a major influence on the development of the new social–liberal thinking in Britain from the 1870s until 1914.

---

liberal political thinker, Green's practical involvement in politics had been largely confined to service as a town councillor in Oxford, where he supported plans for the extension and improvement of secondary and adult education. On a national level, he had also been a supporter in the 1860s of the Reform League's campaign for extension of the suffrage, as well as of the policies of the National Education League.

On the level of political ideas, however, Green played a crucial role in furthering the gradual transition from the old, individualist classical liberalism – a major intellectual and political influence from roughly the late eighteenth century to the 1860s – to the new, collectivist social liberalism, an increasingly influential body of ideas from the 1870s onwards. The emergence of this social liberalism in the late nineteenth century – built around both a positive conception of liberty and a more positive view of the role of the state – was shaped by a growing awareness of poverty and unemployment as acute social and economic problems in British industrial towns and cities. The new liberalism was a response, too, to the practical reality of the rise of an increasingly organized and partly enfranchised working class in industrial society.

These factors gave rise to tensions between the new social liberalism, formulated between the 1870s and 1914 by Green, D.G. Ritchie, Leonard Hobhouse, J.A. Hobson and other liberal thinkers, and the older, more orthodox liberalism. In particular, classical liberal positions such as a celebration of an unregulated capitalist economy, a negative conception of liberty as the absence of constraints on the individual, and a commitment to a limited state, were all subjected to severe scrutiny by the new social–liberal thinkers in the light of the problems generated by industrialization and urbanization.

In response, therefore, to these ideological tensions, there was an increasing trend in British liberal thought from the late 1870s towards an emphasis on greater state responsibility for working and living conditions within the established framework of a capitalist market economy. To some extent that approach was itself a development of liberal arguments for increased state intervention, evident in the practice of Gladstone's administration of 1868–74, that had been strengthened by the extension of representative democracy in Britain. After 1880 this movement towards a more collectivist form of liberalism gathered pace at both policy-making and theoretical levels. In policy terms, for instance, its leading ideas were embodied in Joseph Chamberlain's Unauthorized Programme of 1885 and in Gladstone's Newcastle Programme adopted by the National Liberal Federation in 1891.

In general, the increased state intervention advocated by liberals during this period assumed two principal forms: first, state responsibility for the regulation of industrial working conditions, and second, state involvement in the provision of health, education and welfare services. Among the earliest theoretical justifications for this growth in state activity, and hence for the abandonment of the extreme market individualism of some nineteenth-century liberals, was that provided by the Oxford philosopher, T.H. Green. In his political writings, most notably in his *Lectures on the Principles of Political Obligation* (1882), his major work of political philosophy, and in his highly influential lecture, 'Liberal Legislation and Freedom of Contract', delivered in early 1881, Green attempted to confront two contemporary liberal dilemmas. First, he was aware of the fact that, in the face of the problems generated by industrialization, the older classical liberalism had become vulnerable to the charge that it provided an ideological justification for the interests of the rich and powerful rather than a defence of those of the poor and disadvantaged. Second, he realized, too, that liberal ideas and policies needed to reflect both growing doubts about the social effects of an unregulated market economy, and a continuing awareness of the dangers posed for the individual by a paternalistic or authoritarian state.

Faced, then, by these acute dilemmas, Green believed that it was time to give liberal thought a more positive and social emphasis both in its view of individual liberty or freedom and in its attitude towards the role and functions of the democratic state. By doing so, he maintained that British liberalism could discard its frequent appearance as a vehicle for the interests of the economically dominant classes – the factory-owners, employers and landlords – and become instead a revised and revitalized force for social and industrial reform.

The most concrete expression of this revisionist liberalism favoured by Green emerged in the form of his 1881 lecture, 'Liberal Legislation and Freedom of Contract'. Prompted by Gladstone's proposal to regulate contracts between Irish landlords and tenants, it explored the ideological tension between the Liberal government's imminent legislation and the classical liberal principle, hitherto widely regarded as sacrosanct, of freedom of contract. Specifically, in supporting that legislation Green used his lecture to advance his positive conception of liberty and to champion its practical application by a more active, interventionist state.

The philosophical basis of Green's political thought involved a rejection both of the utilitarianism of Bentham and John Stuart Mill and of the more recent Social Darwinism of Herbert Spencer (1820–1903). In revising liberal theory, Green turned away, too, from Locke's earlier doctrine of natural rights. In their place, he drew upon the German philosophical tradition, represented in particular by Georg Hegel (1770–1831), of idealism, which held that reality is more than a material phenomenon and that ideas, rather than matter, form the substance of ultimate reality.

The most important expression of Green's idealist philosophy is to be found in his *Lectures on the Principles of Political Obligation*, delivered at Oxford between 1879 and 1880, but not put together and published until after his death in 1882. At Oxford he was the most prominent of a group of neo-Hegelian idealist philosophers, who included F.H. Bradley, Bernard Bosanquet, D.G. Ritchie and Edward Caird. Green and his colleagues thus led a revival after 1870 of intellectual interest in late eighteenth-century/early nineteenth-century German philosophy – particularly that of Hegel – that was to be sustained until the 1920s.

The influence of Hegel's idealist philosophy upon Green was evident, first, in his belief in the existence of a spiritual universe, ordered by God, beyond the realm of the purely material; second, in his emphasis on viewing social and political issues from the perspective of spiritual ideals; and third, in his view that individuals participate in the spiritual universe through their capacity for organizing their lives according to moral principles derived from such ideals. Green maintained that liberal theory needed to be revised so that it took account of such idealist assumptions and no longer rested on materialist principles such as Bentham's concept of utility.

Nevertheless, it is also true that many aspects of Green's political thought owed much to non-Hegelian intellectual antecedents or influences. His view, for instance, of the mutual relationship between the individual and the community had been anticipated in the late eighteenth century by the conservative political philosophy of Edmund Burke (1729–97). Green shared, too, in the political discourse of his day, which was suffused with theological concepts derived from evangelical Christianity.[1]

Moreover, he also drew upon a longer tradition of political thought that could be traced back to Aristotle and which had been revived, in different ways, by both Rousseau and Hegel. Such a tradition had emphasized, first, the social nature of the individual, and second, the moral aspect and function of civil society and the state. As adapted by Hegel, this second emphasis involved the depiction of the state as an actualization of an ethical ideal, which in Green's interpretation consisted of the common good, a central notion of idealist political thought.

Shaped, then, by these various intellectual influences, Green's idealist revision of liberalism represented a significant change of direction in the evolution of British political thought during the last quarter of the nineteenth century. Rejecting the extreme individualism and materialism that had often underpinned classical liberalism, his political philosophy attempted instead to revive and adapt to modern industrial conditions fundamental beliefs about the individual and society that had their intellectual roots in classical Greek thought. These concerned not only the social nature of the individual person, but also the moralizing effect of social and political activity upon each individual citizen who wills the common good.

Green's view of the social individual

Green's belief in the social nature of individuals led him, like Rousseau, to the conviction that they could only truly realize themselves within the framework of society and that their very identities were derived from the social roles and relationships in which they were involved. Moreover, that social framework merely facilitated, he maintained, the individual's personal development without directing it, just as the linguistic framework of vocabulary and grammar made possible human speech and communication without dictating their actual content.

Unlike the contractual and utilitarian theories of society that had deeply influenced classical liberal thought, Green's liberalism stressed, too, as Burke had done earlier, the beneficial role of a society's traditions, customs, laws and institutions in helping to bind individuals together into a larger social entity. Furthermore, in Green's view, individuals could only develop as moral beings in a society imbued with such structural features, which were in turn reflections of the capacity of those same individuals for ordering both their own lives and their society's character according to certain rules of moral conduct.

This view of the possibility of moral progress clearly reflected an optimistic view of human nature and potentiality. For Green individuals were thus more than just, as in Bentham's view, self-seeking utility-maximizers dominated by the over-riding desire to promote pleasure and avoid pain. Rather, they were capable, he believed, of moral self-development both through the control of their desires by reason and through the determination of human conduct by will and rational choice.

Finally, since it was within the society of which they were members that individuals developed their moral character, it therefore followed that, in Green's view, active participation in the social and political life of the community represented the highest form of the individual's self-development as well as an important goal of a liberal society. The source of Green's conviction here was not so much Hegel's philosophy, but rather, as George Sabine observed, 'on the one hand his understanding of Christian brotherhood and on the other hand a liberalized conception of Greek citizenship . . .'[2]

Green's positive conception of liberty

In the political context of growing doubts both about a mainly negative view of liberty and about a limited role for the state, Green developed his positive conception of liberty, his most distinctive and important contribution to Western liberal thought. This involved the belief that the state's powers could legitimately be used to widen the individual's opportunity to realize his potentialities. The impulse behind Green's interpretation of individual liberty was essentially ethical, rooted as it was in moral indignation that few of his countrymen shared in the economic and cultural benefits created by industrial society. An 'underfed denizen of a London yard',[3] he remarked, had no more share in the civilization of England than a slave had in that of ancient Athens.

In relation to the liberal tradition, Green's positive conception of liberty was an attempt to move beyond the insights of classical liberalism by reinvolving the individual in society. Classical liberal thinkers such as Bentham had argued that all state legislation was intrinsically a restriction of individual freedom. They had thus promoted a negative view of liberty as the absence of constraint or compulsion. In contrast, Green argued that a society's growth in personal freedom was not measured merely by a reduction of the powers of the state, but rather by the 'greater power on the part of the citizens as a body to make the most and best of themselves'.[4] Moreover, in his view, 'the mere removal of compulsion, the mere enabling of a man to do as he likes, is in itself no contribution to true freedom'.[5]

Developing these points in his 1881 lecture, 'Liberal Legislation and Freedom of Contract', Green stated that:

> We shall probably all agree that freedom, rightly understood, is the greatest of blessings; that its attainment is the true end of all our effort as citizens. But when we thus speak of freedom, we should consider carefully what we mean by it. We do not mean merely freedom from restraint or compulsion. We do not mean merely freedom to do as we like irrespectively of what it is we like. We do not mean a freedom that can be enjoyed by one man or one set of men at the cost of a loss of freedom to others. When we speak of

freedom ... we mean a positive power or capacity of doing or enjoying something worth doing or enjoying, and that, too, something that we do or enjoy in common with others.[6]

As a concrete example of the classical liberal, negative conception of liberty that he rejected, Green drew particular attention to the traditional right of 'freedom of contract' between landlord and tenant or employer and employee. In his view, this so-called 'freedom' was illusory since it merely legitimized unlimited exploitation of the mass of the working population by landlords or employers. For contracts of tenancy or employment were seldom made between free and equal parties. Indeed, the bargaining power of those groups was often grossly unequal. As a consequence, the stark alternatives to such contracts for tenants or employees were frequently eviction, unemployment, poverty or starvation.

In such cases, therefore, the actual coercion exerted by landlords or employers upon tenants or workers under the legal form of contract was a far greater threat to individual freedom, Green argued, than the legal coercion exerted by the state upon landlords or employers when it regulated contracts (as Gladstone's government proposed to do) in order to protect the weaker party.

For these reasons it was an abuse of language to define liberty in terms of such limited arrangements as unequal contracts. As Green pointed out:

> If the ideal of true freedom is the maximum of power for all members of human society alike to make the best of themselves, we are right in refusing to ascribe the glory of freedom to a state in which the apparent elevation of the few is founded on the degradation of the many ... [7]

More broadly, Green did not believe that liberty could be equated, as in Bentham's view, with the absence of legal constraints, or with the lack of state intervention for social purposes. Rather, the ideal should be understood, he maintained, in terms of the individual's opportunity for self-development, a condition that could be promoted not just through the removal of legal and political constraints, but also through the dismantlement of restrictive social and economic barriers.

Green therefore put forward instead his distinctive interpretation of liberty as 'a positive power or capacity of doing or enjoying something worth doing or enjoying'.[8] Liberty thus involved for the individual an effective, rather than purely formal, possibility, in the light of existing social and economic circumstances, of developing one's capacities and realizing one's potentiality. At the same time, 'freedom in the positive sense' for Green also meant 'the liberation of the powers of all men equally for contributions to a common good',[9] a goal that could be pursued by fashioning, and sharing in, the material and cultural goods of modern society.

In formulating his conception of liberty in these terms, Green was thus attempting to advance an ideal of personal self-development that took account of forms of social and economic coercion – poverty, limited educational opportunities, or squalid housing conditions, for instance – that stifled the expression of individuals' capacities, eroding their ability 'to make the best of themselves'. On the practical level of public policy, the promotion of that ideal would therefore entail state legislation to protect from exploitation those least able to pursue their own interests. It would also require various forms of state intervention to remove various social obstacles blocking the path of the individual's material, moral and cultural improvement.

The classical liberal, negative conception of liberty as the absence of legal or political restraints was inadequate, in Green's view, not only because it failed to take sufficient account of those impediments, but also because it paid little attention to the kinds of moral purposes that the unrestricted private individual ought to pursue. Green's positive conception of liberty was therefore both social and *moral* in its focus. It emphasized the individual's capacity for doing something worthwhile in his or her inescapable role as a social and moral being, one who only develops morally through participation in, and membership of, civil society.

Central, then, to Green's positive view of liberty is the notion of moral self-development. For liberty is identified by him with moral conduct and the rational pursuit of moral purposes. Like Rousseau and the classical Greek thinkers before him, Green thus held that true freedom consisted in rational self-direction. Actions that, by contrast, were determined by narrow egoistic drives and impulses could not be said to be truly free. Nor, therefore, could political measures aimed at 'the mere removal of compulsion, the mere enabling of a man to do as he likes', be considered in themselves contributions to 'true freedom'.[10]

Moreover, this moral foundation of Green's conception of liberty is evident, too, in the way in which, in his idealist thinking, individual freedom was indissolubly linked to the common good – a moral purpose which the individual shared with all other members of the community. For it was as members of such a community, with clear duties towards it, that individuals acquired true freedom – their capacity for moral, intellectual and cultural self-development – in pursuit of the common good. 'Freedom in its positive sense' thus involved 'the liberation of the powers of all men equally for contributions to a common good'.[11]

Green's positive view of the state

Green's positive conception of liberty, which, as we have seen, was both morally based and socially orientated, was not just formulated by him at an abstract level of academic political philosophy. For it also provided in his thinking the main theoretical justification for a more positive and interventionist role for the state in the face of the acute social problems generated by industrialization.

Green thus maintained that in certain situations the democratic state was required to make policy decisions and laws that would both protect the weakest and poorest members of society from exploitation and remove social barriers that impeded the individual citizen's capacity for self-development. Collective action, he argued, could therefore contribute towards liberty in its positive sense, particularly by removing obstacles or disadvantages that had been created either by the abuse of economic or social power or by the historically entrenched system of hereditary privilege in English society, which included, notably, landlordism.

The state, in Green's view, should consequently intervene to regulate industrial conditions, enforcing acceptable standards of hygiene and safety. It should also make available to all public health and education services unless they were already supplied by voluntary action. Such measures were justified on the ground that an overworked, unhealthy or under-educated person could not be regarded as free in, for Green, the meaningful, positive sense of a capacity for self-development. The state should therefore be imbued with an active role in promoting conditions conducive to the realization of that ethical ideal.

To that end, in his 1881 lecture, 'Liberal Legislation and Freedom of Contract', Green argued that the state should seek to liberate the poor from ignorance, disease, squalid housing and exploitation at work. In practical policy terms, such collective action should include legal protection for landed tenants in Ireland, the provision of compulsory state education, regulation of public health, control over conditions and working hours in factories, and, controversially from a liberal standpoint, temperance legislation prohibiting the sale of alcohol to workers.

Explaining the theoretical justification for these forms of state intervention, Green maintained that:

> Our modern legislation ... with reference to labour, and education, and health, involving as it does manifold interference with freedom of contract, is justified on the ground that it is the business of the state, not indeed directly to promote moral goodness, for that, from the very nature of moral goodness, it cannot do, but to maintain the conditions without which a free exercise of the human faculties is impossible.[12]

Moreover, the role of the state was not only, in Green's view, an enabling one of this kind, designed to assist, through public policy and legislation, the individual's quest for self-improvement. It was also conceived by him as a means of furthering the other, related moral aspect of his ideal of liberty – the pursuit by individuals of the common good. For a more active, enabling democratic state should also seek, Green believed, to encourage wider participation, by all social classes, in the social and political life of the nation. In the case of the working class, such a process would help to ensure that the British government and parliament took account of its distinctive interests when they made policy decisions and enacted legislation.

More broadly, wider political participation would engender, too, a widespread sense of active citizenship that would both instil in the better-off a conscientious desire to remove social barriers and promote a general harmony of interests between all social groups. The result, Green hoped, would be a shared pursuit of the common good, an ideal that could be realized by the activities of the democratic state within a liberal society.

Conclusion

Green's revised, positive conception of liberty was thus accompanied and reinforced by a revised, positive view of the role of the state both as a means of encouraging the individual's self-development and, in Green's own phrase, as 'an instrument of the common good'. Both these social–liberal stances helped to provide, in the last quarter of the nineteenth century, a theoretical justification for increased state responsibility for improving the working and living conditions of the people. The revision of liberal thinking signalled by Green's positive view of liberty in turn reflected a changing climate of political opinion in Britain that was characterized not only by growing doubts about the social and economic effects of an unregulated capitalist system but also by a greater willingness to deploy the legislative powers of the state to rectify those deficiencies.

Yet in spite of Green's liberal revisionism, he sought to maintain continuity with classical liberalism by reaffirming some of its central individualist concerns, such as a belief in the benefits of private property and in the value of voluntary organization and activity, as well as in the merits of a capitalist economy. He was nonetheless concerned, above all, in his political thought to reformulate the fundamental liberal principle of individual liberty so as to take account of radically changed social and economic conditions in late nineteenth-century Britain.

After 1880, and until about 1920, the influence of Green's political ideas – particularly this positive view of liberty and his support for a more active, interventionist state – was far-reaching. They profoundly affected both practising British Liberal Party politicians and contemporary and subsequent liberal thinkers. Such politicians included Herbert Asquith, British Prime Minister between 1906 and 1915, and a student of Green's at Oxford, as well as contemporaries of Asquith's such as Herbert Samuel, Edward Grey and R.H. Haldane. At the same time, Green's political thought influenced the 'New Liberal' thinkers of the early twentieth century, including, most notably, Leonard Hobhouse (1864–1929) and J.A. Hobson (1858–1940), whose ideas provided a theoretical justification for the social and industrial legislation of the reforming Liberal governments between 1906 and 1914.

Notes

1   On this point, see R. Bellamy, *Liberalism and Modern Society*, Cambridge, Polity Press, 1992, pp. 35–47.

2   G. Sabine and T. Thorson, *A History of Political Theory*, 4th edn, Hinsdale, Illinois, Dryden Press, 1973, p. 657.

3   T.H. Green, *Lectures on the Principles of Political Obligation* (ed. A.D. Lindsay), London, Longmans, Green and Co., 1941, p. 8.

4   T.H. Green, *Lectures on the Principles of Political Obligation and Other Writings* (ed. P. Harris and J. Morrow), Cambridge, Cambridge University Press, 1986, p. 199. Lecture on 'Liberal Legislation and Freedom of Contract' (1881).

5   ibid. ('Liberal Legislation').

6   ibid.

7   ibid. p. 200 ('Liberal Legislation').

8   ibid. p. 199 ('Liberal Legislation').

9   ibid. p. 200 ('Liberal Legislation').

10   ibid. p. 199 ('Liberal Legislation').

11   ibid. p. 200 ('Liberal Legislation').

12   ibid. pp. 201–2 ('Liberal Legislation').

SECTION C

Contemporary debates

In the post-1945 theoretical discussion of liberty, it has been Isaiah Berlin's highly influential distinction between negative and positive views of liberty that has provided the essential starting-point for political philosophers and historians of political thought alike. For with his 1958 essay 'Two Concepts of Liberty', Berlin provided the coherent conceptual framework within which different traditions of thinking about liberty have subsequently been examined.

Moreover, following the example of Gerald MacCallum, in his 1967 article, 'Negative and Positive Freedom', many political philosophers have attempted to combine both negative and positive elements in a neutral, value-free definition of liberty in terms of the 'triadic' formula:

X (the agent) is free from Y (the obstacle or impediment) to do or become Z (the objective).

However, much of the surrounding debate in political philosophy has centred on the question of the true nature of the Y variable. Berlin and other advocates of the liberal, 'negative' view of liberty have maintained that the obstacle facing the individual agent in any given situation derives from deliberate human coercion. By contrast, Rousseau's descendants as advocates of the idealist, 'positive' view have sought to go beyond this position by focusing their attention on economic and social constraints on individual action.

In this philosophical debate, supporters of Berlin's approach have shared his conviction that the negative view of liberty it to be preferred, first, because it is neutral between different theories or interpretations of human nature, and, second, because only such a 'demoralized' conception of liberty can be used in comparative judgements about the relative degrees of liberty in different societies and political systems. The key assumption underlying this line of argument is that the liberal, negative view of liberty is a demoralized one precisely because it is concerned with the absence of deliberate coercion, not with the kinds of values or goals that the individual ought to pursue or with the kinds of capacities that he or she ought to exercise.

More broadly, many political philosophers have attempted to transcend this debate by agreeing that MacCallum established with his triadic formula a single, uncontested *concept* of liberty. They have also insisted, however, that there are many different *conceptions* or interpretations of that concept, all of which rest on different views of society or human nature. Each conception of liberty is thus a contested one since it cannot be said to embody the 'true' essence of freedom.

Since the last quarter of the twentieth century this academic discussion of the nature and meaning of freedom has become more than a matter of conceptual analysis. For since the mid-1970s the contending positions carried increasingly clear implications for the role and scope of the state in the economy and society. They have thus become positions vigorously advanced in an ideological, rather than purely philosophical, debate.

On the one hand, the negative view of liberty has been interpreted by libertarian political philosophers such as Robert Nozick (1938–) and by neoclassical liberal political and economic thinkers such as Friedrich von Hayek (1899–1992) as implying support both for a free-market economy and for a limited or even minimal state. In similar terms economists such as Milton Friedman have emphasized the importance of freedom of economic choice in the market-place – for consumers, employers and employees – and hence the absence of state interference with such choice as central aspects of personal liberty.

By contrast, late twentieth-century advocates of the positive conception of liberty, whose ranks have included democratic socialist thinkers and politicians, tended to be ideologically committed to active state intervention within a market-oriented economy and society in order to reduce economic and social constraints on individual freedom. The principal argument underlying their commitment has been that only through various collectivist measures, such as government redistribution of wealth and resources, may the ideal of liberty in its positive sense – the individual's opportunity for self-development – be truly realized.

Since the 1960s the debate about the connection between law, morality and liberty, which in the mid nineteenth century John Stuart Mill had generated with his essay *On Liberty*, was revived as another area of controversy in contemporary political thought. In Britain, the lawyer Lord Devlin developed what was in a sense an updated version of the response of Mill's most prominent critic, Sir James Fitzjames Stephen, to Mill's distinction between self-regarding and other-regarding actions and hence to his 'harm' principle limiting collective interference with private conduct. Echoing Fitzjames Stephen, Devlin argued that society by means of law ought to seek to punish or prohibit certain kinds of acts widely considered immoral and hence damaging for society at large. Furthermore, he maintained, society ought to do this, thereby upholding certain moral standards, even if those acts inflicted no direct harm on another person's interests or even rested on the mutual consent of all parties concerned.

Lord Devlin elaborated this argument in 'Morals and the Criminal Law' (1957) and in *The Enforcement of Morals* (1965), which were critical reactions to the Wolfenden Report of 1957 which had argued, in the spirit of Mill, that a private sphere of activity, even if widely judged to be immoral, should not be subject to direct legal interference. Such a sphere would encompass various choices of lifestyle and unorthodox forms of sexual behaviour, including homosexual relations between consenting adults.

In a celebrated reply to Devlin, the moral philospher H.L.A. Hart, in his *Law, Liberty and Morality* (1963) attempted to determine theoretically the limits of law in relation to personal morality and purely private activity. Upholding Mill's position, Hart sought to refute Devlin's argument that an act should be punished if it was commonly considered immoral even if it inflicted no direct harm on another's interests or rested on mutual consent. He thus, like Mill, ruled out collective interference with individual freedom on purely moralistic grounds. Unlike Mill, however, Hart did concede that some acts should be forbidden on paternalistic grounds, the state thereby deciding that it had in some cases a responsibility to protect people from themselves – as, for instance, when the criminal law prohibited trade in, and consumption of, hard drugs.

Returning to the debate on the broader distinction between negative and positive liberty, another more recent area of contemporary debate has centred on an alternative criticism of negative liberty that stresses the moral importance of freedom as personal autonomy. This interpretation, advanced, for instance, by the philosopher Joseph Raz in his *The Morality of Freedom* (1986), holds that liberty should be understood not in value-free terms as the mere absence of constraints or coercion, but rather as a means to the pursuit of valuable goals. These would include the enlargement of options and opportunities for individuals through the provision of collective goods, such as education, for instance, or through the redistribution of resources. Liberty is thus depicted in this positive sense as a morally desirable means to the attainment of autonomy, not in a negative sense as a condition derived from a right asserted against collective coercion.

By contrast, liberal critics of this approach have stressed the superior importance, as they regard it, of the absence of coercion and the provision of choice as essential aspects of individual freedom. Indeed, these are viewed from such a perspective as the necessary preconditions for, and hence as prior to, the enjoyment of personal autonomy. However, some of these defenders of the negative view of liberty would concede that its primary emphasis on the absence of coercion should be supplemented by some kind of redistributive principle so that liberty itself remains a valuable idea for socially or economically disadvantaged individuals.

An important example of this modified approach has been the principle of equal liberty expounded by the liberal political philosopher John Rawls (1921–). As part of his attempt to develop a theory of social or redistributive justice, Rawls thus described in his major work of political philosophy, *A Theory of Justice* (1971), the ideal foundations of a society based on his idea of 'justice as fairness'. For him these include the fundamental principle that each person in such a society should have an equal right to the most extensive liberty that is compatible with a similar degree of liberty being enjoyed by others. 'Liberty,' Rawls declares, 'can be restricted only for the sake of liberty.' In other words, as in Locke's interpretation, the individual's liberty is limited only by an obligation to respect the fact that every other individual enjoys an equal right to liberty.

In Rawls's theory of justice as fairness, this principle of equal liberty is complemented by a second principle which holds that social and economic inequalities are only justifiable if they not only operate in such as a way as to confer benefit on the least advantaged, but also are related to positions in society and the economy that are open to all under conditions of equal opportunity. This distinctive fusion of the principles of liberty and social justice raises, however, once again a familiar problem in the history of theorizing about liberty. For is liberty to be understood, as in the Lockean liberal tradition, as the entrenchment of formal rights – political, legal or social – for all individual citizens? Or is liberty to be interpreted, as in the tradition derived from Rousseau, as the opportunity to take advantage of particular rights or freedoms either as a result of a more equal distribution of resources in society or through the provision of collective goods?

Finally, a different line of criticism of the negative view of liberty has been opened up since the 1980s by the communitarian critique of liberalism. Communitarian philosophers such as Charles Taylor, Alasdair MacIntyre, Michael Sandel and Michael Walzer have argued that liberals, by upholding a negative conception of freedom, and by advancing a wider liberal individualism in their political and economic thinking, are adhering to a false ideal of the 'unencumbered self'. For, it is argued, modern liberals have continued to portray an image of the isolated individual pursuing his interests and goals within his own private sphere and without any attachment to the traditions, culture, customs or institutions of his particular society.

In developing this critique, communitarian philosophers were, to a large extent, reacting against the highly individualist theories of both Rawls and Robert Nozick. In place of the primary emphasis on individual liberty or rights inherent in such theories, communitarians, by contrast, have based their alternative vision of society upon the idea of an 'embedded self', a social being whose identity is inextricably linked to the community in which he or she is placed, and whose existence is constrained by social obligations and responsibilities.

Communitarian philosophers have therefore formulated a social conception of freedom, rooted in the social foundation of human personality and in an awareness of the social implications of individual action. Liberal philosophers, however, have responded to such criticisms by arguing that the liberal approach to personal liberty is compatible both with collective activity and with communal values. The affirmation, for instance, of the fundamental freedoms of expression and association involves defending liberties which, whilst attributed to individuals, are essential means of ensuring not only the collective progress of civil society but also its protection from arbitrary incursions by the state.

These, then, are some of the interesting controversies and areas of debate that have arisen from political reflection on liberty in the post-1945 period. Each of them, in distinctive ways, has built upon, or critically responded to, the intellectual traditions, developed over 300 years, surrounding this core political value and ideal.

Further reading

I. Berlin, 'Two Concepts of Liberty' (1958), reprinted in *Four Essays on Liberty*, Oxford, Oxford University Press, 1969.

Lord Devlin, *The Enforcement of Morals*, Oxford, Oxford University Press, 1965.

T. Gray, *Freedom*, London, Macmillan, 1991.

H.L.A. Hart, *Law, Liberty and Morality*, Oxford, Oxford University Press, 1963.

W. Kymlicka, *Liberalism, Community and Culture*, Oxford, Oxford University Press, 1989.

W. Kymlicka, *Contemporary Political Philosophy: An Introduction*, Oxford, Oxford University Press, 1990, Ch. 6.

W. Kymlicka, 'Liberal Individualism and Liberal Neutrality', in S. Avineri and A. De-Shalit (eds), *Communitarianism and Individualism*, Oxford, Oxford University Press, 1992, pp. 29–50.

G.C. MacCallum, 'Negative and Positive Freedom' (1967), reprinted in D. Miller (ed.), *Liberty*, Oxford, Oxford University Press, 1991, pp. 100–22.

A. MacIntyre, *After Virtue*, London, Duckworth, 1981.

D. Miller (ed.), *Liberty*, Oxford, Oxford University Press, 1991. (A collection of some of the most influential analyses of the concept of liberty over the last 120 or so years.)

S. Mulhall and A. Swift, *Liberals and Communitarians*, 2nd edn, Oxford, Blackwell, 1996. (A good introduction to the philosophical debate between liberals and communitarians.)

R. Nozick, *Anarchy, State and Utopia*, Oxford, Blackwell, 1974.

Z. Pelczynski and J. Gray (eds), *Conceptions of Liberty in Political Philosophy*, London, Athlone Press, 1984. (A useful collection of studies of influential interpretations of the concept of liberty in the history of political thought.)

J. Rawls, *A Theory of Justice*, Oxford, Oxford University Press, 1971.

J. Rawls, *Political Liberalism*, New York, Columbia Press, 1993.

M. Sandel, *Liberalism and the Limits of Justice*, Cambridge, Cambridge University Press, 1982.

C. Taylor, 'Atomism', in S. Avineri and A. De-Shalit (eds), *Communitarianism and Individualism*, Oxford, Oxford University Press, 1992, pp. 29–50.

Rights

The term 'human rights' has become a central part of the vocabulary of contemporary political argument and debate. This has been particularly the case since 1945 in the wake of the brutalities and horrors that characterized the dictatorships of Nazi Germany and the Soviet Union. As well as being a major concern of Western political thought since that time, rights have also become embodied both in international declarations and conventions and in the constitutions of nation-states. They have also been the inspirational idea underlying a wide variety of practical claims and demands made not only by political movements and organized groups but also by individual citizens.

'Human rights' as a term is the contemporary member of a family of concepts which includes 'natural rights', 'the rights of man' and 'civil rights'. It has its historical roots in the natural law tradition of seventeenth- and eighteenth-century European political thought. Like the related concept of liberty, the idea of rights has become, since that period, deeply embedded in Western liberal–democratic theory and increasingly exported as a value and ideal throughout the international order – particularly since the mid twentieth century.

Furthermore, the concept of rights has been, as Michael Freeden has noted, 'one of the most reputable and positively connoted in political theory'.[1] The widespread promotion of ideas associated with the concept has thus generated far less ideological or political controversy than the espousal, for instance, of the ideals of equality or social justice. Indeed, as Jeremy Waldron observed, not since the American and French Revolutions of the late eighteenth century have rights been so widely used 'as touchstones of political evaluation'; for 'in the market-place of domestic politics and in international affairs, respect for rights is the new criterion of political legitimacy'.[2]

Reflecting this generally favourable connotation, a broad definition of human rights, considered as both a legal and a political concern, has been offered by one commentator as a set of 'internationally agreed values, standards or rules regulating the conduct of states towards their own citizens and towards non-citizens'.[3] This view itself echoed the tone of the preamble of the most influential declaration of rights since 1945 – namely, the United Nations 1948 Universal Declaration of Human Rights – which had defined rights as 'a common standard of achievement for all peoples and all nations'. Nevertheless, in spite of such agreed critical standards, rights have remained for at least 200 years matters of both theoretical and practical controversy and debate.

SECTION A

Historical development of the concept of rights

The concept of rights first emerged in European thought in the twelfth century[4] and was developed into a theoretical form by the end of the fourteenth century. In particular, it appeared as a prominent idea within medieval Christian doctrine – notably in the thinking of the thirteenth-century Italian theologian and philosopher St Thomas Aquinas (1224–74). His world-view emphasized the importance of God-given 'natural law' as an underlying force in the universe. For Aquinas this amounted to a set of general moral principles laid down by God as the basis for proper human conduct. Though God-given and part of the divine plan, natural law could be discovered by rational human thought and formed a yardstick for judging both political society and the 'positive' laws enacted by mankind.

In Aquinas's conception of natural law, it was the moral duties of human beings – of rulers and subjects alike – that were stressed rather than the rights of the individual citizen. Nevertheless, early modern theories of natural law that were associated with the gradual development in Europe of the modern secular, territorial state emerged from this medieval theoretical background after 1500. Already evident in the writings of the Dutch philosopher Hugo Grotius (1583–1645), such theories, which became increasingly free of medieval theological trappings, were linked in the seventeenth century to two prevailing schools of thought about God-given natural rights.

The first of these, a more conservative one, developed most vividly by the English political philosopher Thomas Hobbes (1588–1679), centred above all on the individual's right of self-preservation. According to Hobbes's theory, individual human beings surrendered the virtually unlimited right to freedom which they enjoyed in the 'state of nature' – man's 'natural', pre-social condition – when they entered civil society. They made this transition, as we have seen,[5] on the basis of a social contract, or 'covenant', formed among themselves out of respect for the principal laws of nature, which were discovered through reason and designed to ensure men's survival in a dangerous world.

In Hobbes's view, then, natural law consisted of certain rules of self-preservation that egoistic individuals came to observe as a result of their enlightened self-interest. Such rules not only imposed certain natural duties – most crucially, the duty not to kill another person – but also conferred certain natural rights – most vitally, the right to preserve and defend one's life – with which human beings were endowed by God.

Hobbes's approach to natural law and natural rights had conservative, and indeed authoritarian, political implications since his interpretation of these ideas was bound up, through his social contract theory, with his advocacy of the virtually absolute authority of the state, entrusted by the individual with ensuring his security of person and property. A more radical and far-reaching school of thought about natural rights emerged, however, later in the seventeenth century, expressed most powerfully in the political philosophy of John Locke (1632–1704).

In his major work of political theory, his *Second Treatise of Government* (1689), Locke shared the contemporary view that natural rights were rights enjoyed by human beings in the state of nature, before the formation of civil or political society. Like Hobbes, too, Locke connected such natural rights to the concept of natural law – to the notion of a set of universal, God-given moral principles entailing both rights and duties for rulers and subjects alike.

Locke's political theory, however, placed particular emphasis upon the rights that individuals held in relation to governments and rulers, rights that were sanctioned or authenticated by natural law. The primary role of governments was viewed from this perspective as one of protecting those fundamental natural rights – namely, the rights to life, liberty and property. Moreover, such rights could be claimed and invoked by the people, Locke asserted, against a tyrannical government that acted in an arbitrary or oppressive manner.

This interpretation of natural rights was thus put forward by Locke as a major part of his theoretical justification for opposition, and even armed resistance, to absolute government. Specifically, he developed his interrelated natural rights and social contract theories as essential elements both of his critique of the absolutist monarchies of Charles II and James II, and of his subsequent intellectual defence of the English Glorious Revolution of 1688.

By the end of the seventeenth century, Locke had therefore become the most articulate and influential exponent of a theory of natural rights that was replete with radical political implications. His position had to some extent already been anticipated in England earlier in the seventeenth century by radical Protestants who sought to challenge established secular and ecclesiastical authorities in the name of the individual rights of the common people.[6] As later developed by Locke, this view of natural rights, though revolutionary in its wider significance, involved the defensive assertion of rights against the invasion by the state of the individual's sphere of private interests. Such a view therefore implied a theory of limited government that both restricted the role of the state to the protection of the individual's fundamental natural rights – to life, liberty and property – and explicitly prohibited the state, on moral grounds, from violating those rights.

Locke's radical, anti-statist view of natural rights was restated a hundred years later by the late eighteenth-century political thinker and activist, Thomas Paine (1737–1809), a major intellectual influence on the American Revolution of 1776–83. Shaped by the prevailing assumptions of European Enlightenment thought, with its emphasis on the capacity of human reason for resolving social problems and for developing new political structures, Paine's defence of individual rights was set out in his classic text, *The Rights of Man*, Part 1 (1791). In its pages he argued that the central purpose of all governments was the protection of what he referred to as the natural and imprescriptible rights of man. Citing the 1789 French Declaration of the Rights of Man and of Citizens, Paine identified these as the rights to liberty, property, security and resistance of oppression. He maintained, too, that all other civil and political rights – to, for instance, limits placed on government, to freedom to choose a government, to freedom of speech, and to fair taxation – derived from those fundamental natural rights.

Paine's views were echoed by the authors of both the American and the French declarations of rights that accompanied the democratic revolutions which he himself had either inspired and actively assisted, as in America, or strongly defended, as in the case of France. Indeed, Paine's phrase, the 'rights of man', the title of his most famous work, was reproduced in the title of the 1789 French Declaration of the Rights of Man and of Citizens. More widely, that phrase had gradually replaced 'natural rights' during the latter period of the eighteenth century, thereby removing the theological assumptions, derived from medieval Christian doctrine, that were still implicit in seventeenth-century natural law theories.

Following the American and French Revolutions, then, the doctrine of the rights of man became embodied in succinct declarations of rights, as well as in new constitutions, which stressed the need to uphold the natural rights of the individual citizen against other individuals and particularly against the state itself. The American Declaration of Independence of July 1776, the revolutionary manifesto of the thirteen newly-independent states of America, formerly colonies of Britain, thus affirmed the individual's 'inalienable rights' to 'life, liberty and the pursuit of happiness', to be safeguarded by the state. The Declaration went on to assert, in the spirit of Locke, that governments, which derived their powers from the consent of the governed, were instituted to secure those 'inalienable' rights, and that any government which sought to violate such rights could legitimately be overthrown by the people.

In a similar vein, the 'Declaration of the Rights of Man and of Citizens', proclaimed by the French Constituent Assembly in August 1789, affirmed as 'natural and sacred' the 'inalienable' rights to 'liberty, security and resistance to oppression'. Moreover, from these fundamental natural rights of man, the French Declaration stressed, stemmed a whole set of democratic political principles – including the accountability of public officials, freedom of speech, and popular participation in government.

Both these revolutionary declarations were products of particular historical circumstances and of popular uprisings against particular regimes – namely, the monarchical governments of George III of Britain and of Louis XVI of France. Yet both documents were presented in a style that invoked universal principles which purported to have a moral objectivity transcending time or place. For the rights of man, so the declarations claimed, belonged to all human beings by virtue of their humanity, and not just to members of a particular nation, race or religion.

Critiques of theories of the natural rights of man

In spite of the profound impact of the doctrine of the rights of man upon the American and French Revolutions, by the end of the eighteenth century a systematic and coherent critique of its central assumptions was being developed from various points on the political spectrum. Directly challenging the French revolutionaries' celebration of the doctrine, the Irish politician and political thinker, Edmund Burke (1729–97) played a major role in this process of critical reaction. In his highly-influential work, *Reflections on the Revolution in France* (1790), Burke argued that the notion of pre-social absolute and fundamental natural rights was meaningless in the context of civil society, which by its very nature was an organic and evolving entity. For him, the only real and meaningful rights were those prescribed by custom or tradition and transmitted from one generation to another.

Moreover, in Burke's view, the concept of the rights of man was also simplistic since it took no account of the complexities of either civil society or civil government. Underlying these criticisms lay Burke's deep conviction that the individual could not be abstracted from his particular community, and that his identity could not therefore be interpreted in merely abstract terms as the possessor of natural rights derived from some fictitious pre-social natural condition.

Shortly after the publication of Burke's *Reflections on the Revolution in France*, Thomas Paine had responded vigorously in his *Rights of Man*, Parts I and

II (1791–2). But in the decades that followed, further critiques of the doctrine of the rights of man were developed from both classical liberal and revolutionary socialist standpoints. In the case of the former, the English utilitarian philosopher Jeremy Bentham (1748–1832) famously dismissed the notion of the rights of man as ' rhetorical nonsense ... nonsense upon stilts',[7] preferring instead the principle of utility – the promotion of the greatest happiness of the greatest number – as a more reliable basis for social and political reform.

Bentham's objections to the idea of the natural rights of man, refined in particular in his work, *Anarchical Fallacies* (1843), were both philosophical and political in character. Philosophically, he rejected the notion that statements about the rights of man were even meaningful. It made no sense, in his view, to refer to abstract rights that existed before, or independently of, particular legal codes or systems. By contrast, only statements about specific rights and corresponding duties embodied in a system of law were considered by him to be truly meaningful. For Bentham, then, it followed that the only real rights in civil society were man-made, positive, legal rights established by actual legal systems or procedures.

Politically, too, Bentham argued that the invocation by would-be reformers or even revolutionaries of the doctrine of the abstract rights of man actually served, for various reasons, as a barrier to the enactment of social and political reform. In place of that hollow doctrine, he therefore urged the application of the principle of utility, with its pragmatic assessment of the beneficial consequences of human actions in terms of their tendency to promote the general happiness or public interest. That principle alone, not the high-flown nonsense of the 'rights of man', would provide the yardstick for judging the desirability of either public policy or government legislation.

Nevertheless, later classical liberal thinkers – notably, John Stuart Mill (1806–73) – did modify this harsh utilitarian critique in several important respects. In particular, Mill accepted the existence in civil society of certain rights-based interests that could be reconciled with the principle of utility. Whilst he rejected both the abstract notion of abstract rights and the conservative idea of conventional or customary rights, he did advance, during the course of his defence of freedom of self-regarding conduct,[8] the alternative notion of rights-based interests protected by law. As he wrote in *On Liberty*:

> [Each person] should be bound to observe a certain line of conduct towards the rest. This conduct consists ... in not injuring the interests of one another; or rather certain interests which, either by express legal provision or by tacit understanding, are considered as rights.[9]

For Mill this area of rights-based interests encompassed the individual's own interest in his or her personal security and safety. It thus amounted to a sphere of private activity within which no form of state interference should be permitted. The protection by law of that private sphere would in turn promote the utilitarian goal of the general happiness. Mill's distinctive conception of rights could thus, he believed, be reconciled with the principle of utility espoused not only by Bentham but also by his own father, James Mill, Bentham's friend and colleague.

Explaining further how he had come to adopt this compromise position on rights, John Stuart Mill pointed out that, whilst rejecting any reliance on 'the idea of natural rights, as a thing independent of utility',

> I regard utility as the ultimate appeal on all ethical questions; but it must be utility in the largest sense, grounded on the permanent interests of a man as a progressive being.[10]

A third highly-influential critique of the doctrine of the rights of man emerged in the writings of the German economic historian and revolutionary socialist thinker, Karl Marx (1818–83). Like both Burke and Bentham, Marx dismissed the doctrine on grounds of its excessively individualistic and abstract nature. However, he advanced his own critical position as part of a wider radical critique of the 'bourgeois' liberal theory of rights. This was developed by Marx in the context of his examination, in his youthful work, *On the Jewish Question* (1844), of the limitations of proposals for extending civil and political rights to Jews in the German Christian state of Prussia.

Whilst exploring this, at the time controversial issue, Marx conceded that in the past the liberal assertion of individual rights within the liberal–constitutional state had led to the emancipation of certain social groups from the oppressive hierarchical structures of feudal society. But the true liberation of mankind, Marx argued, lay in the emancipation of individuals from *all* oppressive class institutions, not just feudal ones, that existed in *all* aspects of civil society and not merely within the apparatus of the state. From this distinctive standpoint Marx observed that:

> the so-called rights of man ... are nothing but the rights of the member of civil society, i.e. egoistic man, man separated from other men and the community.[11]

Moreover, the ideals originally celebrated in the French Declaration of the Rights of Man – liberty, property, equality and security – in reality, he maintained, legitimized the 'withdrawal' of bourgeois man from society, thereby undermining his communal life and eroding his civic responsibilities. In addition, the liberal political rights affirmed in the French Declaration fostered, in Marx's view, not only the illusion of equality in a bourgeois society riven by inequalities of wealth and power, but also the façade of democracy in a bourgeois state characterized by repressive class rule.

For Marx, then, the 'rights of man' formed a central part of the ideology, the prevailing values and beliefs, of the dominant bourgeois-capitalist class of industrialists and entrepreneurs that had risen to power in Western societies since the French Revolution. In wider and more general terms, his critique of liberal declarations and statements of rights rested, like the otherwise very different critiques of Burke and Bentham, on his objection to the universalist and ahistorical character of such revered documents. These needed instead, he insisted, to be viewed against the background of particular economic and social conditions.

Marx's highly restrictive ideological interpretation of the idea of the natural rights of man was to exert a major influence on the thinking of his revolutionary socialist followers in the late nineteenth century and during the first half of the twentieth century. From the 1950s, however, Western Marxists tended to view the concept of human rights in a more favourable light, regarding it as having some value as a means to attaining the broader goal of a socialist economy and society.

Development of the concept of human rights in the twentieth century

In the face of the critiques developed by Burke, Bentham and Marx, theories of the natural rights of man declined in influence during the nineteenth and early twentieth centuries. This process was underlined by the growing political impact of utilitarian philosophy in Britain. For it was its central principle of utility, rather than the doctrine of the rights of man, that provided the main theoretical justification for the gradual movement towards mass democracy in Britain after 1832.

Moreover, the increasing development in Europe of social theory, embodied in the ideas and writings not only of Marx but also of major sociological thinkers such as Max Weber (1864–1920) in Germany and Emile Durkheim (1858–1917) in France, further weakened the intellectual appeal of natural rights theories. Weber, Durkheim and their followers conceived of human society not as the artificial creation of rights-bearing individuals, but rather as an evolving natural process shaped by the interaction between individuals and cultural, social and economic forces.

Later, during the 1920s and 1930s, the idea of natural rights came under pressure from a third intellectual direction – the increasingly influential philosophical school of logical positivism. Developed by philosophers such as Bertrand Russell, G.E. Moore and A.J. Ayer, this theoretical approach insisted that all propositions should consist of statements that could be verified by experience or observation. As a consequence, it rejected as meaningless, in a manner akin to Bentham's critique, any statements about 'natural rights' on the ground that they did not refer to observable phenomena and were therefore empirically unverifiable.

In spite, however, of these concentrated onslaughts from diverse theoretical sources, by the 1940s the concept of rights regained its force and influence, albeit recast in the form of the idea of 'human rights', regarded as belonging to every human being by virtue of his or her humanity. Superseding the traditional conception of rights as based on notions of God-given natural law and of a social contract, the refurbished idea of 'human rights' rested on the underlying assumption that each individual person was entitled to an equal degree of respect as a human being.

The particular historical factor that propelled the idea of human rights back into the foreground of political debate was the growing awareness in the 1940s of the scale of violation of such rights that was being perpetrated by the Nazi dictatorship in Germany. The British and American war leaders, Winston Churchill and Franklin Roosevelt thus stated in the preface to their Atlantic Charter in 1942 that 'complete victory over their enemies is essential to decent life, liberty, independence and religious freedom, and to preserve human rights and justice, in their own land as well as in other lands'. Moreover, at the end of the Second World War, Allied tribunals in 1945, in the course of charging Nazi and Japanese leaders with 'crimes against humanity', invoked the traditional concept of natural law in order to override the defence that those charged with such crimes had only been obeying the laws of the regimes they served.[12]

It was against this historical background that, in 1948, the United Nations Organization published its Universal Declaration of Human Rights. This was a systematic attempt to secure universal recognition of a wide range of human rights. The Declaration thus affirmed, in its Articles 1–21, the importance of civil and political rights such as the rights of life, liberty, property, equality before the law, privacy, a fair trial, freedom of speech and assembly, freedom of movement, religious freedom, freedom to participate in government – either directly or indirectly – the right to political asylum, and the absolute right not to be tortured. The 1948 Declaration also affirmed, more controversially, the importance of certain social and economic rights – including the right to education, to work for a just wage, to social security, and to an adequate standard of living.

The United Nations Declaration was not, however, incorporated in the positive law of its signatory member states, the Soviet Union in particular opposing such a move. Nor was it accorded the status of international law since the document was applicable to all individual citizens rather than to particular nation-states. Nevertheless, publication of the Declaration did lead to the subsequent establishment of various international tribunals and agencies which helped to exert political pressure on countries guilty of violating civil and political rights. Another positive consequence was the establishment in 1950 of the European Convention for the Protection of Human Rights and Fundamental Freedoms (abbreviated to the European Convention on Human Rights), which was designed to translate into practical terms the principles enunciated in the Declaration of 1948.

Problems associated with the concept of human rights

The widespread recognition after 1945 of the political importance of human rights was not confined to these various international declarations and agencies. It was also reflected in various works of political theory, particularly in the period that witnessed the revival of systematic philosophical enquiry about politics from 1970 onwards. Some of these contemporary contributions to theoretical reflection on rights will be broadly outlined at the end of this chapter.

A human right has been defined by Freeden as:

> a conceptual device, expressed in linguistic form, that assigns priority to certain human or social attributes regarded as essential to the functioning of a human being; that is intended to serve as a protective capsule for those attributes; and that appeals for deliberate action to ensure such protection.[13]

From this perspective, then, human rights may be regarded as those fundamental rights that should be protected constitutionally and legally so that they may be enjoyed by all individual human beings regardless of their status in the particular societies in which they live.

A number of problems, however, both theoretical and practical, have arisen from broad definitions of this kind. First, there is the often glaring discrepancy between the apparent universality of human rights as internationally agreed standards, on the one hand, and the cultural relativism apparent in their selective implementation, on the other. Numerous reports of Amnesty International and other human rights organizations, as well as those of United Nations agencies, have thus demonstrated in detail both the absence of universal respect for human rights and the reality of numerous instances of their systematic violation.

Nonetheless, the depressing frequency of such human rights abuses has provided not so much an argument against the universality of standards but rather clear evidence of the difficulty of maintaining and ensuring those standards. As Peter Baehr has observed, nation-states throughout the world affirm certain moral values or norms embodied in national legislation prohibiting, for instance, murder and theft. The frequent occurrence of cases of murder and theft does not constitute grounds either for questioning the value of such norms or for repealing the national laws in which they are embodied. 'The same,' Baer argues, 'is true of international standards: they are insufficiently respected, but that does not mean that no consensus can be reached about the nature of such standards.'[14]

The acute problem, however, of ensuring that those critical standards are universally observed has arisen not only from the actions of oppressive regimes, but also from the wide cultural and religious differences that so evidently exist throughout the international order. The political debate which such differences have generated on the question of human rights has been crystallized, for instance, in Western liberal responses to certain Islamic fundamentalist practices that reflect particular religious, moral or cultural attitudes or beliefs. Such practices have included brutal forms of capital and corporal punishment, as well as highly restrictive treatment of women.

The difficulty, then, inherent in defending the notion of human rights as internationally agreed standards or rules of conduct stems to a large extent from the practical reality that such standards, so far from being universal, have tended to be observed most consistently in Western liberal–democratic societies and cultures. The need for their wider, indeed universal, observance arguably provides grounds for ensuring that human rights, in order to be applicable to all individuals regardless of cultural differences, should be both fairly generalized in nature and not too broad or all-embracing in their scope.

A second problem associated with the definition of the concept of human rights has revolved around the distinction, greatly stressed by Bentham, between legal and moral rights – between, that is, the empirical claim that a person has a legal right to something and the moral claim that he or she has a human right to some benefit or form of treatment. For Bentham, moral rights – in the form of the so-called 'rights of man' – were really a mistaken way of describing legal rights that ought to exist. But 'natural rights' – the conceptual precursor of the 'rights of man' – were called such in seventeenth-century political thought because, like natural law, they were held to be God-given and not dependent on man-made positive law. In Bentham's view, that was the source of the illusory nature of the very concept; for the natural 'rights of man' were rhetorical and metaphysical nonsense, he argued, precisely because they could not be translated into, or enforced by, particular legal systems or codes.

Moreover, ever since the French Declaration of 1789, normative statements about rights – whether described as the 'rights of man' or 'human rights' – which clearly revolved around questions of *value*, have been presented as statements of fact about human beings, as, for instance, in the French Declaration's assertion that 'men are born free and equal'. By contrast, legal rights, as Bentham emphasized, were laid down in law or in a system of formal rules; as a consequence they were also enforceable through the courts of law. For these reasons right was truly, in Bentham's phrase, 'the child of law'.[15]

Britain has provided a clear illustration of this problem of the apparent unenforceability of moral rights. For most individual human rights – including, for instance, the rights to free speech or freedom of assembly – were not embodied in statute law until 1998 when the European Convention on Human Rights was incorporated into British law. Prior to that innovation, individual human rights were instead recognized in Britain as common law principles, established by precedent, custom and tradition. However, the somewhat imprecise legal basis of such arrangements at times meant that individual rights could not be easily upheld in British courts. Examples of such difficulties can be cited as the lack of firm safeguards against government restrictions on press and media freedom during the late 1980s.

Bills of Rights – that is, codified sets of rights 'entrenched' in constitutional law – which have been established in other Western countries (e.g. the USA) have provided the means of preventing such problems by formally protecting individual human rights from the incursions of national governments. However, the introduction of such Bills of Rights has been accompanied by at least two potentially serious drawbacks. First, the codification of sets of rights might well enlarge the powers of the judiciary rather than those of elected politicians since the former would be entrusted with determining the proper scope of individual human rights. Second, the embodiment in legal codes or systems of sets of human rights does not by itself ensure that such rights will actually be respected by the state. As Andrew Heywood has observed, the Soviet Constitutions of 1936 and 1977, which ostensibly entrenched a whole range of human rights, provide a cautionary historical reminder of this grim discrepancy between theoretical commitment and practical realization. Citing, too, an illustration of this point drawn from a Western liberal–democratic state, Heywood further notes that the United States Constitution's Fifth Amendment, enacted in 1870, sought formally to safeguard for American citizens the right to vote regardless of race, colour or previous condition of servitude. Yet in practice, in many Southern states, African-Americans did not exercise the right to vote until the 1960s.[16]

Such grave shortcomings underline the problematic question of the status and hence enforceability of human as opposed to legal rights. Nevertheless, it is worth remembering that much of the theoretical inspiration behind the most influential and systematic embodiments of human rights – notably, the US Bill of Rights, the UN Declaration of Human Rights, and the European Convention on Human Rights – was provided by political thinkers such as Locke, Paine and their successors who strove to defend and promote the cause of the natural, pre-social and pre-legal 'rights of man'.

In addition to this matter of the practical *status* of moral or human rights, their widening *scope* has developed into a further area of controversy and dispute, particularly since 1945. 'To what *kinds* of rights are individual human beings entitled?' has thus emerged as another problematic question – on both practical and theoretical levels. As we have seen, since the seventeenth century an essentially *negative* conception of rights became prevalent in Western political thought. For theories of natural rights, which were gradually secularized in the twentieth century in the form of ideas about human rights, implied the existence of a private sphere of rights enjoyed by the individual – to life, liberty, property, and so on – that ought not to be invaded by other individuals or by the state. Such rights were thus civil and political rights held by the individual citizen against other persons or against the state. They thereby presupposed, too, the liberal idea of limited government – of limits placed upon the state and its institutions for the purpose of protecting the individual's private sphere of activity.

However, in the second half of the twentieth century a more positive conception of social and economic, or 'welfare', rights arose in political and social theory. In his work *Citizenship and Social Class* (1950), the British social theorist T.H. Marshall traced the roots of this development. In an influential analysis, he described the gradual historical evolution of three main sets of citizenship rights – first, from the seventeenth century, *civil* rights, designed to protect individual freedom within civil society, and entailing limited government; second, from the eighteenth century, *political* rights, which conferred upon the individual the right to participate in the processes of government – whether directly or indirectly; and third, and most recently, *social* rights, which aimed to ensure for the individual citizen a minimum social status. This last set of rights included the right to social security and economic well-being and to other conditions conducive to a civilized life. Such social rights would also require the presence of a more active and interventionist state that assumed greater responsibilities for the working and living conditions of the people.

In 1948 the UN Universal Declaration of Human Rights incorporated not only 'negative' civil and political rights but also 'positive' social and economic rights – Marshall's third category – which included the rights to education, social security and employment. However, the addition of such positive 'welfare' rights has generated considerable debate, first, about whether they can truly be treated as rights at all, and, second, about the ideological and policy implications of the implementation of such rights.

D.D. Raphael, for instance, has argued that the Universal Declaration of 1948 'would seem less starry-eyed' and unrealistic if it had confined its list of social and economic rights merely to the rights to social security and education since both those claims were fundamental to a dignified human life and capable, too, of being broadly met by governments. By contrast, the inclusion of welfare 'rights' that were practically unattainable in many states – such as the rights to work or to paid holidays – tended in effect to jeopardize the implementation of fundamental and attainable civil and political rights.[17]

Doubts, then, have been raised in this area of debate about the practical attainability of social and economic rights in view of the severe resource constraints suffered by many, particularly Third World, countries. Such so-called rights have thus been regarded by some political theorists as illegitimate or vacuous since the social and economic conditions necessary for realizing such 'rights' are non-existent in many parts of the world. Maurice Cranston, for example, argued that it was therefore preferable and logically more coherent to regard welfare rights as political and social ideals or recommendations.[18]

A further criticism levelled at the status of social and economic rights has focused on their apparent lack of universality. For such 'rights', it has been argued, really amount to claims made upon governments by citizens of particular societies or nation-states rather than claims made by individuals by virtue of their status as human beings. Moreover, social and economic rights are role based and cannot be universalized. For instance, the right to social security applies mainly to the poor and disadvantaged; the right to holidays with pay applies only to the employed; and so on. In response to this criticism, however, Raymond Plant has contended that 'positive' social and economic rights such as the right to social security are as universal in character as 'negative' civil and political rights such as the right to a fair trial. For the right to social security revolves around how an individual ought to be treated in circumstances – in this case, those involving poverty – in which any human being could potentially find himself or herself.[19]

Turning to the second major area of debate about 'positive' welfare rights of this kind – concerning their broader ideological implications – the major objection raised here is that their implementation would, in practice, require the enlargement rather than the limitation of the powers of the state. Such a development might well lead to invasions of the individual's autonomy – his private sphere of activity. By contrast, it is argued, the protection of civil and political rights requires collective action confined mainly to the establishment of a legal framework ensuring individual freedom and hence autonomy in many areas of conduct.

However, the response to this line of argument from 'positive' rights theorists has been twofold. First, they maintain that while it is true that the promotion of welfare rights has required a more active and interventionist state, it is also the case that the protection of 'negative' rights has, in certain political circumstances, required positive state action – for example, legislation ensuring freedom of association. Second, and perhaps more pertinently in modern liberal–democratic societies, 'positive' rights theorists maintain that the individual's freedom, in the traditional 'negative' sense of autonomy or non-interference, is restricted in society just as much by social and economic barriers as by deliberate state interference. Collective provision of social and economic resources (e.g. education or welfare benefits) is thus viewed from this perspective as just as fundamental to the exercise of human rights as freedom from direct state coercion.

The post-1945 debate, therefore, over the proper scope of human rights has been concerned with the nature and range of the attributes of human beings that should be protected either by general declarations or conventions, or by particular legal codes or procedures. The problem, in particular, of the practical implementation of certain rights that serve, in Freeden's phrase, as 'protective capsules'[20] for particular human attributes is one that appears prominently, as we have seen, in two other major areas of debate about rights – concerning, first, the tensions between universality and cultural relativism, and second, the distinction between moral and legal rights. Perhaps such difficulties underline the need, already suggested, for maintaining the focus of attention – in political theory and practice alike – upon a set of rights that are not only general and universal in nature but also closely and clearly delimited in their scope.

Notes

1   M. Freeden, *Rights*, Milton Keynes, Open University Press, 1991, p. 1.
2   J. Waldron (ed.), *'Nonsense upon Stilts': Bentham, Burke and Marx on the Rights of Man*, London, Methuen, 1987, p. 1.
3   P. Baehr, *Human Rights: Universality in Practice*, London, Macmillan, 1999, p. 1.
4   See R. Tuck, *Natural Rights Theories: Their Origin and Development*, Cambridge, Cambridge University Press, 1979.
5   See Chapters 1B and 2B.
6   See R. Eccleshall, 'Liberalism', in R. Eccleshall *et al.*, *Political Ideologies: An Introduction*, 2nd edn, London, Routledge, 1994, pp. 28–57.
7   J. Bentham, 'Anarchical Fallacies' (1843), in Waldron, op. cit. p. 53.
8   See Chapter 3B.
9   J.S. Mill, *On Liberty* (1859), in *Utilitarianism and Other Writings* (ed. M. Warnock), Glasgow, Collins, 1962, p. 205.
10   ibid. p. 136.
11   K. Marx, 'On the Jewish Question' (1844), in D. McLellan (ed.), *Karl Marx: Early Texts*, Oxford, Blackwell, 1971, p. 102.
12   Waldron, op. cit. p. 154.
13   Freeden, op. cit. p. 7.
14   Baehr, op. cit. p. 19.
15   Bentham, 'Anarchical Fallacies', in Waldron, op. cit. p. 73.
16   See A. Heywood, *Political Theory: An Introduction*, 2nd edn, London, Macmillan, 1999, p. 190.
17   See D.D. Raphael, *Problems of Political Philosophy*, rev. edn, London, Macmillan, 1990, p. 110.
18   See M. Cranston, *What Are Human Rights?*, London, Bodley Head, 1973.
19   See R. Plant, *Modern Political Thought*, Oxford, Blackwell, 1991, pp. 271–2.
20   Freeden, op. cit. p. 7.

SECTION B

Locke's theory of natural rights

Historical context: political and intellectual

Locke's major work of political philosophy, his *Second Treatise of Government*, was originally conceived around 1680 as a theoretical justification for political opposition and resistance to the regimes of absolutist monarchs – specifically, that of Charles II of England – which in Locke's view had betrayed the trust vested in them by the English people to protect their natural rights. By this term Locke, drawing, like Hobbes, on the European natural law tradition, meant the rights with which human beings were equally endowed as creatures of God, rights which consisted in particular, in his formulation, of the rights to life, liberty and property.

Furthermore, Locke's *Second Treatise of Government* was published in 1689 as a theoretical justification, too, for the removal from the English throne of Charles II's successor, his Catholic brother, James II, whom Whigs such as Locke regarded as even more guilty of betraying the people's trust. In his preface to his *Two Treatises of Government*, Locke thus described the English people as having acted, in the 'Glorious Revolution' of 1688, to recover and preserve the rights that had been taken away from them by the usurper James II. For with their 'love of their Just and Natural Rights' and 'their Resolution to preserve them', they had, Locke claimed, 'saved the Nation when it was on the very brink of Slavery and Ruine'.[1] William III, who had replaced James, thereby ushering in for the first time a constitutional monarchy in England, was in similar spirit described by Locke as 'our Great Restorer', the new monarch that would return to the English people their ancient rights.

Locke's concern with the defence of the subject's rights was intimately connected in his political thought both to his theory of political obligation and to his related account of sovereign government as a form of trusteeship.[2] Historically, his preoccupation with the question of rights itself reflected deep anxieties on the part of the English Parliament following the restoration of the Stuart monarchy, and the accession of Charles II, in 1660. These fears revolved to a large extent around the issue of freedom of religious belief and practice in the light of the royal family's evident sympathies with the Catholic religion. They revolved, too, around the contentious issue of property rights, and the associated fear that the new king, like his father, would seek to levy taxes on property without the consent of Parliament. Indeed, these two issues of concern were really, as Iain Hampsher-Monk has noted, closely linked, since:

> The royal claim to rule by prerogative and to tax without the consent of Parliament was effectively seen as a kind of arbitrary government; and arbitrary government in turn was associated in people's minds with Catholicism.[3]

These popular attitudes had been shaped partly by the fact 'that those neighbouring nations which were Catholic – notoriously France and Spain – were also absolutist monarchies', and partly, too, by the fact that 'Catholicism was seen as a kind of religious absolutism', threatening with the aid of the Pope's authority and power men's freedom of religious conscience.[4] In the face, then, of this dual threat of political and religious absolutism crystallized in the form of a Catholic monarchy, with all the dangers it posed both for private property rights and for religious freedom, the Whigs in the English Parliament, led by the Earl of Shaftesbury, Locke's patron, friend and political colleague, had been active in seeking to place parliamentary limits on monarchical power. In particular, they had been strenuously seeking, between 1679 and 1681, to exclude, by means of a Parliamentary Bill, Charles II's Catholic younger brother, James, Duke of York (the next in line of succession) from accession to the English throne.

Following the failure of these attempts, and his consequent accession to power in 1685, James II proceeded to implement a number of legislative and policy measures that deeply alienated Parliament, confirming their worst fears. These included his introducing new laws or repealing old ones without Parliamentary approval, setting up new courts, and appointing Catholics to senior positions in the army and universities.

As the principal intellectual spokesman of the gathering Whig movement of opposition to these autocratic developments, Locke's main theoretical concern when he originally formulated his political theory between 1680 and 1683 had been to justify opposition to absolute government. In exile in the Netherlands after 1683, his main concern when he returned to England in 1689 following the successful uprising against James II the previous year, was to justify theoretically the cause of rebellion against a particular tyrannical government. During both these periods, the grounds on which he based his justification – for both opposition and rebellion – remained consistent: namely, the need to resist, and if necessary remove, any ruler who betrayed the people's trust and violated their natural rights to life, liberty and property.

Locke's conception of natural rights

In developing his theory of natural rights, Locke drew upon the ideas of the natural law tradition that stretched back, in particular, to the thought of the thirteenth-century Italian theologian and philosopher St Thomas Aquinas (1224–74), and which had been revised in a more modern form in the work of the Dutch philosopher, Hugo Grotius (1583–1645).

Moreover, within the context of English politics in the late seventeenth century, Locke was consciously formulating his theory as part of his broader attack on political absolutism. To a large extent, his theory was thus a critical response to other contemporary theoretical accounts of political authority – notably that of Sir Robert Filmer – which sought to justify absolutist regimes in terms of notions or doctrines such as natural hierarchy or the divine right of kings.

Locke therefore drew on the traditional idea of divinely-ordained natural law in rejecting the belief that there was any natural, pre-social basis for political hierarchy. More positively, he also drew on the natural law tradition in claiming that each person, as a creature of God, had a natural right and duty to ensure his own survival and well-being in the world, as well as a related duty to respect the same right in others.[5]

Locke thus rooted his theory of natural rights in this traditional assumption of God-given natural law which, for him, constituted an unwritten code of conduct that regulated man's natural condition, the pre-social and pre-political 'state of nature'. In such a condition individual human beings, as creatures of God, were endowed with certain fundamental natural rights. They were entrusted, too, with certain natural duties to respect the same rights in others. In the state of nature, before the formation of either civil society or civil government, those rights specifically included, according to Locke, the natural rights to life, liberty and property, and hence the right of each individual to be free from violent death, from arbitrary restrictions on his person and from theft of his property.

Moreover, the God-given law of nature, which could be discovered by human reason, 'teaches all Mankind ... that being all equal and independent, no one ought to harm another in his Life, Health, Liberty or Possessions'.[6] For, since human beings were, in Locke's view, capable of understanding certain fundamental and universally valid rules of moral conduct, they were therefore able to recognize the need to treat other people as free, independent and equal. After all, in the state of nature all individuals were equally concerned with ensuring their own survival and well-being, and thus with preserving their lives, liberties and properties.

With regard to the particular fundamental natural rights that he identified, Locke clearly extended their scope beyond Hobbes's emphasis on the right to self-preservation. Locke thus maintained that, in addition to that first basic right to survive, to remain free from violent death, human beings were endowed by God with a natural right to freedom. This condition of 'natural liberty', as Locke called it, was enjoyed by human beings in the state of nature before the formation of civil society. Its essential meaning, he explained, was that:

> The Natural Liberty of Man is to be free from any Superior Power on Earth, and not to be under the Will or Legislative Authority of Man, but to have only the Law of Nature for his Rule ...[7]

The third fundamental natural right was specified by Locke as the right to property. In its most elementary form, this was depicted as springing from the fact that:

> Men, being once born, have a right to their Preservation, and consequently to Meat and Drink, and such other things, as Nature affords them for Subsistence.[8]

However, it should be stressed that Locke referred to property in both a narrow and a broad sense. In its more restricted usage, the term was used by him to denote the exclusive private use of external possessions. In this narrow sense, property for Locke was a necessary condition of, or means to, liberty, since it was a safeguard of personal independence. But in its broader sense he also referred to property as 'life, liberty and estate', thereby embracing all three fundamental natural rights. Every person, he maintained, had 'a Property in his own Person which no Body has a right to but himself'.[9] In this sense property thus signified for Locke a person's ownership and control of his life rather than merely his possession of material goods. It could therefore be equated both with self-preservation and with freedom of thought and action.

In Locke's theory, then, these three fundamental natural rights – to life, liberty and property – along with their corresponding obligations, derived from God-given natural law. In the state of nature such rights were limited only by men's natural obligation to respect the same rights in others. Any further limitations of the natural rights to liberty or property, Locke insisted, required the consent of the person who possessed those rights.

However, two harsh 'inconveniences', as Locke calls them, unfortunately arise from the state of nature in ways that adversely affect the exercise of natural rights. First, since the law of nature is an unwritten code of moral conduct, it might on occasion be ignored if the personal interests of certain individuals are involved. Second, without any written laws, and without any established judges or magistrates, certain individuals might well interpret the unwritten law of nature in a highly subjective manner, becoming judges in their own cases.

Such circumstances justified, therefore, in Locke's view, the establishment of civil government upon the basis of a social contract founded on trust or consent. This collective agreement between rulers and subjects was the culmination of a process that had been initiated with the formation of civil society. It was thus a contract that had been created in two stages and in response to the 'inconveniences' and uncertainties of the state of nature.

Three important consequences flowed from this theoretical account of the origin of civil government and of its significance for the natural rights of individual subjects. In the first place, the fact that under the law of nature individuals, as creatures of God, were equally endowed with natural rights to life, liberty and property, and yet enjoyed those rights in an uncertain or precarious manner, provided for Locke the original justification for the establishment of civil government. It thus followed that for him the central, overriding purpose of civil government was to protect and preserve the individual's natural rights. For just as the formation by individuals of civil or political society had arisen from their desire 'to unite for the mutual Preservation of their Lives, Liberties and Estates, which I call by the general name, Property',[10] so, too, did the same motive underlie – in the second stage of the social contract – their collective decision to institute civil government. Locke thus maintains, again using the term property in this larger sense, that:

> The great and chief end therefore, of Mens uniting into Commonwealths, and putting themselves under Government, is the Preservation of their Property.[11]

A second major implication of Locke's account of the origin of civil government is that this central purpose that has brought it into existence – the protection of the individual's natural rights – also sets firm limits on the political authority of civil government. For Locke insists that any government that violates the natural rights of its subjects has betrayed their trust, vested in it when it was first established. That government has thereby undermined its own authority, forfeiting its claim to the subjects' obedience.

Such a grave situation might arise if, for instance, a government seeks to imprison an innocent person, or if it allows any individual to assault another without punishment. In those circumstances a ruler or government has violated the individual subject's natural right to liberty. Similarly, it will have infringed his natural right to property if it seeks to seize his possessions in an arbitrary manner that does not involve an approved system of taxation, or if it allows any individual to seize another's property without due punishment. For those natural rights were God-given and inherent in the very character of living human beings as God's creatures. Prior to both civil society and man-made law, they could not be taken away by governments without the individual subject's consent.

Finally, these constraints placed in Locke's theory upon the authority of government implied, too, that individual subjects had in the last resort a right of collective resistance to, or even rebellion against, unjust or oppressive rulers. For if a government failed to discharge its responsibilities to the people by protecting their natural rights, or if it abused its powers by acting in an arbitrary or tyrannical manner, then the people had in those circumstances the right to overthrow that government. Moreover, this collective act, which should be based on a majority decision, would have the effect, Locke maintained, of dissolving an unjust or tyrannical government, as it did in 1688, without leading also to the dissolution of civil society, which had originally come into being before the establishment of civil government.

Locke's account of the right to property

Locke's theory of natural rights clearly, then, had radical implications for his view of the role of civil government – in terms of both its central purpose and its limited or conditional political authority. That view was confirmed, he believed, by the removal of James II in the revolution of 1688. Another aspect, however, of Locke's theory of natural rights turned out to have more conservative social and political implications – namely, his account, set out in Chapter 5 of the *Second Treatise of Government*, of the right to property. This concentrated mainly on property in Locke's narrow, more restricted use of the term – that is, the possession of land and other goods, such as houses, furniture and other personal belongings, that could be sold or exchanged for money.

In this account of property, Locke begins by maintaining that both divine revelation and reason have demonstrated that God gave the earth to mankind in common for their use and enjoyment. Since all human beings have an equal right to life, it follows that they therefore have an equal claim to the fruits of the earth, which will ensure their self-preservation. This universally felt need of human beings to survive provides for Locke the first argument in defence of his idea of a natural right to property. For individuals have, in his view, a right to the private appropriation of what was originally common property – the earth and all its fruits – in order to preserve their lives, to stay alive.

The second argument that Locke deploys in justification of this transition from common to private property rights revolves around the application of human labour. For the exclusive right to private property stems, in his account, directly from the individual's own labour, which in turn is the essential basis of man's property in Locke's broader sense of a person's ownership and control of his own life. As Locke explains:

Though the Earth, and all inferior Creatures be common to all Men, yet every Man has a Property in his own Person. This no Body has any Right to but himself. The Labour of his Body, and the Work of his Hands, we may say, are properly his. Whatsoever then he removes out of the State that

Nature hath provided, and left it in, he hath mixed his Labour with, and joyned to it something that is his own, and thereby makes it his Property. It being by him removed from the common state. Nature placed it in, it hath by this labour something annexed to it, that excludes the common right of other Men . . .[12]

When, therefore, an individual 'mixes his labour' with what was previously an object of common property, then, according to Locke, that object becomes his private property. For example, the transformation, through a person's labour, of a natural object such as a wooden log into a human artifact such as a chair creates the right to acquire that chair as an item of private property, and with it the associated rights of use and of transfer to others by sale or gift.

These, then, were the two principal arguments that Locke advanced in making his case for the exclusive right to private property – that such a right derived from the fundamental right to life, to self-preservation; and that it was the product, too, of the individual's labour, the essence of his productive human activity. However, these two arguments in turn raised the problematic question of what limits should be placed on the private appropriation of property. In response to this question, Locke qualified his arguments for private property acquisition by conceding that there must be two important conditions limiting that process. First, he stresses the limitation of sufficiency, based on the need to make sufficient property available for others to acquire through their own labour in order to preserve themselves. Private acquisition should thus be limited by what is sufficient for the individual's own use. Second, Locke stipulates the limitation of non-wastage. The individual must not, he maintains, acquire more property than he can actually cultivate, in the case of land, or consume, in the case of its products. For if he does so, thereby allowing what he acquires to go to waste, then he is depriving another person of what could be used for his own survival and well-being.

In Locke's account of property, these two limitations of sufficiency and non-wastage were thus really interconnected since his strictures against waste were designed to ensure that sufficient property – particularly land – was left for the use of others. However, the invention and introduction of money as a means of exchange drastically affected both of these limitations placed by Locke on the private acquisition of property. In the first place, money allowed men to acquire far more property than was sufficient for their immediate use. Second, it enabled them to store wealth in a non-perishable form, thereby avoiding the problem of waste.

The introduction of money, therefore, appeared to render obsolete Locke's two limitations on the private acquisition of property. It also gave rise to wide inequalities in the distribution of wealth, producing in Locke's words a 'disproportionate and unequal Possession of the Earth'.[13] Such inequalities were clearly apparent in England at the time that Locke was writing, characterized as it was by large accumulations of wealth in the hands of a small landed minority.

In Locke's view, however, the private acquisition of property, and the inequalities which, in a money-based economy, that principle inevitably generated, were justified also because of the value-added effect of this process. For the private cultivation of land would, he maintained, lead to improved land use, thereby increasing its productivity and raising the living standards of all, landowners and labourers alike. Moreover, inequalities in the distribution of property were justifiable, too, on grounds of effort and hence desert since:

> God gave the World to men in Common; but since he gave it to them for their benefit, and the greatest Conveniences of Life they were capable to draw from it, it cannot be supposed he meant it should always remain common and uncultivated. He gave it to the use of the Industrious and Rational, (and Labour was to be his Title to it;) not to the Fancy or Covetousness of the Quarrelsom and Contentious.[14]

In deploying these arguments, Locke did not appear to address directly the objection that the accumulation of great estates, by removing so much from the common stock of land, might well have the effect of preventing other industrious individuals from exercising their own property rights. More specifically, Plamenatz drew attention to the implications of a logical flaw in Locke's account of property.[15] For the assumption underlying Locke's justification of private acquisition is, Plamenatz noted, that because someone was the *first* to 'mix his labour' with land, then that fact confers on him the right to the exclusive use of that land regardless of who later applied their own labour to it. In the case, for instance, of the owner of a large estate who employs labourers, it could be argued that, according to Locke's own underlying assumptions, those labourers, by applying their labour to the land, have a right to appropriate their own share of it in order to preserve their lives and liberties. It would thus have been more logically consistent for Locke to have argued that a person has a right to own land or some other external object if he *alone*, rather than he as the *first* person, applied his labour to it.

In Locke's account of property, therefore, it is clear that, with the invention of money, the natural right to property was severely limited in its effective exercise by the unequal distribution of property ownership. For such inequalities had the effect both of weakening the originally strict limitations that Locke placed on the accumulation of property, and of diluting the radical implications of his fundamental notion that property is essentially the product of the application of individual labour. Indeed, some political theorists, notably C.B. Macpherson, have claimed that in Locke's translation of an inclusive right to common property into an exclusive right to private property lies an early-modern justification for capitalist property relationships.[16]

Nevertheless, an effort should be made here to recover the political and intellectual contexts within which Locke was developing his account of property. His primary concern in the *Second Treatise of Government* was to demonstrate that *all* individual subjects – landowners and labourers alike – had a common interest in the formation of civil society and in the establishment of civil government in order to preserve their lives, liberties and possessions from the uncertainties of the state of nature. They also had a common interest, he argued, in resisting unjust and tyrannical rulers who threatened or violated their natural rights to life, liberty and property.

The defence of those rights required, in Locke's view, certain institutional mechanisms – notably, an assembly of property owners to authorize taxation, and more broadly, a system of limited and constitutional government rather than an absolutist monarchy. In circumstances of extreme conflict and tension, such as those of England in the 1680s, the defence of the interrelated rights to liberty and property even required the right to resist autocratic rulers who abused their political authority. The capacity, moreover, for inspiring and exercising that resistance in defence of civil society, however unequal its nature, lay, as Plamenatz observed, with 'the educated and propertied classes'[17] represented by the English Parliament, and not with the common people as a whole.

Conclusion

Locke's theory of natural rights has exercised a profound influence on the Western liberal-constitutional tradition. In particular, it shaped and guided the ideas of the founders of the American republic in the late eighteenth century, inspiring the authors of both the Declaration of Independence and the American Constitution. With his emphasis on popular consent, limited government and the right of resistance, if necessary, against autocratic rulers, Locke provided the American revolutionaries with, in Waldron's words, 'the paradigm of a theory of natural rights'.[18]

More broadly and recently, Locke's account of rights may be viewed as directly related to, and a major influence upon, the assumptions and arguments of modern liberal theory. For Locke may justifiably be regarded as, in Schapiro's description, 'the founder of modern liberal conceptions of individual human rights'.[19] The liberal tradition of reflection on, and defence of, individual rights, which was in decline during the nineteenth and early twentieth centuries but revived sharply after 1945, both in political thought and in formal declarations and national constitutions, has thus clearly demonstrated the lasting impact of Locke's at times flawed, yet nonetheless powerful and inspiring arguments.

Notes

1   J. Locke, *Two Treatises of Government* (ed. P. Laslett), Cambridge, Cambridge University Press, 1988, p. 137.
2   See Chapters 1B and 2B.
3   I. Hampsher-Monk, *A History of Modern Political Thought*, Oxford, Blackwell, 1992, p. 69.
4   ibid.
5   For an extended discussion of these influences, see J. Waldron (ed.), *'Nonsense upon Stilts': Bentham, Burke and Marx on the Rights of Man*, London, Methuen, 1987, pp. 7–13.
6   Locke, op cit. p. 271 (*Second Treatise*, Ch. 2, sect. 6).
7   ibid. p. 283 (*Second Treatise*, Ch. 4, sect. 22).
8   ibid. p. 285 (*Second Treatise*, Ch. 5, sect. 25).
9   ibid. p. 287 (*Second Treatise*, Ch. 5, sect. 27).
10   ibid. p. 350 (*Second Treatise*, Ch. 9, sect. 123).
11   ibid. pp. 350–1 (*Second Treatise*, Ch. 9, sect. 123).
12   ibid. pp. 287–8 (*Second Treatise*, Ch. 5, sect. 27).
13   ibid. p. 302 (*Second Treatise*, Ch. 5, sect. 50).

14   ibid. p. 291 (*Second Treatise*, Ch. 5, sect. 34).

15   See J. Plamenatz, *Man and Society*, Vol. 1 (revised by M.E. Plamenatz and R. Wokler), London, Longman, 1992, p. 373.

16   See C.B. Macpherson, *The Political Theory of Possessive Individualism*, Oxford, Oxford University Press, 1962. For a critique of Macpherson's interpretation, see, for instance, I. Shapiro, *The Evolution of Rights in Liberal Theory*, Cambridge, Cambridge University Press, 1986, pp. 137–48; and R. Ashcraft, *Locke's Two Treatises of Government*, London, Unwin Hyman, 1987, Ch. 7.

17   Plamenatz, op. cit. p. 376.

18   Waldron, op. cit. p. 7.

19   Schapiro, op. cit. p. 82.

Burke's case against the 'rights of man' and for 'prescriptive' rights

Historical context: political and intellectual

A hundred years after the exposition of Locke's theory of natural rights, its central tenets were largely incorporated into the highly emotive doctrine of the rights of man. This was one of the principal ideals that inspired the French Revolution of 1789 and was subsequently embodied in the Declaration of the Rights of Man and of Citizens proclaimed by the French Constituent Assembly in August 1789. This document affirmed as 'natural and sacred' the 'inalienable' rights to 'liberty, security and resistance to oppression', whilst emphasizing, too, a whole set of democratic political principles depicted as stemming from those natural rights.

The Irish politician and conservative political thinker, Edmund Burke (1729–97) wrote his most influential work, *Reflections on the Revolution in France* (1790) in direct and challenging response to these momentous developments. In its pages Burke denounced the inspirational doctrine of the rights of man as meaningless, simplistic, excessively individualistic and politically dangerous.

Nevertheless, it should be stressed that Burke had not always opposed the idea of rights per se. Indeed, as an active member within the British Parliament of the liberal faction of the Whig party under the leadership of Charles James Fox, he had taken a stand on several notable occasions in the cause of the traditional, or what he referred to as the 'prescriptive', rights of British subjects whenever those rights were being infringed by the autocratic actions of King George III and his appointed ministers or officials. Burke had actively campaigned, for instance, between 1788 and 1794 for the impeachment of Warren Hastings, the Governor-General of Bengal, on the grounds that he had violated the traditional rights, laws and customs of the Indian subjects of the East India Company.

In similar spirit, Burke had also been a longstanding admirer of the English Glorious Revolution of 1688 which had sought, in his words, to 'preserve our ancient indisputable laws and liberties, and that ancient constitution of government which is the only security for law and liberty'.[1] Furthermore, in the dispute between the American colonists and the British government of George III which led to the American Revolution of 1776–83, Burke had argued in the British Parliament that the colonists were defending the ancient rights affirmed in the English

Edmund Burke (1729–97)

Dublin-born Irish statesman and political thinker, often regarded as a founding-father of the Western conservative tradition. After being educated at Trinity College, Dublin, Burke moved to London in 1750 with a view to beginning a legal career, but became instead an obscure and impoverished writer for a while. His fortunes, however, gradually changed, particularly after he became a Whig member of the British Parliament in 1765 as well as Secretary to Lord Rockingham, leader of the Whig Party and subsequently Prime Minister.

By courtesy of the National Portrait Gallery, London

Burke became a leading member of the liberal faction of the Whig Party from that period until 1790, playing an important role in parliamentary affairs. Among his contributions to political debate during those years were a number of speeches and writings both on matters relating to the British Constitution and on issues arising from British, Irish and American politics. In particular, Burke was concerned with defending the customary rights of British subjects – in Ireland, India and America – in the face of infringements of those rights by ministers or officials of George III's governments.

Although Burke had been sympathetic on those grounds to the American Revolution of 1776–83, he fiercely opposed the French Revolution of 1789, and its English sympathizers, in his most famous work of political theory, *Reflections on the Revolution in France,* published in 1790. Burke's opposition was based on his conviction that the revolution had been inspired by abstract principles such as the 'rights of man' rather than by legitimate grievances.

The publication of Burke's *Reflections* provoked passionate responses from radical thinkers such as Thomas Paine and Mary Wollstonecraft. It also led to a permanent breach between Burke and other prominent liberal members of the Whig Party, including Charles James Fox. Burke nonetheless attempted to defend his position, and his apparent departure from the advocacy of political reform, in his *Appeal from the New to the Old Whigs* (1791).

Burke's importance in the history of modern political thought is assured not only by the debate generated by his *Reflections on the Revolution in France,* but also by his profound influence on the later development of Western conservatism.

Constitution.[2] For the Americans were seeking to preserve certain long-established rights – particularly the right to property, as well as independent institutions and commercial practices, which they had inherited from England and carried over into their new country.

However, in fiercely opposing the French Revolution, Burke distinguished it clearly from those two other, essentially defensive, as he saw them, revolutions in England and America. For, in his view, the French Revolution was a foolish and misguided attempt to destroy the old order in France and to build a new one on the artificial foundations of abstract principles such as the rights of man, popular sovereignty and abstract rationality. Those principles were all the products of eighteenth-century Enlightenment rationalism, which Burke deplored. That current of thought promoted the goal of human emancipation, by means of the application of reason, from both traditional values and established social and political institutions. In the political writings of Rousseau and others this radical ideal of the individual's liberation from the chains of traditional society also required for its fulfilment if not, in the case of the anti-rationalist Rousseau, the elevation of human reason, then certainly the need for the reconstruction of society and government through the realization of such innovative ideas as the general will and popular sovereignty. Moreover, within this theoretical climate American politicians and political thinkers such as Thomas Jefferson and Thomas Paine popularized the powerful idea of the 1789 French Declaration of the Rights of Man and of Citizens, drafted by the Marquis de Lafayette, a young liberal noble-man, after consultations with Jefferson, by that time the American ambassador in Paris.[3]

Burke's critique of the doctrine of the 'rights of man'

Burke's reaction against the ideas and doctrines that inspired the French Revolution was thus also a reaction against the Enlightenment thinking that had generated them. In his *Reflections on the Revolution in France*, in which for the first time he sought to develop his own conservative principles in an extended forum, he turned his critical scorn in particular upon the most emotive of the French revolutionaries' leading ideas – their espousal of the universal, natural rights of man. Burke's critique was based on three principal objections – first, that the idea of the rights of man was abstract and hence even meaningless and simplistic; second, that it was excessively individualistic and hence unrelated to the particular circumstances of actual, existing communities; and third, that it was politically dangerous since it threatened to subvert and destroy established laws, institutions and, indeed, customary or 'prescriptive' rights.

With regard to his first charge, Burke rejected the French revolutionaries' idea of the 'rights of man' as an abstract conception of rights. Such an idea derived, he argued, from the false notion of 'natural' rights possessed in some artificial 'state of nature' conceived by political thinkers such as Locke as existing prior to civil society. The 'rights of man' derived, too, from the Enlightenment view, which Burke also rejected, of the exercise and application by individuals of abstract reason in pursuit of social and political reconstruction.

These abstract ideas were, in Burke's view, inherently flawed since they failed to take account of the complex and specific nature of existing societies, which had been shaped by a shared historical experience. Such ideas were flawed, too, because their proponents erroneously implied that their promulgation would bring about the creation of a new social and political order. In truth, however, Burke insisted, human societies evolved organically through a gradual process of collective experimentation.

In such societies, therefore, rights could not exist in some abstract and universal sense, but rather only in a practical, concrete form. This point led directly and logically to Burke's second, related objection to the notion of the 'rights of man'. For, in his view, it was meaningless to talk of the universal, natural rights of individuals abstracted from their particular communities. Rights were social in their foundation and character, he argued, since human beings were social creatures moulded by their communities, with their particular social relationships and communal obligations. Individuals were not, then, isolated beings who entered into a civil society artificially created for the purpose of securing the 'natural' rights that they once enjoyed in some fictitious, pre-social 'state of nature'.

For Burke, moreover, the 'real' rights which actually existed in civil society were made legitimate by the fact that, like its established institutions, they had been recognized over time by the members of that particular society as satisfying their human wants and needs. Such rights were thus inherited or 'prescriptive' in character since they were given or prescribed by civil society as a result of the forces of custom or tradition.

Real, 'prescriptive' rights were therefore attuned to the particular circumstances of society. This was of immense practical importance since it was Burke's conviction that:

> Circumstances (which with some gentlemen pass for nothing) give in reality to every political principle its distinguishing colour, and discriminating effect. The circumstances are what render every civil and political scheme beneficial or noxious to mankind.[4]

By contrast, the doctrine of the 'rights of man' – 'a metaphysical abstraction', in Burke's dismissive phrase – ignored all the 'infinite modifications' of time and circumstance which determined the practical feasibility of any particular political proposal. Indeed, the zealous exponents of that doctrine appeared to consider 'their speculative designs as of infinite value, and the actual arrangement of the state as of no estimation'.[5]

One important consequence of this neglect was that universalist theories of the rights of man paid insufficient attention to the specific national differences – in terms of shared histories, institutions and legal and constitutional traditions – that existed between different civil societies. By underestimating the significance of those differences, the natural rights theorists overlooked the fact that the actual 'arrangement of the state' in particular national societies would have profound practical implications for the implementation of 'their speculative designs'.

For all these reasons, then, Burke regarded the doctrine of the universal rights of man as not only abstract and metaphysical but also excessively individualistic. For it was a radical conception of rights divorced from the particular histories, institutions and laws, and hence from the actual workings, of existing national societies.

Finally, Burke also regarded 'the rights of man' as a politically dangerous doctrine for several reasons. In the first place, the all-important distinction between the status of abstract, universal rights, on the one hand, as proclaimed in the French Declaration, and their translation into political practice on the other, was one that contained within itself destructive possibilities. As Burke explained, the abstract, natural rights of man were 'metaphysically true', but also 'morally and politically false'.[6] For any attempt to apply such rights to civil society would, in his view, have only the practical effect of destroying the inherited, 'prescriptive' rights that were actually recognized in society.

For example, any attempt to impose by political means the goal of equality of civil and political rights upon the basis of the principle, derived from the European natural-rights tradition, that all human beings were created equal by God, would in practice undermine established, traditional rights such as the right to private property – which were, and always had been, unequally distributed in civil society. In other words, there was a basic contradiction between, on the one hand, the attempted implementation of the abstract principle of abstract rights and, on the other, the continuing recognition of real, prescriptive rights, which could be safeguarded only by a respect for custom and historical continuity.

Burke also considered the idea of universal claims to natural rights to be a destructive force in society because of the indiscriminate and potentially far-reaching nature of such claims; for 'by having a right to everything [men] want everything'.[7] Furthermore, Burke rejected as equally pernicious the notion, again drawn from the natural-rights tradition, that the universal rights of man provided a theoretical perspective from which individuals could critically evaluate the existing social and political institutions of their particular society, and in the last resort, justify their engaging in violent rebellion against it. For the French revolutionaries had employed the doctrine of the rights of man in precisely that manner, thereby generating disruptive political consequences that simply could not be predicted or perhaps even controlled.

Burke's defence of inherited, 'prescriptive' rights

On the basis of these arguments, then, Burke regarded the doctrine of the natural rights of man as an ahistorical, individualistic and dangerous abstraction. As he argued in his later work, *An Appeal from the New to the Old Whigs* (1791), in which he vigorously restated his critical position:

> The pretended rights of man ... cannot be the rights of the people. For to be a people, and to have these rights, are things incompatible. The one supposes the presence, the other the absence, of a state of civil society.[8]

Nevertheless, it must again be borne in mind that Burke's critique of these 'pretended rights' was developed expressly from the standpoint of his own conservative conception of rights, as expressed, in a fairly extended manner, both in his *Reflections on the Revolution in France* and in his *Appeal from the New to the Old Whigs*. His attack was thus directed at the abstract *basis* of the French revolutionaries' radical conception of rights, not at the idea of the existence of rights per se.

In Burke's view, the real rights that certainly did exist in late eighteenth-century England did not therefore consist of abstract and speculative claims to the 'rights of man'. Rather, they amounted to the historically-based rights and liberties of Englishmen that had been handed down from one generation to another as what he called 'an entailed inheritance'. Whilst celebrating this principle of inheritance embodied in various English charters and laws, Burke thus noted that:

> from Magna Charta to the Declaration of Right, it has been the uniform policy of our constitution to claim and assert our liberties, as an entailed inheritance, derived to us from our forefathers, and to be transmitted to our posterity; as an estate specially belonging to the people of this kingdom without any reference whatever to any other more general or prior right . . .[9]

From this premise Burke proceeded to identify those real, 'prescriptive' rights, which had been inherited, along with established customs, laws and institutions, and transmitted in this manner within an evolving society. He thus claimed that:

> Men have a right to live by that rule [the rule of law]; they have a right to justice, . . . They have a right to the fruits of their industry; and to the means of making their industry fruitful. They have a right to the acquisitions of their parents; to the nourishment and improvement of their offspring; to instruction in life, and to consolation in death.[10]

Burke completed this list of 'prescriptive' rights enjoyed in civil society with the affirmation of a joint-stock principle of individual entitlements to its material resources, maintaining that:

> each man . . . has a right to a fair portion of all which society, with all its combinations of skill and force, can do in his favour. In this partnership all men have equal rights, but not to equal things. He that has but five shillings in the partnership, has as good a right to it, as he that has five hundred pounds has to his larger proportion. But he has not a right to an equal dividend in the product of the joint stock . . .[11]

Each individual, as a partner in the national community, therefore possessed, in Burke's view, an equal right to the resources of civil society in proportion to his own contribution to their development. But each individual did not possess a right to an equal share of those resources regardless of the differential contributions made by himself and his fellow-countrymen. What was being affirmed here was thus the prescriptive right to the fruits of one's industry within the partnership between the generations that comprised civil society. What was certainly not being upheld in Burke's exposition was the abstract, egalitarian principle of *equality* of property rights. Indeed, the recognition over time of inherited rights such as the right to private property necessarily entailed in their practical application, Burke maintained, the unequal distribution of such rights.

It was Burke's conviction that these recognized 'prescriptive' rights constituted the only meaningful basis for an empirically valid conception of rights in existing civil societies and states, and alone corresponded, too, to the experienced needs and wants of the people who belonged to, and identified with, those national communities. Moreover, prescriptive rights, together with inherited institutions, laws and customs, formed the only secure context within which, in Burke's view, gradual, incremental change within the existing social and political order was either feasible or desirable.

Notes

1   E. Burke, *Reflections on the Revolution in France* (1790) (ed. C. O'Brien), Harmondsworth, Penguin, 1968, p. 117.
2   See Burke's 'Speech on Conciliation with America' (1775), in E. Burke, *Pre-Revolutionary Writings* (ed. I. Harris), Cambridge, Cambridge University Press, 1993, pp. 206–69.
3   See J. Waldron (ed.), *'Nonsense upon Stilts': Bentham, Burke and Marx on the Rights of Man*, London, Methuen, 1987, pp. 22–5.
4   Burke, *Reflections on the Revolution in France*, p. 90.
5   ibid. p. 155.
6   ibid. p. 153.
7   ibid. p. 151.
8   E. Burke, 'An Appeal from the New to the Old Whigs' (1791), in L.I. Bredvold and R.G. Ross (eds), *The Philosophy of Edmund Burke: A Selection from His Speeches and Writings*, Ann Arbor, University of Michigan Press, 1960, p. 49.
9   Burke, *Reflections on the Revolution in France*, p. 119.
10   ibid. p. 149.
11   ibid. pp. 149–50.

Paine's defence of the rights of man

Historical context: political and intellectual

Burke's attack on the French Revolution and on the ideas and doctrines that inspired it proved to be the catalyst for a fierce and prolonged ideological debate in Britain during the 1790s. Of the various critical responses to his *Reflections on the Revolution in France*, the most influential emerged in the form of Thomas Paine's *The Rights of Man*, Part 1 (1791). The debate generated by these two works did not involve any direct exchange of arguments between the two authors. Rather, it amounted to the exposition of radically different approaches both to the French Revolution itself and to its inspirational doctrine of the rights of man. By implication, too, this controversy, which was sustained by numerous subsequent contributions from other authors, among them, conservatives, liberals and radicals, focused on the additional, highly contentious issue of whether political reforms should be introduced in Britain following the precedent and spirit of the French Revolution.

Published in February 1791, Thomas Paine's *The Rights of Man*, Part 1 soon became an extremely popular work, selling 300,000 copies in its first six months of publication in a British population of 10 million, of whom 4 million were at that

Thomas Paine (1737–1809)

English-born radical thinker and international revolutionary activist. After a varied yet largely unfulfilled early life in England, Paine emigrated in 1774 to Philadelphia, America. There he rapidly became known as a radical supporter of the American cause during the revolutionary war of independence, even joining the rebels' army.

In America Paine also became a prolific and widely-read political writer. Among his early works the best-selling pamphlet, *Common Sense* (1776) had the greatest impact. This provided a theoretical justification for American independence from Britain and for the subsequent American Revolution of 1776–83, of which Paine was one of its intellectual leaders.

By courtesy of the National Portrait Gallery, London

After holding several appointments in America, Paine returned to Europe in 1787, living mainly in France where he was increasingly drawn to the revolutionary cause. In 1791–2 he published his most famous work of political theory, *The Rights of Man*. Part 1 of this (1791) was in large part an attempt to refute the traditionalist arguments underlying Burke's attack on the French Revolution of 1789, as memorably set out in his *Reflections on the Revolution in France* (1790).

Because of the radical and anti-monarchical views expressed in *The Rights of Man*, Paine was charged in England with sedition in 1792 and forced to flee France to avoid prosecution. Whilst in exile, he became active in French politics, being elected as a representative for Calais in the French Convention. However, in the political turmoil of the Terror that began late in 1793, Paine was imprisoned in Paris and narrowly escaped execution.

He spent his remaining years in France engaged in writing, and there completed his last major work, *The Age of Reason*, Part 1 (1794) and Part 2 (1796), which contained a bitter attack on the foundations of Protestant Christianity. Partly because of the controversy generated by such views, and in the light, too, of developments in France after 1793, Paine's influence as a radical political thinker declined in Europe and America in his later years.

Nevertheless, Paine's importance as an influential political thinker lies both in his role as a radical defender of the democratic revolutions in America and France, and in the influence that his leading ideas have exerted on the Western liberal–democratic tradition.

time illiterate. Part 2 of *The Rights of Man* was published in February 1792. Later that year, Paine was charged with sedition in London, with his trial set for December. In September he fled England for France, where he was soon elected as a representative for Calais in the French Convention. In December 1792 he was declared an outlaw in England.

This was in no way, however, Paine's first taste of political controversy and conflict. After a chequered and largely successful early life in England, working in turn as a corsetmaker, exciseman, schoolteacher and tobacconist, he had emigrated to America in 1774 in order to escape imprisonment for debt in England. Whilst working in Philadelphia, as editor of *The Philadelphia Magazine*, Paine had published in 1776 his first political work *Common Sense,* which soon became a bestseller in the American colonies. This amounted to a theoretical justification for the increasingly popular cause of the American independence from England, as well as a critique of the English monarchy and its underlying principle of hereditary succession. Within the space of two years, then, Paine 'had been transformed from an oppressed and impoverished English artisan of no significance into an internationally recognized intellectual leader of the American Revolution'.[1]

From this turning-point onwards Paine became a prolific author of influential revolutionary pamphlets, all composed in a direct, persuasive and accessible style, which gave them a wide popular appeal. At the same time, he became actively involved in the revolutionary cause itself, joining the American army and associating with the Founding Fathers of the Revolution – George Washington, Thomas Jefferson and James Madison.

After returning to Europe in 1787, Paine lived mainly in France, although with some time spent in his native England. In France he became increasingly drawn to the revolutionary cause that eventually provoked Edmund Burke into publishing his sustained, rhetorical attack on French republicanism, *Reflections on the Revolution in France* (1790). Paine's vigorous response, *The Rights of Man,* Part 1 (1791), was in large part an attempt not only to refute the traditionalist arguments and claims underlying Burke's critique of the French Revolution, but also to dissect the selective historical interpretation upon which that critique rested. In sharp contrast, Paine presented not so much an elaboration of natural-rights theory, but rather a restatement of his radical case, already advanced in *Common Sense*, against the principle and practice of hereditary monarchy, exemplified by the traditional English political order that Burke revered.

As both a radical democrat and a republican, Paine drew a favourable contrast between the new political systems that he saw emerging in America and France and the deeply flawed character and operation of British government. In defending and praising the American and French Revolutions, he was influenced by two important sets of political ideas. The first of these consisted of the central tenets of eighteenth-century Enlightenment rationalism, most notably its belief in the application of reason to the social and political worlds, and in the possibility of social and political reform and reconstruction as a result of that process. The titles of some of Paine's principal political writings – for instance, *Common Sense* and *The Age of Reason* – reflected this Enlightenment influence.

Second, Paine's advocacy of the revolutionary cause in America and France was influenced, too, by English radical Whig ideas, articulated most compellingly by John Locke and his followers. These included an emphasis on the need to place constitutional limits on the growing power of the English monarchy. In his hostility, however, to all forms of hereditary privilege, and in his subsequent celebration of the French Revolution as the overthrow of a regime based on that outmoded principle, Paine clearly went beyond the radical Whig commitment to restoring constitutional balance within the existing order. Nonetheless, other radical Whig influences did seem to Paine to have revolutionary implications. These included leading Lockean ideas such as the fundamental natural rights of the individual and the right, too, of collective resistance to, and even rebellion against, tyrannical government.

Harnessing all these ideas to the revolutionary cause required the literary resources of Paine's clear, direct and polemical style. Aimed at a mass readership, this was a more striking feature of his political writings than any great intellectual originality or sophistication. As Bruce Kuklick has observed:

> Paine was an influential political thinker not because he had new ideas, but because he could commandingly express old ones.[2]

Paine's distinction between natural and civil rights

Paine was a supporter of the French Revolution because he regarded it as not only the overthrow of a decayed political regime but also the realization of the principle of universal natural rights, possessed by all people, regardless of their wealth or social status, by virtue of their essential humanity. This moral belief, instilled by his English Quaker family, and strengthened by the influence of ideas derived both from Locke and from the eighteenth-century Enlightenment, provided the theoretical basis for Paine's opposition to hereditary monarchies, as well as for his advocacy of republican and even democratic forms of government founded on the principle of universal suffrage.

In developing his own version of radical natural-rights theory in *The Rights of Man*, Part 1, Paine bagan with an important conceptual distinction between 'natural rights' and 'civil rights'. For him 'natural' rights were those rights that 'appertain to man in right of his existence'.[3] These were fundamental rights with which human beings, as creatures of God, had been equally endowed by their Creator – a truth recognized in various religious traditions.

Among the equal 'natural' rights of individuals Paine identified 'all the intellectual rights, or rights of the mind, and also all those rights of acting as an individual for his own comfort and happiness, which are not injurious to the natural rights of others'.[4]

'Civil rights', on the other hand, were defined by Paine in *The Rights of Man* as those rights that 'appertain to man in right of his being a member of society'.[5] Such rights, however, derived from the natural rights of individuals since:

> Man did not enter into society to become *worse* off than he was before, nor to have fewer rights than he had before, but to have those rights better secured. His natural rights are the foundation of all his rights.[6]

Moreover, in Paine's account civil rights were those natural rights – in particular, rights to security and protection – which individuals could not safeguard by themselves, requiring instead for that purpose the collective support of civil society and government. As Paine put it:

> Every civil right has for its foundation, some natural right pre-existing in the individual, but to the enjoyment of which his individual power is not, in all cases, sufficiently competent.[7]

On the basis of these propositions, Paine elaborated further the distinction between natural and civil rights as being one 'between that class of natural rights which man retains after entering into society, and those which he throws into the common stock as a member of society'.[8] These natural rights which the individual retained after entering civil society were 'all the intellectual rights, or rights of the mind'[9] – in other words, the rights to freedom of thought, to freedom of religious belief and to freedom of expression in its various forms. Such retained rights could be freely exercised by the individual without the assistance of government.

In Paine's view, it was, however, the role of government to protect these natural rights from interference by others and to desist, too, from any attempts to infringe such rights through its own collective activity. It was also the role of government to enable individuals to exercise more effectively the natural rights which they had exchanged for civil rights – for example, the rights to security and protection – when they entered civil society. But since no-one had the right to subject another human being to his will without his consent, the authority of government must, by the same token, Paine added, be based on the consent of those who chose to place some of their natural rights within its collective agencies of interpretation and enforcement.

Towards the end of *The Rights of Man*, Part 1, Paine reinforced this interpretation of the distinction, and yet at the same time the continuity, between natural and civil rights with a favourable discussion of the 'French Declaration of the Rights of Man and of Citizens', whose main authors, including, for example, Layafette, he had previously advised and influenced. Of its seventeen articles Paine observed that the first three in particular 'comprehend in general terms, the whole of a declaration of rights' and that 'all the succeeding articles either originate from them, or follow as elucidations'.[10] These first three articles stated that:

> I. Men are born, and always continue, free and equal in respect of their rights. Civil distinctions, therefore, can be founded only on a public utility.
> II. The end of all political associations, is, the preservation of the natural and imprescriptible rights of man; and these rights are liberty, property, security, and resistance of oppression.
> III. The nation is essentially the source of all sovereignty; nor can any individual, or any body of men, be entitled to any authority which is not expressly derived from it.[11]

Paine further observed that those articles 'are the basis of Liberty, as well individual as national; nor can any country be called free, whose government does not take its beginning from the principles they contain, and continue to preserve them pure . . .[12]

Paine's status as a radical popularizer of natural-rights theory

Without any particularly rigorous theoretical analysis, Paine had thus provided a persuasive exposition for a mass audience of certain fundamental ideas drawn from natural-rights theories. These consisted, in particular, of the beliefs, first, that all individuals, regardless of their station in life, possessed as creatures of God equal natural rights; second, that as a consequence they should be treated equally before the law; and third, that they should be provided with equal opportunities in determining the way in which they and their society should be governed. Those essential beliefs in turn reflected the confident assumptions of eighteenth-century Enlightenment rationalism – such as an unswerving faith in the capacity of the common people for self-government, and in the desirability of applying the test of reason to all existing social and political institutions.

Paine's interpretation of the rights of man also reflected, as we have seen, the influence of radical Whig ideas derived from Lockean notions of natural rights, government by consent, and the subjects' right of resistance to tyrannical rulers. Paine, however, with his stress on the natural equality of all individuals, as well as on equality of political rights, understood as the right of all citizens to participate in government either directly or indirectly, unquestionably conceived of natural rights in more egalitarian terms than had Locke. In addition, the favoured political framework within which Paine advanced the case for equal natural and civil rights was one of popular sovereignty, universal suffrage and republican government. For Locke, by contrast, that framework had consisted of parliamentary sovereignty combined with a constitutional monarchy. In both these respects, then, Paine's conception of universal natural rights was essentially more radical, even if he shared with Locke an awareness of the doctrine's potentially revolutionary implications.

In spite, however, of the radical emphases that characterized Paine's interpretation of the concept of natural rights, its political impact did not lie in its theoretical originality, but rather in its lucid summary of the Enlightenment and Lockean, Whig ideas that underlay it. As Freeden has observed:

> Paine's contribution to the natural-rights tradition was not as an innovator but as a popularizer who made the traditional accessible.[13]

In popularizing such ideas, the lack of rigorous analysis of their underlying premises and assumptions left certain theoretical problems unresolved in Paine's account of the nature and scope of natural rights. For example, the grounds on which he derived the existence of universal natural rights appeared, as in the French Declaration of 1789, to be a general deistic belief, common among eighteenth-century thinkers, in a Supreme Being, and in the equality of men before God. But this belief was justified by Paine, a fierce critic of Protestant Christianity, in only a somewhat cursory manner in *The Rights of Man*.[14]

In addition, Paine's account of natural rights, again like the French Declaration, succeeded in conflating natural and civil rights, thereby precluding the possibility of conflicts between them. Instead, he tended to cherish the optimistic assumption that the rational and enlightened individual would be prepared to accept constraints on his individual rights for the sake of either social order or the public interest.

Paine's long-term influence

Yet in spite of such theoretical limitations, some of which the English utilitarian philosopher, Jeremy Bentham (1748–1832) was shortly to expose, Paine's influential and populist defence of the natural rights of man established his reputation as the leading antagonist of conservative critics of the French Revolution such as Burke. It also solidified his position as a major intellectual influence on the late eighteenth-century democratic movement in America and France. That achievement was marked symbolically by the fact that, in 1789, he was given the key of the Bastille prison in Paris by Layafette to take to George Washington.

Soon afterwards, however, Paine's fortunes changed rapidly for the worse. As an associate of the moderate Girondin Party, he was imprisoned in Paris at the end of 1793 when the more radical Jacobins gained control of the French Convention, thereby ushering in the French Terror. (Paine had urged the Convention against the execution of Louis XVI.) Although he was released ten months later and was re-admitted to the Convention in 1795, his remaining years in France were devoted mainly to writing and publishing his last major work, *The Age of Reason,* Part 1 (1794) and Part 2 (1796), which contained a bitter attack on the foundations of Protestant Christianity.

During this period, the influence of Paine's radical republican ideas in England was eroded by public reaction to the French Terror and to the execution of Louis XVI. These events caused widespread alarm and unease, even among radical Whigs such as Charles James Fox and his supporters. To many English observers, moreover, the developments to the 1790s appeared to vindicate Burke's critique of the French Revolution and to discredit Paine's optimistic defence. Certainly the practical political effect was that the French Terror could be used by English aristocratic leaders to repress any radical proposals for extension of the franchise or for parliamentary reform.

For these reasons the periods after 1793 and later, after 1802 when he returned to America, were years in which Paine's prestige and influence as a radical political thinker declined in both Europe and America. But this historical fact should not be allowed to obscure his major long-term impact on the Western liberal–democratic tradition. For Paine's ideas and arguments concerning not only individual rights, but also the nature of representative government, universal suffrage, citizenship and the importance of constitutions as means of guaranteeing the rights of citizens, have all been among the most significant theoretical influences on both the thought and practice of liberal–democratic societies and political systems.

Notes

1   T. Paine, *Political Writings* (ed. B. Kuklick), Cambridge, Cambridge University Press, 1989, p. viii.
2   ibid.
3   T. Paine, *The Rights of Man* (ed. H. Collins), Harmondsworth, Penguin, 1969, p. 90.
4   ibid. p. 90.
5   ibid.
6   ibid.
7   ibid.
8   ibid.
9   ibid.
10   ibid. p. 135.
11   ibid. p. 132.
12   ibid. p. 136.
13   M. Freeden, *Rights*, Milton Keynes, Open University Press, 1991, p. 18.
14   See Paine, *The Rights of Man*, pp. 90–1.

SECTION C

Contemporary debates

In the post-1945 period the widespread agreement about the fundamental import-ance of human rights has been reflected in the revival of contemporary political philosophy – particularly in Britain and the USA. A number of systematic theories have been expounded to explain or justify the basis on which individuals can make rights claims against their societies or governments. Robert Nozick (1938–), for example, in his major work, *Anarchy, State and Utopia* (1974), pro-ceeded from the assertion that:

> Individuals have rights, and there are things no person or group may do to them (without violating those rights). So strong and far-reaching are these rights that they raise the question of what, if anything, the state and its offi-cials may do.[1]

With a similar anti-collectivist emphasis, Friedrich von Hayek (1899–1992) argued in Vol. II of his *Law, Legislation and Liberty* (1973) that the liberal idea of rights had been undermined by state collectivists' preoccupation with the illusory pursuit of distributive justice.[2]

From an opposing, social–liberal standpoint John Rawls (1921–), though less directly concerned with the issue of rights than with the ideal of social or dis-tributive justice, argued in his highly influential work, *A Theory of Justice* (1971) that the underlying basis for human rights is the principle of the equal right to liberty which can be claimed and upheld equally by all individuals. This, Rawls's 'first principle of justice', holds that 'each person is to have an equal right to the most extensive total system of liberties compatible with a similar system of liberty for all'.[3]

From a similar social–liberal perspective Ronald Dworkin in his *Taking*

Rights Seriously (1977) stressed the moral priority of rights claims over any utilitarian considerations as a basis for public policy. He also sought to develop his conception of rights on the foundations of both constitutional–legal theory and a commitment to the principle of equality of rights, derived from the idea of the unconditional worth of each person.

In broader theoretical terms, much of the contemporary debate over Rawls's 'first principle of justice' – the equal right to liberty – has been conducted by those who have formed either 'negative' or 'positive' conceptions of liberty. In practice, these rival schools of thought have thus been composed of, on the one hand, market–liberal or libertarian thinkers – such as Hayek and Nozick – who favour a limited state and a market economy, or, on the other, of social–liberal or democratic socialist thinkers – such as Rawls, Nozick or Plant – who favour a more activist and interventionist state promoting distributive justice.

This ideological division has been apparent, too, in the long-running dispute over the scope and extent of human rights. For since 1945, as we have seen,[4] a new range of social and economic, or 'welfare', rights has been added to the traditional liberal range of civil and political rights. This development, which has been both embodied in international declarations of rights and expressed in political thought, has reflected underlying collectivist assumptions about the need for greater state intervention in the economy and society. However, the resulting disagreements that it has generated among political theorists have raised problematic questions that are both ideological and practical in nature – concerning the proper role of the state in modern society, as well as the feasibility of translating social and economic ideals into practice in materially-deprived countries or regions.

A distinctively communitarian critical response to modern restatements of rights theory – whether libertarian, market–liberal or social–liberal in character – emerged in political philosophy during the 1980s and after. Communitarian theorists such as Charles Taylor, Alasdair MacIntyre and Michael Sandel thus developed a critique of the notion of the primary importance of individuals as rights bearers – an idea that pervades all of these modern rights theories, regardless of their contrasting ideological implications. Such critics depict the modern liberal conception of rights, presented as prior to any society or state, as one that rests on an empirically false notion of an 'unencumbered self', separated from the individual's particular society or culture.[5]

Modern liberals have responded to such communitarian criticisms by arguing that the defence of traditional civil rights (for example, to freedom of speech or freedom of association) is concerned with rights and liberties which, whilst ascribed to individuals, nonetheless serve two vital communal purposes. First, the defence of civil rights is essential for fostering the processes of voluntary interaction and cooperation between individuals that lie at the heart of civil society. Second, the safeguarding of civil rights is fundamental to the protection of those very processes from arbitrary or oppressive political interference.[6]

Since the 1960s much reflection on, and writing about, rights has focused on the particular problems and issues surrounding women's rights. At first the attention of feminist thinkers and activists was directed towards the need for equal civil rights for women on the grounds that such rights (for example, the right to property or the right to vote), which properly belonged to all individual citizens, had been denied to women in the past on the basis of irrelevant or unreasonable criteria, such as women's alleged inferiority or secondary social status.

Since the 1980s the emphasis of the debate shifted to the advocacy of additional, special rights for women. These were claimed in order both to take account of women's distinctive interests, characteristics, capacities and needs, and to overcome past inequalities or disadvantages, built into various social institutions and practices.[7] Such claims have led in practice to the advocacy of equal opportunities policies or programmes, such as, for example, measures establishing the right to perinatal maternity leave in order to ensure security of employment.

More controversially, some feminist thinking on rights has moved beyond the advancement of additional special rights for women by means of such corrective or compensatory policy measures. Some feminists have thus also advocated 'positive' or 'reverse' discrimination in favour of women. This approach, also known as 'affirmative action' in the United States, has been designed to offset past injustices or unequal treatment by conferring on women particular advantages – through, for example, the operation of quota systems that deliberately reserve certain positions for women in the field of employment.

In addition to the debate surrounding that approach, which has been promoted, too, by other disadvantaged social groups such as ethnic minorities, a final area of controversy emerging since the 1960s may be briefly discussed here. This concerns the extension of the range of entities regarded as possessing rights. Moral philosophers such as Peter Singer have thus argued that animals, since they not only have bodily needs but also as sentient beings feel pain, should be treated with the same respect as human beings in many areas.[8]

This debate, however, has been carried beyond this commitment to animal welfare, involving a benevolent concern with the well-being of animals, to a more radical and vehement advocacy of 'animal rights'. According to this view, animals, too, have rights in the same sense that human beings do, and are therefore entitled as rights bearers to equal treatment.[9] Against this position it has been argued that a clear moral distinction exists between human beings and animals with regard to rights claims.[10] For since human beings are demonstrably capable of both rational thought and moral judgement and conduct, they alone are entitled to claim rights, and they alone are required, too, to fulfil certain corresponding obligations. Such arguments clearly raise fundamental questions about the very nature and content of rights in general.

Notes

1   R. Nozick, *Anarchy, State and Utopia*, Oxford, Blackwell, 1974, p. 5.
2   See F. von Hayek, *Law, Legislation and Liberty*, Vol. II, 'The Mirage of Social Justice', London, Routledge and Kegan Paul, 1973, Ch. 7.
3   J. Rawls, *A Theory of Justice*, Oxford, Oxford University Press, 1971, p. 302.
4   See Chapter 4A.
5   See, for example, C. Taylor, 'Atomism', in S. Avineri and A. De-Shalit (eds), *Communitarianism and Individualism*, Oxford, Oxford University Press, 1992, pp. 29–50.
6   See, for example, W. Kymlicka, 'Liberal Individualism and Liberal Neutrality', in Avineri and De-Shalit (eds), op. cit. pp. 165–85.

7   See A. Carter, *The Politics of Women's Rights*, London, Longman, 1988.
8   See P. Singer, *Animal Liberation: A New Ethics for our Treatment of Animals*, rev. edn, London, Cape, 1990.
9   See, for example, T. Regan, *The Case for Animal Rights*, London, Routledge and Kegan Paul, 1983.
10   For an example of this viewpoint, see R.G. Frey, *Interests and Rights: The Case Against Animals*, Oxford, Oxford University Press, 1980.

Further reading

P. Baehr, *Human Rights: Universality in Practice*, London, Macmillan, 1999.
D. Beetham (ed.), *Politics and Human Rights*, Oxford, Blackwell, 1995.
D. Bellamy, 'Citizenship and Rights', in D. Bellamy (ed.), *Theories and Concepts of Politics*, Manchester, Manchester University Press, 1993.
A. Carter, *The Politics of Women's Rights*, London, Longman, 1988.
A. Cassese, *Human Rights in a Changing World*, Cambridge, Polity Press, 1990.
M. Cranston, *What Are Human Rights?*, London, Bodley Head, 1973.
R. Dworkin, *Taking Rights Seriously*, London, Duckworth, 1977.
M. Freeden, *Rights*, Milton Keynes, Open University Press, 1991.
R.G. Frey, *Interests and Rights: the Case Against Animals*, Oxford, Oxford University Press, 1980.
A. Gewirth, *Human Rights: Essays in Justification and Applications*, Chicago, Chicago University Press, 1982.
P. Jones, *Rights*, London, Macmillan, 1994.
T. Regan, *The Case for Animal Rights*, London, Routledge and Kegan Paul, 1983.
I. Schapiro, *The Evolution of Rights in Liberal Theory*, Cambridge, Cambridge University Press, 1986.
P. Singer, *Animal Liberation: A New Ethics for our Treatment of Animals*, rev. edn, London, Cape, 1990.
H. Steiner, *An Essay on Rights*, Oxford, Blackwell, 1985.
J. Waldron (ed.), *Theories of Rights*, Oxford, Oxford University Press, 1984.
J. Waldron (ed.), *'Nonsense upon Stilts': Burke, Bentham and Marx on the Rights of Man*, London, Methuen, 1987.

Equality

Throughout the history of modern political thought the idea of equality has constituted a highly contentious political ideal, arousing high hopes among its advocates and deep-seated fears among its critics. Since the era of democratic revolutions in the late eighteenth century it has consequently been the source of fierce and sustained ideological controversy – far more so than has been the case with the concepts of liberty or even rights. It is true that as a moral procedural principle – concerning the right to equal consideration or treatment – equality has commanded broad support across the political and ideological spectrum. But as a distributive principle – concerning the equal distribution of opportunities or public goods or wealth or power – the egalitarian idea has been, and still is, hotly contested, particularly since 1945 within the debate on the implications of the related concept of social justice.

Historically, three main concepts of equality may be identified in Western political thought from the seventeenth century onwards: first, formal or foundational equality – particularly of individual rights; second, equality of opportunity; and third, equality of outcome. The first two of these concepts were developed within the broad framework of the Western liberal tradition; the third has been associated closely, but not always consistently, with the European socialist tradition. Moreover, each of these three concepts of equality has given rise to particular methods or strategies for ensuring or attaining their respective goals.

SECTION A

Formal or foundational equality

Formal or foundational equality, the least contentious formulation of the ideal, was also the first idea of equality to shape the development of modern political thought. Essentially the concept rests upon the assumptions, first, that all people are endowed with equal moral worth by virtue of their shared humanity, and, second, that each human being is consequently entitled to be treated equally unless relevant or reasonable grounds can be cited for differential treatment.

These twin assumptions were embedded in natural-rights theory during the seventeenth and eighteenth centuries. In Western political thought they were first articulated and developed in a coherent form in England after 1680 by John Locke and other Whig thinkers who stressed the equal capacity of all men to discover and recognize God-given natural law – the unwritten moral code guiding human conduct in the world. This belief in turn led to the emphasis upon the notion that all men, as creatures of God, were equally endowed with identical natural – that is, God-given – rights to life, liberty and property. Such rights, however, could only be guaranteed in civil society, Locke argued, by limited, constitutional government based on popular consent.

Locke's formal egalitarianism, which was, however, accompanied by acceptance of a high degree of social and economic inequality in the England of his day, had already been anticipated since the 1640s by the radical Puritan groups, the Levellers and the Diggers, who sought to challenge the established centres of monarchical and ecclesiastical authority within the English state. Popularized and adapted in the late eighteenth century by the radical political thinker, Thomas Paine, this central concern with the equal natural rights of all human beings became embodied in the first major declarations of rights, proclaimed and published after the democratic revolutions in America and France in the late eighteenth century. The American Declaration of Independence of 1776 thus stated that 'All men are created equal', while the French Declaration of the Rights of Man and of Citizens of 1789 asserted that 'Men are born, and always continue, free and equal in respect of their rights'.

From a very different philosophical standpoint, Jeremy Bentham and other utilitarian thinkers during the following period affirmed the procedural principle of formal equality not in the sense of equal natural rights, but rather in terms of the notion that all human beings were equally capable of experiencing pleasure or pain. Each person, Bentham maintained, should therefore be considered equally as an individual capable of maximizing his or her happiness or well-being. Everybody should thus 'count as one, and nobody as more than one'.

The foundations, therefore, of the concept of formal equality – built from both natural-rights theory and utilitarian philosophy – were laid in the seventeenth and eighteenth centuries. Since that time there has been broad agreement across the ideological spectrum – amongst liberals, conservatives and socialists alike – about the moral desirability of this procedural principle. This has led in turn to widespread acceptance of the notions implicit in formal equality – in particular, equality before the law and equal rights to other civil and political liberties such as, for instance, the right to participate, directly or indirectly, in the processes of government.

However, the procedural principle of formal equality historically has been applied mainly in a negative manner – as a means, that is, of removing special aristocratic privileges as well as restrictive barriers erected in the past on the basis of irrelevant criteria such as gender, race or religion. Formal equality has also been regarded as in some respects a limited concept since its implementation has at times taken little account of individuals' effective capacity for exercising their formal rights. Karl Marx in his youthful essay, *On the Jewish Question* (1844), was thus scornful about proposals for granting to Jews in the German Christian state of Prussia equal civil and political rights. He argued that these apparent liberal gains within the structure of the Prussian state were merely superficial since they masked the continuing oppression of Jews in all parts of bourgeois civil society.

Nevertheless, a more positive interpretation of the principle of equal rights had earlier been advanced by the English feminist writer and thinker, Mary Wollstonecraft (1759–97). In her most famous work, *A Vindication of the Rights of Woman* (1792), she argued the case for equal rights for women in the legal, political and social fields on the ground that women should be entitled to such rights regardless of any irrelevant 'distinction of sex'. The liberal philosopher, John Stuart Mill (1806–73), in his essay, *The Subjection of Women* (1869), later deployed similar arguments, albeit from a modified utilitarian standpoint, for the equal status of women in all areas of civil society.

Mill, himself a major figure in the Western liberal tradition, rejected the idea of natural rights (though not the notion of rights-based interests).[1] Nevertheless, the concept of formal equality in its most familiar form – namely, equality of civil and political rights – has played a central role in the development of the liberal tradition since the seventeenth century. As Robert Eccleshall has pointed out:

What emerges from the varieties of liberalism is a persistent image of the good society as an association of free persons who are equal in their possession of basic rights.[2]

Liberalism itself as a political ideology has thus, in this view, endorsed 'a succession of strategies for extending the freedoms to which everyone is considered to be equally entitled'.[3]

Equality of opportunity

A second major concept of equality – the distributional idea of equality of opportunity – developed historically in the climate in which the concept of formal or foundational equality had become well established. Most historians of political thought have traced the first usage of the idea to the political writings of the ancient Greek philosopher, Plato (427–347 BC). Within the framework of an essentially authoritarian political philosophy, Plato advocated in one of his major works, *The Republic*, an educational system designed to give equally talented children an equal opportunity to realize their potentialities. This aim would require the removal of all social factors or institutions – including the family – which had the effect of conferring arbitrary advantages upon one person or another. For Plato the wider consequence of these arrangements was that the resulting social positions occupied by men and women would derive entirely from their individual talents and abilities.

In the history of modern political thought, however, this concept of equality of opportunity, like the earlier notion of formal equality of rights, has been closely associated with the developing liberal tradition. Liberals have thus embraced the concept as a theoretical basis both for their attack on arbitrary advantages or privileges and for the practical realization of the older foundational notion, derived from Locke and his contemporaries, of the equal right to liberty.

In the early modern period, the essential force of the idea can be discerned in the impassioned critique of existing social and economic inequalities developed by Jean-Jacques Rousseau (1712–78). Indeed, Norman Barry has described Rousseau as unquestionably 'the intellectual ancestor of modern thinking on equality of opportunity'.[4] In his *Discourse on the Origin of Inequality* (1755), Rousseau argued that the establishment in civil society of the institution of private property, reinforced by law and government, had been the real source of inequality of both opportunity and condition. Central to his argument was the distinction he drew between, on the one hand, acceptable and unchangeable human inequalities – of physical strength, intellectual ability, physical attractiveness, and so on – and, on the other, unacceptable and alterable social inequalities, which were the products of social convention.

From this starting point, Rousseau proceeded in *The Social Contract* (1762) to advance the case for a small-scale agrarian society of interdependent equals, one that would be characterized by a broad measure of, though not absolute, equality of property ownership. This was viewed by Rousseau as one of the necessary conditions for realizing his key concept of the general will, the common view that society holds about what promotes the common good.

Rousseau's examination of the origins of social inequality is one of the earliest and most influential theoretical accounts in the history of modern political thought. Moreover, his subsequent espousal in *The Social Contract* of greater equality of economic condition through a redistribution of private property was central to his ideal of a free society – one in which individuals would have the opportunity to participate directly in governing their society. In this sense, Rousseau was, as Barry suggests, 'the intellectual ancestor' of modern notions of equality of opportunity.

Yet in spite of his legacy, that concept in its modern form has evolved more clearly out of that part of the Western liberal tradition which has stressed the individual's equal right to liberty, a tradition with which Rousseau bears a somewhat uneasy or ambivalent relationship. Although, as we have seen, John Stuart Mill rejected the idea of natural rights, an essential aspect of his conception of liberty was that individuals should be equally able to develop their moral, intellectual and cultural capacities without regard to the particular circumstances of their birth or social background.

This idea acquired a more egalitarian emphasis after 1870 with the emergence in Britain of a more collectivist form of liberalism in the face of a growing awareness of the scale of poverty and unemployment as acute social problems in industrial towns and cities. This reality, combined with the rise of an increasingly organized and partly enfranchised industrial working class, gave rise to a new social liberalism which emphasized the need for greater collective responsibility for working and living conditions. The key ideas that provided the theoretical justification in liberal terms for increased state intervention – involving both regulation of industrial conditions and state involvement in the provision of health, education and welfare services – were twofold. First, a more positive conception of liberty was formulated by new liberal thinkers, and, second, alongside it, a more positive role for the state was prescribed.

The democratic state was thus envisaged as an agency for removing social and economic barriers that lay in the path of its citizens. At the same time, liberty, the fundamental principle and core value of liberalism, was interpreted as the individual's opportunity for self-development, morally, intellectually and culturally, in pursuit of the common good. For the liberal philosopher, T.H. Green (1836–82), the ultimate political ideal was therefore 'freedom in its positive sense: the liberation of the powers of all men equally for contributions to the common good'.[5]

These ideas pervaded the political thought of later New Liberals such as Leonard Hobhouse and J.A. Hobson, as well as providing the main ideological justification for the ambitious programme of social and industrial legislation enacted by the Liberal governments between 1906 and 1914. Hobson, in particular, gave the more positive conception of liberty an egalitarian resonance by stating that the New Liberalism involved 'a fuller appreciation and realization of individual liberty contained in the equal opportunities for self-development'.[6] A greater role for the state would be necessary, in his view, in order to promote such opportunities. However, 'Liberals must ever insist,' he stressed, 'that each enlargement of the authority and functions of the State must justify itself as an enlargement of personal liberty, interfering with individuals only in order to set free new and larger opportunities.'[7]

In the last quarter of the nineteenth century these ideas about a positive role for the state in the promotion of wider opportunities for the individual generated intense ideological debate and fragmentation among liberals. Nevertheless, during this period such notions became firmly embedded in social–liberal thinking, articulated in opposition both to conservative commitments to hierarchy and tradition and to conservative fears about the perils of mass democracy that were posed from that perspective by the advance towards universal suffrage.

Moreover, the increasingly propagated liberal ideal of equality of opportunity also gave rise to a merit- or desert-based conception of the related ideal of social justice. That principle hinges on the belief that the distribution of rewards and benefits in society should be based on certain morally-acceptable principles. Liberal thinkers have sought to justify differential rewards in society upon the basis of different levels of talent, ability, effort and individual contribution. Their conception of social justice has rested on the underlying ideal of equality of opportunity since it presumes that everyone should have an equal chance to exercise his or her talents, thereby making his or her particular contribution to society.

Historically, this was a distributive idea that challenged traditional conservative justifications for a hierarchical distribution of rewards and privileges based on the notion of entitlement through either inheritance or acquisition. In terms, too, of economic philosophy, this liberal ideal of reward according to merit presupposed that a market economy provided the most effective mechanism for rewarding merit or desert, operating as it did upon the basis of the market-determined value of goods or services.

Essentially the ideal of equality of opportunity has been concerned, as Andrew Heywood has noted, not so much with the moral, legal and political *status* of individuals – as in the case of the ideal of formal equality – but rather with 'the circumstances in which they live and the chances or prospects available to them'.[8] This interpretation of equality has, however, raised a number of problematic questions. First, as many socialists have pointed out, the promotion of the ideal might well lead in practice to unequal outcomes. It would thus, as the British socialist thinker R.H. Tawney observed, mean in effect 'not the absence of violent contrasts of income and condition, but equal opportunities of becoming unequal'.[9] Indeed, in Tawney's view, the liberal ideal amounted to a conception of society that could be described as 'the Tadpole Philosophy, since the consolation which it offers for social evils consists in the statement that exceptional individuals can succeed in evading them'.[10] For that and other reasons the later British socialist thinker and politician Anthony Crosland argued in his major work, *The Future of Socialism* (1956), that the ideal of equality of opportunity could only be meaningful and realizable if accompanied by fiscal and social policy measures that effectively and radically redistributed wealth and resources in society.[11] Certainly the idea of equality of opportunity has implied a meritocratic rather than egalitarian society which, as Crosland's friend Michael Young pointed out in his *The Rise of the Meritocracy* (1961) might in its most rigorous application merely produce new, more inflexible and inescapable forms of 'merited' social stratification rather than some eminently desirable model of social organization.[12]

Furthermore, a systematic application of the ideal of equality of opportunity might well raise problematic questions about the balance between equality and liberty. This dilemma might arise either from widespread state intervention in many areas of economic and social life (for example, taxation of property incomes derived from inheritance), or from compensatory policies or programmes designed to offset unequal family or personal circumstances. The latter might require the removal of factors that are the result of fortuitous circumstances – for instance, as Barry has suggested, the fact of being the daughter of a successful entrepreneur.[13] In the process, this would lead to an erosion of personal liberties – such as the right of inheritance – rather than a maximization of the equal right to liberty. Compensatory policies might involve, too, reverse or 'positive' discrimination in favour of certain disadvantaged groups (e.g. ethnic minorities or women) which, whilst aiming to offset past injustices, might violate the principle of formal equality by denying rights to other citizens in, for example, the fields of educational or employment opportunities.

The attempt, therefore, to realize the ideal of equality of opportunity by eradicating either contingent factors – such as luck, family circumstances or genetic differences – or environmental factors – such as inequalities of wealth or disparities in the quality of educational provision – which in their various ways promote inequality, might thus entail policies that would endanger or even infringe individual rights or liberties. For this reason, and in the light, too, of the negative aspects of a meritocratic society, there is, as Barry has noted, 'something deeply unsatisfactory at the heart of the doctrine of equality of opportunity'.[14]

The ideal may still, however, be stated in more limited terms which stipulate the removal of the most overt kinds of discrimination based on race, religion or gender, rather than an unrealistic elimination of all kinds of arbitrary advantage. Equality of opportunity may thus be promoted in a more coherent and sensible manner which its earlier liberal advocates, such as Leonard Hobhouse and J.A. Hobson, would have appreciated. Combined, too, with an emphasis on the need for certain basic minimum social conditions – of education, healthcare, housing and welfare – as a starting-point for individual citizens, arguably it constitutes the form of equality that appears most compatible with the liberal principle of the equal right to liberty.

Equality of outcome

A third and manifestly more radical concept of equality, involving another distributional usage of the term – namely, equality of outcome – was developed after the French Revolution of 1789, mainly within the European socialist tradition. The concept was expressed in its starkest form by the early French socialist, Gracchus Babeuf, who, in his *Manifesto of the Equals* (1796), asserted the case for absolute equality in the distribution of goods and for uniform treatment of individuals within a communist society. Since then, the concept has been understood as implying, if not literal equality of that kind, then at least the ideal of achievement either of similar levels of wealth or resources or welfare in society, or of equal satisfaction of human needs.

This radical concept has thus revolved around the attempt to equalize outcomes or end-results in society rather than mere opportunities or initial circumstances in life. In terms of its practical realization, the idea of equality of outcome has therefore required, in the view of its socialist advocates, the redistribution of wealth and income, either through public, or common, ownership of industry or through progressive direct taxation. It has also entailed the redistribution of resources through social policies – concerning education, healthcare, housing and welfare – financed by direct taxation and high levels of public expenditure. The underlying goal in various schools of socialist thought has consistently been one that posits a far higher degree of social equality, sometimes expressed in terms of 'a classless society'.

The socialist concept of equality of outcome emerged from the early nineteenth century onwards in response to the perceived inadequacies of earlier liberal ideas of equal rights and equality of opportunity. Formal equality – of legal, civil and political rights – was thus disdained by Marx in his *On the Jewish Question* (1844) as a superficial idea since it concealed, he believed, the inequality and oppression that pervaded all areas of bourgeois–capitalist society.

Equality of opportunity, too, was viewed by successive generations of socialists of varying complexion – both Marxist and evolutionary or democratic socialists alike – as a partial and limited ideal that could be invoked to justify wide economic and social inequalities. The British socialist thinker and historian, R.H. Tawney, thus characterized the ideal, as we have seen, as 'the Tadpole Philosophy', which in effect legitimized a competitive, market-based race in which, whilst all were equal at the starting line, some succeeded but many others fell badly behind. This was a view that later democratic socialist thinkers such as Anthony Crosland endorsed and elaborated.

In addition to forming such critical responses to earlier, more restrictive notions of equality, socialists of various kinds have advanced the case for equality of outcome, based on both negative and positive grounds, as a more desirable social and political ideal. Here, however, it should be stressed that not all socialist thinkers have adhered to this radical form of egalitarianism. Early French 'utopian' socialists such as Charles Fourier and Henri Saint-Simon thus accepted the existence within a future socialist society of hierarchical orders with wide inequalities of wealth and position that reflected different levels of talent or individual contribution. Marx, with his contrasting, allegedly 'scientific' vision of socialism, was in some respects scarcely more radically egalitarian. Whilst rejecting the ideal of equal rights as a bourgeois–liberal sham, he wrote little about the likely egalitarian character of a future communist society on the ground that theoretical speculation of that sort was unscientific, indeed 'utopian', in the absence of the appropriate economic conditions which, in time, would produce new social relations and hence new patterns of social organization.

Marx did, however, formulate, in his *Critique of the Gotha Programme* (1875), a needs-based conception of social justice which in the socialist tradition has been closely linked to the concept of equality of outcome. In his famous formula he thus declared that, in the future communist society, characterized as it would be by a condition of material abundance, its distributive principle would be: 'from each according to his ability, to each according to his needs'. Nevertheless, Marx qualified this statement by conceding that in the transitional socialist society, which in his vision would span the period between the fall of capitalism and the emergence of communism, the distributive principle would be, as Saint-Simon had earlier maintained, 'from each according to his capacity, to each according to his works'. The individual worker in a socialist society would thus be rewarded for his particular contribution shaped by his physical or intellectual capacities.

Since Marx promoted such ideas, generations of socialists have regarded the ideal of greater equality of outcome – and hence of more equal economic and social circumstances – as inseparable from their image of a post-capitalist, socialist society. To some extent this ideal was expressed in negative terms as a repudiation of the wide inequalities of wealth and power inherent in a capitalist economy and society. But more positively it was a goal cherished as one that complemented and enhanced other socialist ideals – notably, community and social cohesion, social justice and equity, and liberty in its positive sense of opportunity for self-development.

From this ethical perspective Tawney thus characterized an egalitarian society as one that attached 'a high degree of significance to differences of character and intelligence between different individuals, and a low degree of significance to economic and social differences between different groups'. It would seek, 'in shaping its policy and organization, to encourage the former and to neutralize and suppress the latter, . . .'[15] In similar, but more specific, theoretical terms, Crosland later defined the ideal of social equality, which had been 'the strongest ethical inspiration of virtually every socialist doctrine', as one that implied the goal of 'a distribution of rewards, status and privileges egalitarian enough to minimize social resentment, to secure justice between individuals, and to equalize opportunities'.[16]

In the late nineteenth and early twentieth centuries, most schools of socialist thought were united in the belief that, as far as strategy was concerned, the indispensable condition for realizing an egalitarian society of that kind was a fundamental change in the underlying form of economic organization. That would involve the elimination of private ownership of the most significant means of production – the root-cause of wide inequalities of wealth and power – and its replacement by large-scale public ownership of productive wealth. Since the 1950s, however, revisionist socialists such as Crosland and his followers have argued that the most effective and desirable method of pursuing greater equality, of both condition and opportunity, consisted not in the large-scale extension of public ownership, but rather in the implementation of redistributive fiscal and social policy measures. Progressive taxation, educational reform and the expansion of the welfare state, rather than nationalization of industry, were thus viewed as providing the routes to the classless society.

Since the nineteenth century, the socialist ideal of equality of outcome, whether formulated in a literal material sense or in more qualified ethical terms, has generated a high degree of ideological controversy. Both liberals and conservatives of various kinds have maintained that the concept itself, in its practical application, is incompatible with other, more important values and ideals – including, in particular, liberty, interpreted both negatively as the absence of coercion and positively as the presence of opportunity. These liberal and conservative critics have argued that a rigorous commitment to the ideal of equality of outcome would involve a process of social 'levelling' that would have a corrosive effect on individual liberty in its various aspects. Attempts, for instance, to abolish private education in the interest of promoting greater social equality have been viewed from this critical perspective as an assault on the individual's freedom of choice regarding the manner of schooling of his or her children.

Since the mid-1970s, much of this critique of the radical egalitarian position has been developed by New Right theorists – particularly in Britain and the USA. A crucial intellectual influence here has been the Austrian market–liberal political thinker and economist, Friedrich von Hayek, who in his various writings, notably *Law, Legislation and Liberty*, Vol. 2 (1976), drew special attention to the detrimental effects of egalitarian policies implemented within a market economy. For example, steeply-progressive and redistributive direct taxation, of both income and capital-wealth, has been portrayed by Hayek and others as a policy instrument that in effect both erodes incentives and penalizes or stifles talent and enterprise. In broader terms, egalitarian measures have been depicted as breeding a collectivist society that is standardized, economically stagnant and politically coercive.

With the apparent ascendancy of market–liberal ideas and policies in the West since the 1980s, and with it the decline of traditional socialism, there has unquestionably been a retreat on the centre-left from previous commitments to radical egalitarianism. In its place, however, there has been a widespread reaffirmation of the earlier liberal ideals of equal rights and equality of opportunity. Furthermore, the revival of analytical political philosophy since 1970 has combined with these developments to shift the ideological debate away from equality in its radical sense towards the related concept of social justice, thereby focusing on its meaning, its theoretical strengths and difficulties, and its practical implications.

Notes

1   See Chapter 4A.
2   R. Eccleshall, 'Liberalism', in R. Eccleshall *et al.*, *Political Ideologies: An Introduction*, 2nd edn, London, Routledge, 1994, p. 37.
3   ibid. pp. 37–8.
4   N. Barry, *An Introduction to Modern Political Theory*, 4th edn, London, Macmillan, 2000, p. 174.
5   T.H. Green, *The Works of Thomas Hill Green* (ed. R.L. Nettleship), London, Longmans, Green and Co., 1888, Vol. 3, p. 372.
6   J.A. Hobson, *The Crisis of Liberalism* (1909) (ed. P.F. Clarke), Harvester Press, 1974, p. xii.
7   ibid. p. 94.
8   A. Heywood, *Political Theory: An Introduction*, London, Macmillan, 2000, p. 290.
9   R.H. Tawney, *Equality*, London, George Allen and Unwin, 1931 (1964 edn), p. 103.
10 ibid. p. 105.
11 See C.A.R. Crosland, *The Future of Socialism* (1956) rev. edn, London, Jonathan Cape, 1964, Ch. VIII.
12 See Barry, op. cit. pp. 176–7.
13 ibid. p. 174.
14 ibid. p. 177.
15 Tawney, op. cit. p. 58.
16 Crosland, op. cit. p. 77.

SECTION B

Rousseau's vision of democratic equality

Historical context: political and intellectual

Rousseau first developed his ideas on equality at length in his *Discourse on the Origin and Foundations of Inequality Among Men*, to give the work its full title in English. (It has usually, however, been referred to as the *Second Discourse*, or the *Discourse on the Origin of Inequality*.) Published in 1755, Rousseau's *Second Discourse* followed the publication four years earlier of his *First Discourse*, the *Discourse on the Arts and Sciences*, which had won the prize from the Academy of Dijon and made its author famous throughout Europe.

In his *Discourse on the Arts and Sciences*, Rousseau had challenged much of Enlightenment opinion, expressed by Voltaire, Diderot and others, about the progressive development of European society through the advancement of knowledge and science and the application of reason. In rejecting such optimistic beliefs, Rousseau appeared to be turning away from the cause of progress and modern civilization, and celebrating instead a primitive, pre-modern golden age of human innocence.

In his *Second Discourse*, Rousseau developed this perspective further by elaborating the speculative history of mankind that he had begun in his earlier, prize-winning work. In one of the earliest and most influential accounts of social inequality in the history of modern political thought, he argued that the pursuit of inequality had been the root-cause of mankind's moral corruption and decline. In particular, he maintained that the acquisition of the earth by some to the exclusion of others, and the subsequent institutionalization of private property, had paved the way, through deception and injustice, for the establishment of civil society. From this starting point Rousseau traced the development of the other key features of modern civil society – the family, an agricultural economy, government and laws – explaining their character and purpose in terms of the unequal distribution of private property, and the relations of power and authority built around it.

In its impassioned critique of both modern civil society and modern systems of government, Rousseau's *Discourse on the Origin of Inequality* thus directed its fire at the gross inequalities of wealth and power that disfigured most contemporary European states. His major work of political philosophy, *The Social Contract* (1762), was later to provide an alternative vision of how such states might be radically transformed in order to realize what were, for Rousseau, the fundamental political principles of liberty and equality.

The inequality of civil society

In his *Second Discourse* Rousseau began his examination of the origin of human inequality with a celebration of man's natural liberty in a state of primitive innocence. This condition, in his view, had been enjoyed before the formation of modern civil society, and involved the individual's ability to satisfy basic and immediate needs without being subject to the will of another person. Motivated both by the instinct of self-preservation and by pity or compassion, solitary, primitive man, the wandering hunter, possessed this natural liberty, according to Rousseau, in the natural, pre-social state.

However, with the gradual development of civil society, man's natural instinct of self-preservation was transformed into an egoistic drive for self-advancement. Rousseau depicted this impulse as the basis for the acquisition of private property, with all its destructive effects. This major social change was itself the consequence of the growing productive capacity and wealth of society, evident in the emergence, through a process of collective labour, of an agricultural economy, and with it a system of production and distribution. This collective productive activity, in turn, led to the desire of some individuals for effective control over that process for the sake of personal gain and self-aggrandizement. In such a manner, Rousseau contended, the institution of private property had been reinforced and entrenched.

Moreover, Rousseau went on to argue, this institution of private property gave rise to deeply unequal relationships of power and position, which fractured the particular communities built around them. Private property was thus the foundation-stone of civil society, with all its subsequent distortions and abuses. As Rousseau explained in the *Second Discourse*:

> The first person who, having enclosed a piece of ground, to whom it occurred to say *this is mine*, and found people sufficiently simple to believe him, was the true founder of civil society. How many crimes, wars, murders, how many miseries and horrors Mankind would have been spared by him who, pulling up the stakes or filling in the ditch, had cried out to his kind: Beware of listening to this impostor; You are lost if you forget that the fruits are everyone's and the Earth no one's . . .[1]

By contrast, in man's primitive, pre-social state, with its common conditions of life, there could have been no such desire on the part of some individuals to acquire property and consequently no unequal relations of domination and subordination bred by property ownership. But in the first stage of development of civil society, Rousseau observed, inequalities in the distribution of private property had been reinforced by the enactment of laws that recognized and guaranteed property rights. This process had firmly established the division of civil society into the propertied and the propertyless, the rich and the poor.

The second stage in the evolution of civil society, according to Rousseau, involved the establishment of government in order to enforce laws, thereby preventing the increasingly widespread practices of usurpation of property by the rich and robbery by the poor. This political development led, in turn, to an increasing division of civil society into the powerful and the weak, which legalized the existing domination of the rich over the poor.

Rousseau explained this process in terms of a fraudulent social contract. By this method the rich and powerful persuaded the poor and weak, through deception and specious argument, that it would be to the advantage of all members of society to legalize and stabilize property relations that were really to the advantage of the rich and propertied alone. Grossly unequal relationships of domination and subservience were thus legitimized and institutionalized in civil society. As Rousseau observed:

> Such was, or must have been, the origin of Society and of Laws, which gave the weak new fetters and the rich new forces, irreversibly destroyed natural freedom, forever fixed the Law of property and inequality, transformed a skillful usurpation into an irrevocable right, and for the profit of a few ambitious men henceforth subjugated the whole of Mankind to labor, servitude and misery.[2]

In the final stage of development of civil society, Rousseau depicted its division into, first, the rich and poor, and later, the powerful and weak, as being eventually reinforced by a third unequal relationship – namely, that between master and slave. Indeed, the poorest and weakest person had even become 'proud of his slavery', pandering to the whims of the rich and powerful, whilst at the same time regarding them with envy and disdain. This for Rousseau was the ultimate stage of a corrupt, unequal and unfree civil society which rested on the foundations of vanity, on the one side, and widespread envy, on the other.

'Natural' and 'artificial' inequalities

In Rousseau's speculative historical account, social inequality thus stemmed partly from psychological factors – from egoistic feelings of pride which arise when individuals seek to procure advantages over others. Inequality also sprang, as we have seen, from external factors such as the collective process of productive labour which, with the advent of agriculture and metallurgy, gave rise to and established private property.

Central to this historical account was a clear distinction which Rousseau drew between two kinds of inequalities – first, 'natural' inequalities, of physical strength, intellectual endowment, etc., which he regarded as both acceptable and immutable, and second, 'political' inequalities, which he considered to be the artificially created products of convention, and therefore, in his view, both unacceptable and alterable.

Rousseau thus drew attention to:

> two sorts of inequality in the human Species; one which I call natural or Physical, because it is established by Nature, and which consists in the differences in age, health, strength of Body, and qualities of Mind, or of Soul; The other, which may be called moral or political inequality, because it depends on a sort of convention, and is established, or at least authorized by Man's consent. It consists in the different Privileges which some enjoy to the prejudice of the others, such as to be more wealthy, more honored, more Powerful than they, or even to get themselves obeyed by them.[3]

Furthermore, Rousseau insisted that it made no sense

to inquire whether there might not be some essential connection between the two inequalities; for that would be to ask in different terms whether those who command are necessarily better than those who obey, and whether strength of Body or of Mind, wisdom or virtue, are always found in the same proportion to their Power, or their Wealth: A question which it may perhaps be good for Slaves to debate within hearing of their Masters, but not befitting rational and free Men who seek the truth.[4]

In Rousseau's view, the attempt to equate social and political inequalities – of wealth, position and power – with natural or physical inequalities therefore amounted to a theoretically unsound and worthless basis for justifying the existing social and political order throughout Europe. For in reality, he argued, social and political inequalities, the products of convention, had been generated by institutions of private property and inheritance and sustained by the protective political power of modern states. Such artificially-created inequalities had been legitimized, too, not only by bogus doctrines that offered explanations in terms of innate endowment but also by natural-law theories that had depicted private property as a God-given, natural right rather than as a product of forceful acquisition.

This distinction between 'nature' and 'convention' underlying Rousseau's stark contrast between acceptable natural inequalities and unacceptable political inequalities has subsequently been questioned by some political theorists. Norman Barry, for example, has regarded it as a problematic and seldom clear-cut distinction since there are many areas of social life where the use of the terms 'nature' and 'convention' has little meaning or significance. A natural distinction, for instance, such as that based on intelligence is widely considered 'relevant only because society has conventionally regarded it as such for many purposes'. Moreover, Rousseau's broader argument that inequalities are created by 'society' is generally invalid 'since we have no useful conception of man abstracted from society which can form a touchstone for the legitimacy or otherwise of various distinctions'.[5]

The harmful effects of inequality

In spite of these problems associated with Rousseau's distinction between natural and socially-produced inequalities, he was nonetheless in no doubt about the harmful effects of social inequality. First and most obviously, it involved, he argued, both a widespread loss of personal independence and a great deal of human misery by making the many dependent on, and subservient to, the few. For throughout existing civil society, Rousseau observed, 'one sees a handful of powerful and rich men at the pinnacle of greatness and fortune while the masses grovel in obscurity and misery . . .'[6]

Second, inequality was an essentially corrupting force. It eroded man's innate goodness by generating both competition for scare resources and a struggle for power and status. In the process, it magnified personal vanity on one side of the social divide, and envy and resentment on the other.

Third, inequality undermined political liberty in at least two respects. In the first place, it stifled the individual's capacity for independent political judgement concerning the making of laws and policy decisions. This situation arose as a result of the power of the propertied few to dominate the propertyless majority. In addition, the social divisions created by the wide differences of wealth and power between the few and the many destroyed any sense of community. Such divisions thereby weakened, too, the individual's ability to identify with the society of which he was a member, and hence his willingness to play an active part in its civic affairs.

Rousseau's egalitarian remedy

Rousseau's remedy for these social ills bred by inequality, which he so graphically exposed in the *Second Discourse*, was essentially one that was both collectivist and egalitarian. He advocated nothing less than a radical reconstruction of existing eighteenth-century European societies and states, corrupt, unequal and unfree as he claimed they were. This process would require the creation of a new form of social and political organization that would no longer be dominated by relationships of domination and subservience. Within this new order individuals would be politically free, living under laws which they themselves had helped to make as participants in sovereign legislative assemblies. Those laws would be expressions of the general will, the common view that society held about what was in the public interest, rather than in the interests of particular individuals or groups.

Rousseau's prescription for the new social and political order was thus collectivist in this sense. It was directed towards the common good, the shared interests of individuals as active members of a community that assumed collective responsibility for its own affairs. It was at the same time an egalitarian course that he commended since his desired social and political model – namely, a small, self-governing, agrarian society – would be characterized by a broadly equal distribution of property.

This did not mean that Rousseau advocated the abolition of private property. Nor did he seek the achievement of absolute equality in the distribution of property. Indeed, while he rejected Locke's notion of a natural right to accumulate private property, he nonetheless supported the idea of private property, opposing early proto-socialist notions of common property. He adopted this position on the ground that depriving individuals of their chance to acquire property through their own labour would merely make them dependent upon the state rather than upon rich property-owners.

Rousseau's own egalitarian approach was to advocate instead an agrarian society of self-reliant property smallholders. The laws and government of such a society should therefore seek to ensure that all citizens owned enough property of their own to prevent any one of their number being dependent upon the rich. At the same time, government should also seek to control and reduce extreme accumulations of wealth. Rousseau's goal was thus *approximate* rather than absolute equality in the distribution of property. As he explained later in *The Social Contract*:

equality ... must not be understood to mean that degrees of power and wealth should be absolutely the same, but that, as for power, it stop short of all violence and never be exercised except by virtue of rank and the laws, and that as for wealth, no citizen be so very rich that he can buy another, and none so poor that he is compelled to sell himself.[7]

As well as seeking this more equal distribution of wealth, Rousseau's egalitarian remedy for the ills of existing civil society also embraced the ideal of political, and indeed in a sense democratic, equality. His ultimate aim was the creation of a society in which individuals would actively participate as free and equal citizens in the making of laws, by means of sovereign popular assemblies, that governed their communities.

Such an objective could be attained, in Rousseau's view, not just through a redistribution of property along the lines he prescribed, but also through a radical decentralization of political power. This would involve the vesting of sovereignty – of supreme legal authority – in legislative assemblies whose laws and policy decisions were reflections of the general will. As a corollary of this process, both representative government and sectional interest-groups would be discarded as anachronistic barriers in the path of popular sovereignty.

In this envisaged political utopia each male citizen (since Rousseau considered that women were by nature unsuited to the responsibilities of citizenship)[8] would be a politically-independent participant in the popular legislative assembly. For, as a member of an agrarian society of roughly equal smallholders, he would thus be in a position to debate and deliberate in the assembly in an independent manner. Because he was not dependent economically upon a rich property owner, he would also not be required to vote for any policy proposal that was more to the advantage of another citizen than to his own. By the same token, no rich and powerful citizen would be able to persuade others to support policy decisions and laws that conferred special advantages upon that privileged individual.

As a consequence of these new conditions of political equality, support for purely personal or sectional interests in the law-making process would be eliminated. The resulting policy and legislative decisions would thus embody the general will, thereby reconciling the individual's interests with the common good and securing in the process his 'true' moral and civil freedom.

Conclusion

The account of the origin of human inequality presented by Rousseau in his *Second Discourse* was thus the theoretical basis both for his diagnosis of the social and political ills of civil society and for the egalitarian remedy that he offered for them in *The Social Contract*. Indeed, as Robert Wokler has suggested:

The principles of his *Social Contract* are perhaps best understood in contradiction to the terms of agreement recounted in the second *Discourse*.[9]

For the loss of liberty and the creation of deep inequalities that for generations had marred European societies had been the consequences, in Rousseau's view, of a fraudulent and pernicious social contract designed by the rich and powerful to secure their privileges. By contrast, the alternative social and political order described in his later masterwork was conceived on the basis of a *legitimate* social contract that aimed to restore in a new social milieu man's natural liberty and equality that had been lost with the introduction of private property and the other institutions of civil society.

But the various difficulties that surround both Rousseau's notion of a primitive state of human innocence and his vision of ideal self-governing communities have serious implications for his own conception of 'true' liberty and equality. As John Gray has observed, in the light of the social and political developments that have taken place since Rousseau developed his political philosophy:

> We know that liberty and equality are not natural conditions but fragile artefacts of civilized government. They are threatened by social divisions arising from wide differences of wealth, as Rousseau warned; but they are also endangered by social conflicts that arise from the pursuit – by nationalists, fundamentalists and others – of homogenous communities of the kind that Rousseau admired inordinately.[10]

Nevertheless, in spite of the flawed vision of his 'suffocating rural arcadia',[11] Rousseau did at least present a compelling and highly-influential account of the harmful effects of deep economic and social inequalities. He did advance, too, a powerful case for his egalitarian thesis that a reduction of such inequalities, and indeed, the achievement of a much more equal distribution of property, were preconditions for realizing his ideals of both political equality and civil liberty – the capacity for self-government – within a society of independent equals.

Notes

1   J.-J. Rousseau, *Discourse on the Origin of Inequality* (1755), Part II, sec. 1, in *The Discourses and Other Early Political Writings* (ed. and trans. by V. Gourevitch), Cambridge, Cambridge University Press, 1997, p. 161.
2   ibid, p. 173.
3   ibid, p. 131.
4   ibid.
5   N. Barry, *An Introduction to Modern Political Theory*, 2nd edn, London, Macmillan, 2000, p. 175.
6   Rousseau, op. cit. p. 184.
7   J.-J. Rousseau, *The Social Contract and Other Later Writings* (ed. and trans. by V. Gourevitch), Cambridge, Cambridge University Press, 1997, p. 78 (Book 2, Ch. 11).
8   On this point see S.M. Okin, *Women in Western Political Thought*, Princeton, NJ, Princeton University Press, 1992, pp. 144–5.
9   R. Wokler, 'Jean-Jacques Rousseau: Moral Decadence and the Pursuit of Liberty', in *Plato to Nato: Studies in Political Thought* (intro. by B. Redhead), London, Penguin, 1995, p. 128.
10   J. Gray, 'The Desolate Utopian', *New Statesman*, 11 April 1997.
11   ibid.

Wollstonecraft on equal rights for women

Historical context: political and intellectual

Mary Wollstonecraft's arguments in favour of equal legal, political and civil rights for women were advanced most explicitly in her most famous work, *A Vindication of the Rights of Woman* (1792). This followed the publication two years earlier of her *A Vindication of the Rights of Men* (1790), which was the first critical response to Burke's *Reflections on the Revolution in France* (1790), and at the same time an attempt to defend those radical principles – in particular, the doctrine of the rights of man – which Burke had denounced.

Both of Wollstonecraft's political works emerged after a prolific period of writing during the 1780s when she had produced a tract on education entitled *Thoughts on the Education of Daughters* (1787), as well as works of literature, including two novels. After an unhappy and disrupted childhood and youth she had dedicated herself to a literary career under the protective patronage of the publisher, Joseph Johnson, who later introduced her to various radical artists and political thinkers, such as the anarchist philosopher, William Godwin, to whom she was married for the last five months of her life. She died at the young age of 38, days after giving birth to her second daughter, Mary, who was later to marry the poet Shelley and become the author of the celebrated novel, *Frankenstein*.

Mary Wollstonecraft's political writings, in which she forcefully expounded her radical views, were shaped, like Thomas Paine's (1737–1809), by the turbulent revolutionary era in which they both lived. Like Paine, too, she was subject to the same intellectual influences – the rights-based early liberalism of Locke and his contemporaries; the progressivist assumptions of eighteenth-century Enlightenment rationalism; and the radical and republican attitudes that accompanied and underlay the democratic revolutions of the late eighteenth century in, first, America and, later, France.

Against this political and intellectual background, Wollstonecraft's *A Vindication of the Rights of Men* was a rapidly-produced attempt to defend the French revolutionary cause against what she considered to be the inflated and irrational critique of it developed by Burke in his *Reflections*. Her pamphlet was also in part an attempt to defend her friend, the Rev. Richard Price, who had preached a sermon praising the French Revolution, from Burke's disdainful comments in the pages of the *Reflections*. In her response to Burke's views, she claimed that, in repudiating the idea of the rights of man, he was ignoring the oppression, injustice and human misery that had originally ignited the revolution in France.

More broadly, Wollstonecraft claimed that, in his critique, Burke was relying on deep-rooted conservative prejudices instead of rational argument. He had thus revered flawed English laws, customs and political institutions as though they were not only part of God's divine purpose but also products of the collective wisdom of successive generations. In reality, Wollstonecraft argued, those laws and institutions had been designed for the protection of the private property of the rich, not for the defence of the lives and liberties of the wretched poor.

By contrast, Wollstonecraft followed Locke and his successors in claiming

Mary Wollstonecraft (1759–97)

British radical political thinker and feminist writer. Mary Wollstonecraft was the author of a wide range of educational, literary, religious and political works, and was associated with the influential dissenting Protestants in late eighteenth-century England.

Her political writings were shaped, like Thomas Paine's, by the turbulent revolutionary era in which she lived. Intellectually, she was influenced by the theoretical assumptions of Lockean liberalism and Enlightenment rationalism, as well as by the radical democratic ideas of Rousseau.

By courtesy of the National Portrait Gallery, London

Wollstonecraft's first major political work was *A Vindication of the Rights of Men* (1790), written in critical response to the conservative arguments underlying Burke's *Reflections on the Revolution in France,* published earlier in the same year. In her own work she welcomed, as Paine did, the French Revolution of 1789 and defended the ideal of the 'rights of man' that in large part inspired it.

Her most famous work of political theory, *A Vindication of the Rights of Woman* (1792) addressed broad cultural issues concerning the status of women in the England of her day. Specifically, it advanced the radical cause of equal political and civil rights for women. Its impact as a statement of the case for gender equality – conceived in liberal terms of equal status and opportunities for women – was not to be surpassed until the publication of John Stuart Mill's *The Subjection of Women* in 1869.

Though a longstanding supporter of liberal causes, Wollstonecraft was drawn deeply into radical politics by the French Revolution. She became part of a radical intellectual circle that included the anarchist philosopher, William Godwin, whom she married towards the end of her life in 1797.

By that time Wollstonecraft had established her reputation both as a prominent radical defender of the French Revolution and as a significant female political thinker writing within the British liberal tradition. Since her death she has been widely viewed, too, as an important early pioneer of feminist thought.

that all human beings were endowed with God-given, and hence 'sacred', inviolable rights which could be discovered by reason. Like Locke, too, she argued that those natural rights entailed natural obligations, but that no individual should be required to fulfil such obligations if his own rights were not recognized. Human laws and institutions should therefore be respected and obeyed only if they were founded on reason and designed to protect the individual's natural rights.

Wollstonecraft's defence both of the French Revolution and of its inspirational doctrine of the rights of man lacked either the sustained theoretical argument or the rhetorical power of Paine's later, more influential work, *The Rights of Man*, Part 1 (1791). But the political impact of Wollstonecraft's book was considerable, nonetheless. It firmly established her name as a prominent radical defender of the French Revolution and as a significant female political thinker writing within the European liberal tradition. This reputation was enhanced by the publication in 1792 of her most famous work, *A Vindication of the Rights of Woman*.

The case for equal civil and political rights for women

Wollstonecraft's *A Vindication of the Rights of Woman* had essentially a dual purpose. First, during the course of an extended critique of Rousseau's tract on education, *Emile* (1762), it set out to explore the nature and social implications of womanhood. Second, it sought to critically examine the social position of women in a traditional, male-dominated society, focusing attention on their evident lack of legal, political and civil rights within such a society.

In the first place, therefore, Wollstonecraft proceeded to attack the theoretical justification that Rousseau had provided in *Emile* for the differential treatment of boys and girls by the educational system. Boys, according to Rousseau, were to be educated with an overriding emphasis on developing their rational capacities. Girls, by contrast, were to be encouraged to develop and fulfil their natural maternal role and obligations.

Wollstonecraft argued that women were neither emotional by nature nor intellectually inferior to men. Indeed, women were just as capable as men of thinking and acting in a rational manner. Recognition of this fundamental truth should therefore apply also, she maintained, to the debate about the exercise of natural rights. For if the possession of reason was not gender-related, then there could be no rational basis for discrimination against women in the recognition of legal, political and civil rights.

From this theoretical starting-point, Wollstonecraft developed an attack on the English educational system, arguing that it was in need of radical reform so that women could develop and exercise their own rational faculties on the same basis as men, thereby enjoying equal educational opportunities. For the existing educational system, like the other institutions of civil society, had the pernicious effect of reinforcing both man's dominant position and woman's subordinate role within society. The educational system, like English society at large, thus instilled in women characteristics of dependency, weakness, frivolity and inferiority, as well as expectations of life based on their subservient position. Furthermore, this process was reinforced in adulthood, and particularly in marriage and the family, by a particular view of women's sexual role and conduct, defined for them by men for their own advantage.

Expressed, then, in terms of these critical observations, Wollstonecraft's *A Vindication of the Rights of Woman* consisted to a large extent of a moral critique both of the nature of women in a male-dominated society and of the social influences that had shaped the characteristics which she so despised and wished to transform. As Sylvana Tomaselli has written:

Few writers of her day were as critical of women as she was. She did not like women as they were ... What she wanted above all was a trans-formation of women into their opposite. She wanted women to become ratio-nal and independent beings ...[1]

In order to 'effect a revolution in female manners',[2] as Wollstonecraft put it, radical charges were needed, she believed, in the educational system, within the family and in civil society at large. In education she thus argued that the govern-ment should establish day schools, for particular ages, in which boys and girls could be educated together, with appropriate changes in the curriculum ensuring that both sexes would be encouraged to develop their rational faculties.[3]

In general, Wollstonecraft contended that the goal of achieving equality of status and opportunity for women should be pursued both in education and within the family. To further that goal, the development and application of genderless reason was for Wollstonecraft the desired means. Just as the traditions of both Lockean liberalism and Enlightenment rationalism had invoked reason in the cause of checking absolute political power and authority, so, too, could reasoned argument be deployed in the family as a means of ending the excessive power of men over women. As Wollstonecraft remarked in an optimistic spirit:

The divine right of husbands, like the divine right of kings, may, it is to be hoped, in this enlightened age, be contested without danger ...[4]

Moreover, the development of women into rational and independent beings would, in her view, both strengthen marriage and the family and result in more harmonious relations between men and women. She thus maintained that:

If marriage is the cement of society, mankind should all be educated after the same model, or the intercourse of the sexes will never deserve the name of fellowship, nor will women ever fulfil the peculiar duties of their sex, till they become enlightened citizens, till they become free by being enabled to earn their own subsistence, independent of men ...[5]

Finally, Wollstonecraft called upon constitutional reformers in Britain and France to acknowledge that the case for universal civil and political rights for men should be applied also to women within civil society at large. She asked, at the beginning of her *A Vindication of the Rights of Woman*:

If the abstract rights of man will bear discussion and explanation, those of woman, by a parity of reasoning, will not shrink from the same test: though a different opinion prevails in this country ... Consider ... whether, when men contend for their freedom, and to be allowed to judge for themselves respecting their own happiness, it be not inconsistent and unjust to subju-gate women ...[6]

Indeed, in contemporary society those who failed to treat men and women equally in respect of their rights were in effect forcing 'all women, by denying them civil and political rights, to remain immured in their families, groping in the dark'.[7]

Wollstonecraft therefore advocated political and constitutional reform in order to grant such rights to women, including the right to have their own political representatives, 'instead of being arbitrarily governed without having any direct share allowed them in the deliberations of government'.[8] Furthermore, she believed that the recognition of civil and political rights for women was a necessary means not only to 'the progress of knowledge and virtue'[9] in civil society, but also to the transformation of women themselves. For Wollstonecraft was convinced that, in a future climate of political and social reform women 'will change their character, and correct their vices and follies, when they are allowed to be free in a physical, moral, and civil sense',[10] thereby assuming, too, the civil duties that accompanied the rights they had justly been granted.

Conclusion

Wollstonecraft was not a systematic political thinker and her political writings consequently do not contain a rigorous theoretical exposition of the concept of formal equality of rights in relation to women. Indeed, her major work of political theory, *A Vindication of the Rights of Woman*, is both fragmented and in places disjointed and diffusive.

Nevertheless, Wollstonecraft's influence upon the subsequent development of liberal and, in particular, liberal feminist thought has been profound. That is not to say that her legacy has been a matter devoid of controversy. Some later feminist writers have maintained, for instance, that her advocacy of equal treatment and rights for women was rooted not only in the assumptions of liberal natural-rights theory, but also in a tendency to deny the distinctive characteristics and insights of women, submerging them instead in her overriding desire that woman should 'emulate the virtues of man'.[11]

But in spite of such reservations, Wollstonecraft's reputation as an early intellectual pioneer of liberal feminism has since her premature death become firmly established. In large part, that reputation derives from her impassioned, persuasive and often innovative promotion of the ideal of gender equality in her *A Vindication of Woman*. Her case was formulated, as we have seen, mainly in terms of the ideas of equality of educational opportunities and of equality of moral and legal status within the family and civil society at large.

In making that case, her primary emphasis was not so much upon the theoretical arguments for equal civil and political rights for women as upon the moral, social and political consequences that would arise from their eventual recognition by a male-dominated society. Driven by the force of her moral and cultural critique of the nature and position of women within such a society, Wollstonecraft's vigorous advancement of the cause of their emancipation was not to be matched in its influence until the publication of John Stuart Mill's essay on *The Subjection of Women* in 1869.

Notes

1 S. Tomaselli, introduction to M. Wollstonecraft, *A Vindication of the Rights of Men with A Vindication of the Rights of Woman* (ed. S. Tomaselli), Cambridge, Cambridge University Press, 1995, p. xxvi.
2 M. Wollstonecraft, *A Vindication of the Rights of Woman* (1792), in Wollstonecraft, op. cit. p. 117.
3 See Wollstonecraft, *A Vindication of the Rights of Woman*, Ch. 12, in Wollstonecraft, op. cit. pp. 251–75.
4 ibid. p. 112.
5 ibid. p. 260.
6 ibid, pp. 68–9.
7 ibid. p. 69.
8 ibid. p. 237.
9 ibid. p. 68.
10 ibid. p. 294.
11 ibid.

John Stuart Mill on equality of opportunity and on equal status for women

Historical context: political and intellectual

The liberal philosopher John Stuart Mill's views on equality were expressed mainly in two areas of his political and social thought. In the first place, they evolved in the light of his growing conviction that liberalism as a tradition of thought needed to be revised to take account of the changing realities of mid-nineteenth-century English society – including, in particular, the scale of poverty and unemployment in industrial towns and cities. This conviction was reinforced, too, by his sympathetic awareness of the interests and aspirations of an increasingly organized and partly enfranchised industrial working class, as well as of a rapidly developing socialist movement throughout Europe that sought to articulate those interests.

Mill's desire to revise liberalism in the face of these major social and economic changes was evident from 1852 onwards in the third and subsequent editions of his work, *Principles of Political Economy*, first published in 1848. His revisionist project was apparent, too, in his *Chapters on Socialism*, begun in 1869, but not published until after his death. Later in his *Autobiography* (1873), he explained why, partly under the influence of his wife, Harriet Taylor, he had moved towards a more egalitarian form of social liberalism, or 'qualified socialism', as he referred to it. This ideological journey was to be carried a stage further in the 1870s and subsequently, albeit from a different philosophical standpoint, by Thomas Hill Green (1836–82) and other 'new' social–liberal thinkers.

In his *Autobiography*, Mill recalled that:

while we repudiated with the greatest energy that tyranny of society over the individual which most Socialistic systems are supposed to involve, we yet looked forward to the time when society will no longer be divided into the idle and the illustrious … when the division of the produce of labour … instead of depending … on the accident of birth, will be made by concert on an acknowledged principle of justice; … The social problem of the future we considered to be, how to unite the greatest individual liberty of action, with a common ownership in the raw materials of the globe, and an equal participation of all in the benefits of combined labour.[1]

In developing these insights, Mill had been influenced by the writings of early English and French socialist thinkers, such as Robert Owen (1771–1858), Henri Saint-Simon (1760–1825) and Charles Fourier (1772–1837), as well as by the sociological thought of Auguste Comte (1798–1857). This intellectual process was part of Mill's broader movement away from the orthodoxies of classical Utilitarianism, itself a product of the eighteenth-century European Enlightenment. As we have seen, his essay *On Liberty* (1859) was the clearest expression both of his gradual liberation from past commitments and of his attempt at achieving an intellectual synthesis of a modified utilitarian position with those later influences which, in a pluralist spirit, he had subsequently embraced.[2] The egalitarian views which from 1852 Mill increasingly espoused within his 'qualified socialism' were thus another expression of his search for such a synthesis.

The second major area of Mill's political thought in which his egalitarianism was strongly promoted concerned the issue of the legal, social and political status of women in mid-Victorian England. In making a powerful case in his essay on *The Subjection of Women* (1869) for the equal status of women in all areas of civil society, Mill deployed similar arguments to those which Mary Wollstonecraft (1759–97) had advanced seventy-seven years earlier in her *A Vindication of the Rights of Woman* (1797). Philosophically, however, Mill's arguments were based on his utilitarian and libertarian viewpoints rather than on natural-rights theory.

Mill's *The Subjection of Women*, the most developed statement of his views on gender equality, was written during the winter of 1860–1 in Avignon, France. It articulated opinions which he had long held. The essay had also been strongly influenced by the feminist attitudes of his wife, Harriet Taylor, who died in 1858 of tuberculosis, a disease from which Mill also suffered. After a long journey through France, Italy and Greece, begun in 1854 for convalescence, Mill eventually recovered. Following the publication in 1859 of *On Liberty*, which he dedicated to the memory of his wife, he proceeded to complete *The Subjection of Women* just over a year later. It was not to be published, however, until 1869 when, as William Thomas has noted, 'events (notably the 73 votes for his amendment to the second Reform Bill proposing votes for women, in May 1867) made him feel opinion was turning his way'.[3] Composed by Mill in a reasoned yet also impassioned, often subjective style, the work constituted 'his final attempt to reconcile utilitarianism with the most romantic experience of his life'.[4]

Reward according to desert in industrial society

In developing his views on equality, Mill began, as in the rest of his political philosophy, from a Benthamite, utilitarian standpoint which he then sought to modify.

Bentham's conception of equality had been crystallized in the proposition: 'Everyone is to count for one, and no one for more than one.' For in his utilitarian view, each person should be considered equally as an individual capable of experiencing pleasure, and hence of maximizing his or her happiness or well-being. However, Bentham also believed that the principle of security, which for him was, along with equality, subsistence and abundance, one of the four guiding principles of civil law, ought to take precedence over equality. He formed this view on the utilitarian ground that, with regard to the distribution of property, the pain of frustrated expectations or disappointment on the part of the property-owner would generally exceed the pleasure of unexpected gratification on the part of the recipient.[5]

From this Benthamite starting point, Mill interpreted the principle of equality as implying an equal claim by the individual upon society for equality of treatment as a means to happiness. As he argued in his essay on moral philosophy, *Utilitarianism* (1863), which presented his revision of the utilitarian doctrine in which, since his childhood, he had been steeped:

> The equal claim of everybody to happiness in the estimation of the moralist and the legislator, involves an equal claim to all the means to happiness, except in so far as the inevitable conditions of human life, and the general interest, set limits to the maxim . . .[6]

Formulated in these terms, the principle of equality was also viewed more broadly by Mill as a means to individual liberty, which he interpreted in *On Liberty* (1859), in the course of his radical revision of utilitarian theory, not just as a means to happiness but rather in the sense of the individual's moral, intellectual and aesthetic self-development. The development of these fundamental egalitarian principles, derived from classical utilitarianism, and their application to changing economic and social conditions, became evident when Mill began to revise some of the major assumptions of classical liberal thought in the light of those changes. This process was particularly marked from 1852 onwards in the third and later editions of his textbook on economic theory, *Principles of Political Economy*, first published in 1848. Based on the liberal–individualist assumptions of David Ricardo's (1770–1832) economic theory, which Mill had absorbed in the 1820s, the first edition of this work firmly defended the principles of private property and of a free-market economy.

After the French Revolution of 1848, however, which Mill strongly endorsed along with the subsequent, yet short-lived, Second Republic, Mill revised some of these market–liberal assumptions, expressing sympathy for some of the ideas of early French socialist thinkers such as Henri Saint-Simon and Charles Fourier. Consequently, in the third edition of the *Principles of Political Economy*, published in 1852, the year of Napoleon III's coup d'état in France, Mill rewrote his chapter, in Book II, dealing with socialism in recognition of where his political sympathies lay with regard to recent developments on the Continent.

In the course, therefore, of a wide-ranging comparison of communism or socialism, on the one hand, and a free-market economy on the other, Mill employed an egalitarian yardstick for judging their respective merits and flaws as rival forms of economic organization. In the third edition of the *Principles of Political Economy*, he thus maintained that the principle of private property underlying a market economy had not been applied in an equitable manner. For, in practice, the distribution of private property bore no relation to the liberal principle of reward according to merit or desert. Indeed, Mill believed that:

> If ... the choice were to be made between Communism with all its chances, and the present [1852] state of society with all its sufferings and injustices; if the institution of private property necessarily carried with it as a consequence, that the produce of labour should be apportioned as we now see it, almost in an inverse ratio to the labour – the largest portions to those who have never worked at all, the next largest to those whose work is almost nominal, and so in a descending scale, the remuneration dwindling as the work grows harder and more disagreeable, ... if this or Communism were the alternative, then all the difficulties, great or small, of Communism would be but as dust in the balance.[7]

Mill, however, with his underlying acceptance of the precepts of a market economy, argued that:

> The principle of private property has never yet had a fair trial in any country; ... The social arrangements of modern Europe commenced from a distribution of property which was the result, not of just partition, or acquisition by industry, but of conquest and violence ...[8]

Moreover, the enactment of laws of property had violated any notion of equality of opportunity. For in reality they 'have not held the balance fairly between human beings, but have heaped impediments upon some, to give advantage to others; they have purposely fostered inequalities, and prevented all from starting fair in the race'.[9]

However, if such inequalities had been tempered by legislation, the tendency of which had been 'to favour the diffusion, instead of the concentration of wealth', then Mill contended that 'the principle of individual property would have been found to have no necessary connexion, with the physical and social evils which almost all Socialist writers assume to be inseparable from it'.[10]

Mill therefore advocated legislation that would both further the wider dispersal of wealth in society, and seek to relate reward to merit and effort. To that end, he proposed a limit on the amount of inherited wealth, with inheritance taxation levied on the recipient rather than the donor. He continued to believe, however, that individuals should retain control of property which they had accumulated by their own labour or acquired through inheritance.

As another distinctive feature of the 'qualified socialism' to which he was increasingly sympathetic, Mill also advanced the case in *Principles of Political Economy* for co-partnership and profit-sharing in industry and for an extension of the cooperative movement, originally founded in England in 1844, in which there would be competing, self-managed workers' cooperatives with:

the association of the workers themselves on terms of equality, collectively owning the capital with which they carry out their operations, and working under managers elected and removable by themselves.[11]

Mill's advocacy of such proposals, designed to adapt his liberal–egalitarian ideas to contemporary economic and political conditions, underlined the fact that, along with early socialist thinkers such as Owen, Saint-Simon and Fourier, he recognized that the workings of the capitalist system had severe consequences in terms of social injustice. However, Mill repudiated many of the collectivist remedies – including a large-scale extension of state ownership of industry, or direct state intervention in the economy – which French and other radical socialists were offering as the proper response to such ills. In general, he feared, too, the conformist and intolerant effects of state paternalism inherent in many contemporary forms of socialism. He thus wondered:

> whether there would be any asylum left for individuality of character; whether public opinion would not be a tyrannical yoke; whether the absolute dependence of each on all, and the surveillance of each of all, would not grind all down into a tame uniformity of thoughts, feelings and actions.[12]

Such fears clearly underlined his opposition both to the radical egalitarian aims and to the collectivist methods that he discerned in communist and socialist doctrines. He had made it clear in 1849, however, that he was sympathetic to socialist arguments on two conditions: first, if they accepted the liberal notion of allocation of reward according to merit, and second, if they provided a critique of the existing distribution of property on the basis of that liberal principle. He thus believed that the socialist ideas of both Robert Owen and Louis Blanc (1811–82) were 'the modern form of the protest ... against the unjust distribution of social advantages'[13] and therefore fundamentally in harmony with liberal principles.

Saint-Simon and his followers also had, in Mill's view, attempted to apply the liberal notion of reward according to merit in the sense of effort or labour. For they had advocated economic arrangements in which 'every individual [would be] required to take a share of labour ... [and] all [would be] classed as according to their capacity and remunerated according to their works'.[14] However, Mill recoiled from the benevolent authoritarianism inherent in Saint-Simon's broader socialist philosophy, which he regarded as an approach that was both impracticable and unacceptable in a liberal society.[15]

In general, then, Mill sought to strike a balance between, on the one hand, the ideal of equality of opportunity that underlay the notion of reward according to desert and, on the other, his deep-seated commitment to the ideals of individual liberty and individuality. Such a balance could be achieved, he believed, within the context of a competitive market economy based on private property and on the incentive of personal gain. Nonetheless, Mill was prepared to qualify this classical liberal view by endorsing what he considered to be those valid aspects of the socialist critique of the distribution of capitalist property. For such insights underlined the glaring discrepancy between the liberal idea of reward according to desert and the prevailing, grossly unequal conditions of production and distribution in England. Moreover, Mill recognized that removing such injustices also required a more positive and enabling role for the state. In practice, that meant, he argued, that the state 'ought to be considered as a great benefit society or mutual insurance company for helping the large proportion of its members who cannot help themselves'.[16] By intervening, therefore, in such fields as education, welfare and working conditions, the state should thereby seek to widen the individual's opportunities for self-development within an unequal industrial society.

Equality of status for women

Mill's liberal–egalitarian views also found strong and eloquent expression in his advocacy of the improved legal, social and political status of women in the England of his day. Developed in his essay on *The Subjection of Women* (1869) in terms that combined abstract reasoning with a subjective, often impassioned tone, Mill's case for equality of status for women rested on a strong personal conviction which he had 'held from the very earliest period when I had formed any opinions at all on social and political matters'.[17] That conviction amounted to the belief:

> That the principle which regulates the existing social relations between the two sexes – the legal subordination of one sex to the other – is wrong in itself, and now one of the chief hindrances to human improvement; and that it ought to be replaced by a principle of perfect equality, admitting no power or privilege on the one side, nor disability on the other.[18]

In advancing that egalitarian principle, Mill began his essay by seeking to refute those arguments that sought to justify women's legal and political subordination on the ground of their supposed 'natural' inferiority. Indeed, Mill rejected as unscientific any statements about female 'nature' or 'natural' female behaviour. For the word 'natural' in such statements in reality, he argued, meant 'customary', and hence 'what is now called the nature of women is an eminently artificial thing'.[19]

In Mill's view, therefore, assertions about the 'natural' differences between men and women had no intellectually coherent basis since he denied 'that any one knows, or can know, the nature of the two sexes, as long as they have only been seen in their present relation to one another'.[20] Moreover, until there were further developments in 'the most important department of psychology, the laws of the influence of circumstances on character',[21] statements about 'natural' differences between the sexes would remain, he believed, vacuous and subjective reflections of a male-dominated society. Certainly they could provide no sound justification for the existing legal and political disabilities of women in Victorian England.

Mill thus deployed these environmentalist arguments in his reaction against traditional opinions about the alleged 'natural' inferiority of women. In addition, he maintained that there was no significant evidence drawn from experience in support of such prejudices. On the contrary, any relevant evidence that did exist supported, he claimed, his own arguments. Here he drew particular attention to the historical record of highly-effective female monarchs who had exercised their political rule in the face of acute difficulties.

Whilst attacking, then, in the first part of *The Subjection of Women* justifications for the unequal treatment of women based on 'natural' differences between the sexes, Mill had argued, as a central part of his case, that any existing, limited knowledge of such differences had been formed within the context of a male-dominated society. For women in general the conditions that prevailed in such a society were the ones of near-servitude into which they plunged upon getting married. In Mill's view, the family was in fact a 'school of despotism',[22] a realm of male domination, in which women's liberty was sacrificed – sometimes for the sake of comfort or convenience, but sacrificed nonetheless.

Marriage was thus viewed by Mill as central to women's unequal status. For he was writing at a time when, under English marriage laws, women not only lost all legal title to their property upon getting married, but also had no legal protection or redress against the misconduct of husbands, including assault. In short, women were treated as little more than legal appendages of their husbands. Critically observing, then, this subordinate status of the married Englishwoman of the 1860s, Mill wrote:

> She vows a lifelong obedience to him at the altar, and is held to it all through her life by law ... She can do no act whatever but by his permission, at least tacit. She can acquire no property but for him: the instant it becomes hers, even if by inheritance, it becomes ipso facto his. In this respect, the wife's position under the common law of England is worse than that of slaves in the laws of many countries ...[23]

Mill was therefore reinforcing his argument for the equal legal status and treatment of women with the aid of an analogy between the contemporary position of women in England and the historical situation of slaves in other societies. Arguments similar to those currently advanced in justification of women's unequal status had once been deployed and accepted, he pointed out, with regard to the position of slaves. From this broad historical perspective, too, Mill viewed the progress of modern civilization as a gradual process of recognizing the legitimate claims of various suppressed groups, such as slaves, vassals and wage-labourers. In time, he believed, that process would be extended to embrace the belated recognition of the legal and political claims of women. But at the present time, he declared, it remained the case in England that:

> Marriage is the only actual bondage known to our law. There remain no legal slaves, except the mistress of every house.[24]

On the basis of this strongly emphasized analogy between the respective positions of women and slaves, Mill then proceeded to advance the case for firmly establishing the legal rights of women within both marriage and civil society at large. Such reforms would serve to provide necessary legal protection for women, particularly for those vulnerable to the worst, most abusive kind of husband. Mill's underlying assumption here was that 'laws and institutions require to be adapted, not to good men, but to bad'.[25] In addition, securing the legal rights of women would both provide the basis for extending their opportunities within society and create a climate which, by prohibiting certain kinds of unacceptable male conduct, might help to change for the better social and cultural attitudes towards the role of women.

As a response, therefore, to women's legal subordination within the family, society's 'school of despotism', Mill advocated full equality of married persons before the law. This would be the first essential step towards the social recognition and acceptance of marriage as an association of equal partners. Within the framework of such an arrangement, the mutual obligations and benefits of husbands and wives would be clearly identified as the implications of a freely-contracted relationship. Furthermore, these major changes in women's legal status – with regard to marriage, property and person – would be accompanied by a recognition, too, of their political rights, including their right to vote in national and local elections. For in respect of the 'right to suffrage', the same practical considerations that underlay the recent advance towards male suffrage also applied in the future movement towards female suffrage that Mill himself championed in the British Parliament in 1867.[26] As he wrote in clarification of this fundamental point:

> under whatever conditions, and within whatever limits, men are admitted to the suffrage, there is not a shadow of justification for not admitting women under the same.[27]

Mill also argued in favour of equality of opportunity for women 'to hold offices or practise professions involving public responsibilities'[28] on the basis of individual merit and regardless of irrelevant and outdated considerations of gender. He believed, too, that this liberal principle of equality of opportunity should be realized within the workings of a competitive market economy, arguing that:

> so long as competition is the general law of human life, it is tyranny to shut out one half of the competitors. All who have attained the age of self-government have an equal claim to be permitted to sell whatever kind of useful labour they are capable of, for the price it will bring.[29]

Underlying such arguments for the radical improvement of women's legal, social, political and economic status, and hence for the equal treatment of women in all those respects, was the ethical foundation that supported the case for individual freedom of self-regarding conduct which Mill had so eloquently advanced in *On Liberty*. For the pursuit of equality of status and opportunity for women was, in his view, a means above all to liberty, which was in turn valuable not just in itself, but as the means to the individual's self-development, to the enlargement of his or her capacities. The personal independence of women as much as of men, which involved 'the free direction and disposal of their own faculties', was therefore for Mill both the necessary condition of attaining freedom in this sense of self-development and hence a 'clear source of individual happiness'.[30]

Alongside this libertarian basis, Mill's case for gender equality rested, too, on the utilitarian foundation that philosophically he had never entirely abandoned. The existing situation regarding the position of women in Victorian England was unacceptable to Mill not just because it withheld from women all the benefits of liberty, but also because it impeded the moral and intellectual growth of society as a whole, thereby undermining the pursuit of the general happiness. For under the prevailing conditions of grossly unequal status and opportunity, reflected in both legal arrangements and social conventions, the moral and social attitudes of men and women alike, as well as their individual characters, were distorted by the force of such pressures.

The progress of society was obstructed, too, by the harm inflicted upon men by women's lack of status and opportunities in existing society. For as a consequence of women's social exclusion, men were deprived of the beneficial effects of both intellectual stimulation and companionship. By contrast, Mill argued, improving the status of women and extending their opportunities would confer such benefits on men, thereby promoting the common good. In particular, 'great accession to the intellectual power of the species, and to the amount of the intellect available for the good management of its affairs, would be obtained, partly through the better and more complete education of women ...'[31] More broadly, Mill concluded in this utilitarian spirit that:

> The moral regeneration of mankind will only really commence, when the most fundamental of the social relations is placed under the rule of equal justice, and when human beings learn to cultivate their strongest sympathy with an equal in rights and in cultivation.[32]

Conclusion

We have seen that in two major areas of concern within John Stuart Mill's political thought – regarding, first, the need to revise liberal ideals in the light of economic and social changes within industrial society, and, second, the need to apply liberal insights to an examination of the unequal status of women within such a society – certain common themes are discernible. The most significant of these are: the central importance of the ideal of personal liberty understood in the sense of the individual's moral and intellectual self-development; the value of equality of opportunity as a distributive principle that seeks to ensure the allocation of rewards according to merit; and the desirability of a competitive market economy as the framework within which that principle can be realized.

In the first of these areas of concern, Mill was prepared to incorporate much of the contemporary socialist critique of the distribution of capitalist property into his otherwise generally favourable analysis of the workings of a market economy. His approval of the egalitarian thrust of socialist arguments led him to endorse a more positive role for the state with regard both to the redistribution of wealth and to the regulation of the working and living conditions of the people. This movement towards a more collectivist form of liberalism was to be sustained and developed after Mill's death by Thomas Hill Green and other social–liberal thinkers. Ultimately, however, Mill's egalitarianism in this area rested on a belief in a principle of equality of opportunity that could be reconciled not only with his overriding concern with personal liberty interpreted in terms of self-development and individuality, but also with his general, albeit qualified, approval of a competitive market economy as the most desirable form of economic organization.

In Mill's second area of egalitarian concern – involving his fervent advocacy of equal legal, political and social status for women – the compatibility of his espousal of that cause with his underlying liberal philosophy is again clearly apparent. That is to say that the egalitarian ideals that he was advancing with regard to the position of women were consistent both with the utilitarian principles that he had imbibed and modified and with the libertarian commitment that pervaded *On Liberty*.

Mill's sexual egalitarianism thus consisted, first, in his affirmation of the procedural principle of formal equality, understood in the utilitarian sense that all persons, men and women alike, as individuals capable of maximizing their happiness, ought to be treated equally before the law and within civil society at large. Second, he affirmed, too, the distributive principle of equality of opportunity, holding that rewards and opportunities should be allocated on the basis of individual merit and regardless of irrelevant factors such as gender, or indeed, race or religion. Both those concepts of equality, procedural and distributive, Mill considered to be inseparable from the preservation and promotion of personal liberty and individual happiness, his central philosophical and political preoccupations and goals.

Notes

1   John Stuart Mill, *Autobiography* (1873) (ed. J.M. Robson), London, Penguin, 1989, p. 175.
2   See Chapter 4B.
3   W. Thomas, 'Mill', Oxford, Oxford University Press, 1980; reprinted in Q. Skinner, R. Tuck, W. Thomas and P. Singer, *Great Political Thinkers*, Oxford, Oxford University Press, 1992, p. 350.
4   ibid.
5   See E. Halévy, *The Growth of Philosophic Radicalism* (1928), London, Faber & Faber, 1972, pp. 45–6, 50–1.
6   J.S. Mill, *Utilitarianism* (1863) (ed. R. Crisp), Oxford, Oxford University Press, 1998, pp. 105–6.
7   J.S. Mill, *Principles of Political Economy* (1871), 7th edn, London, Longmans, Green and Co., 1923, p. 208.
8   ibid.
9   ibid. p. 209.
10   ibid.
11   ibid. p. 773.
12   ibid. pp. 210–11.
13   J.S. Mill, 'Vindication of the French Revolution of February 1848' (1849), in *Dissertations and Discussions, Political, Philosophical and Historical*, 2nd edn, London, Longmans, Green and Co., 1875, II, p. 388.
14   Mill, *Autobiography*, p. 133.
15   J.S. Mill, 'Considerations on Representative Government' (1861), reprinted in J.S. Mill, *Three Essays: On Liberty, Representative Government, The Subjection of Women*, Oxford, Oxford University Press, 1975, p. 175.

16   J.S. Mill, 'Essay on Coleridge', in *Dissertations and Discussions, Political, Philosophical and Historical*.

17   J.S. Mill, *The Subjection of Women* (1869), in Mill, *On Liberty, The Subjection of Women and Chapters on Socialism* (ed. S. Collini), Cambridge, Cambridge University Press, 1989, p. 119.

18   ibid.

19   ibid. p. 138.

20   ibid.

21   ibid. p. 140.

22   ibid. p. 160.

23   ibid. p. 147.

24   ibid. p. 196.

25   ibid. p. 151.

26   As noted above, Mill's amendment to the Second Reform Bill in May 1867, proposing votes for women, won 73 votes in its favour in the British Parliament. This was a significant advance in British politics at that time.

27   Mill, *The Subjection of Women*, p. 169.

28   ibid.

29   J.S. Mill, 'Enfranchisement of Women' (1851), in *Dissertations and Discussions, Political, Philosophical and Historical*, II, p. 429.

30   Mill, *The Subjection of Women*, p. 214.

31   ibid. p. 199.

32   ibid. p. 211.

Marx on equality in a communist society

Historical context: political and intellectual

Karl Marx, economic historian and economist, political philosopher, radical journalist and revolutionary organizer, is probably the most controversial figure in the history of modern political thought. His unorthodox interpretation of the ideal of equality reflects that distinctive status. For Marx largely rejected the prevailing notion of equality, particularly the early liberal concept of formal equality of rights, regarding it in general not as a timeless value and ideal, but as the intellectual product of a particular stage of historical development and the reflection of particular class interests.

Born in 1818 of Jewish parents in the German state of Prussia, Marx studied history, law and philosophy at German universities, obtaining his doctorate in philosophy at Jena in 1841. Unable to get a university lectureship in Prussia because of his radical political views, he became a radical journalist in Cologne, but, after the newspaper for which he was writing was suppressed, was forced to flee Prussia in 1843. After travelling to Paris, then the centre of the European socialist movement, Marx in 1844 formed what was to prove a lasting friendship with the German radical writer, Friedrich Engels (1820–95), who became not only a friend in the years ahead, but also a colleague, benefactor and co-author of three of Marx's fifty or so philosophical, economic and political works.

Forced to leave Paris in 1845, at the insistence of the Prussian government, again because of his radical political opinions and activities, Marx next moved to Brussels, where in 1848 he and Engels were commissioned to write a doctrinal

Karl Marx (1818–83)

German philosopher, economist, political thinker and revolutionary socialist activist. Born in the German state of Prussia, Marx studied history, law and philosophy in German universities. After working as a radical journalist, he was forced to flee Prussia in 1843 because of his political views.

By courtesy of Hulton Archive

After travelling to Paris, then the centre of the European socialist movement, Marx formed in 1844 a lasting friendship with the German radical writer, Friedrich Engels, who was to become Marx's colleague and benefactor, as well as co-author of three of Marx's fifty or so philosophical, economic and political works.

Marx first described his vision of a communist society in his *Economic and Philosophical Manuscripts,* written in Paris in 1844, but not to be published until 1932. In this work he developed his concept of alienation of labour under capitalism, which he contrasted with the scope for the free development of the individual that would exist, he believed, in a future communist society based on cooperative production.

After leaving Paris in 1845 at the insistence of the Prussian government, Marx moved to Brussels where over the next two years he wrote with Engels *The German Ideology,* which set out at length his materialist conception of history, or theory of historical materialism, as Engels called it. This theory constitutes Marx's major and most distinctive contribution to modern political thought. It provided both the historical foundation for his early communist views and the theoretical basis of the global ideology that later became known as Marxism. In Brussels, too, Marx and Engels wrote *The Communist Manifesto* (1848), one of the classic and most widely-read works of modern political thought.

In 1849 Marx moved with his family to London, where he spent the remainder of his life. After helping in 1864 to found the First International, an association of early socialist and trade union groups, he devoted most of his time in London to theoretical work. This involved, in particular, the completion of his major treatise on economics, *Capital,* Vol. 1 of which was published in 1867.

Marx's varied writings provided the theoretical framework for the revolutionary socialist movement of the nineteenth and early twentieth centuries. More broadly, his theories and arguments constitute an essential reference point for any discussion of the development, interaction and eventual divergence of the diverse currents of socialist thought during that period and since. Marx remains one of the most controversial figures in the history of modern Western political thought.

statement for the Communist League, a small, semi-secret organization of which they were both active members between 1847 and 1852. The result of their literary and intellectual collaboration was *The Communist Manifesto* (1848), one of the classic works of modern political thought. Both celebrated and denounced ever since as a powerful critique, formulated in revolutionary terms, of the Western capitalist system, *The Communist Manifesto* also contains most of the central themes of Marx's political and economic thought as a whole. Indeed, many Marx scholars, including, for example, Leszek Kolakowski, have argued that this short work in many ways provides the most succinct statement of Marx's revolutionary socialist theory and strategy. Kolakowski thus maintained that:

> With the appearance of *The Communist Manifesto*, we may say that Marx's theory of society and his precepts for action had attained completion in the form of a well-defined and permanent outline.[1]

At the time of the publication of *The Communist Manifesto* in 1848, much of Europe – from France to Prussia and Hungary – was convulsed by a series of revolutionary upheavals. All of these, however, were eventually suppressed and the overthrow of the capitalist system by the industrial working class, which Marx and Engels had at first expected, never materialized. Marx himself soon moved with his family to London where he remained for the rest of his life until his death in 1883.

After helping in 1864 to found the First International or, to give it its full title, the First International Workingmen's Association, which brought together a number of early socialist and trade-union groups from various countries, Marx devoted most of his time in London to theoretical work rather than to political activism. In particular, he completed his major treatise on economics, *Capital*, Vol. 1 of which was published in 1867. Volumes 2 and 3 were edited and published by Engels in 1884 and 1894, after Marx's death.

The wider significance of Marx's philosophical, economic and political writings was that they provided the surrounding theoretical framework for the revolutionary socialist movement in the nineteenth and early twentieth centuries. Arguably, it was the powerful economic and social critique of Western capitalism which animated his writings, rather than particular Marxian theories or doctrines, that exercised the most decisive influence on the growth of that movement. Marx's writings also constitute an essential reference point for any discussion about the development of the diverse schools of socialist thought that emerged in the nineteenth century and which diverged sharply and irrevocably into communist and democratic socialist camps after the Russian Revolution of 1917.

The historical context in which Marx's writings acquired their urgency was shaped, first, by the economic and social consequences of the industrial revolution that were so starkly evident in Europe by the mid nineteenth century. These included large-scale production of manufactured goods by means of the factory system; large-scale distribution of such goods through international trade and markets; and the creation and oppressive concentration in industrial towns and cities of a massive labour force in the form of an industrial working class, or proletariat as Marx called it, employed by the dominant economic class: the capitalist bourgeoisie. The latter were the owners of the means of production – capital, factories and machinery – in industrial society. Meanwhile, according to Marx, the institutions and apparatus of the state in capitalist society operated in such a way as to protect and promote the wealth and interests of the bourgeois–capitalist class. The state was thus, in Marx's words, no more than 'a committee for managing the common affairs of the whole bourgeoisie'.[2]

Furthermore, the dominant ideas – political, philosophical and cultural – that were developed and propagated in industrial capitalist society were depicted as largely reflections of the forces of production – the available or new technology or resources – that prevailed in such a society. For such forces, together with the corresponding social relationships, or 'property relations' as Marx termed them, formed the 'mode of production', or economic base, that underlay society itself. The ideas, morality, culture and religion which prevailed in that society were, therefore, in Marx's view, merely 'superstructural' factors that derived from, and reflected, the underlying economic base of capitalist society. The idea of equality – in particular, the early liberal idea of equality of 'natural rights' or of the 'rights of man' – was thus, according to Marx, an example of this socio-economic reality. For it was an idea, he maintained, that expressed the interests of a rising or dominant class at a particular historical period.

These arguments and assumptions pervaded a central and highly influential theory within Marx's economic and political thought – namely, what Engels later described as Marx's 'materialist conception of history' or his theory of 'historical materialism'. This theory hinged on three principal propositions. First, the key to understanding human history was held to lie in the material conditions of man's production; in the way, that is, man acts upon, and changes, the material world through the development of productive forces, involving new technology or resources. Second, the main types of human society throughout history, and particularly within European civilization, which comprised Marx's primary intellectual focus, could be distinguished primarily in terms of their economic systems, their 'modes of production' consisting of both their productive forces and 'property relations', or social relationships. And third, the major changes throughout history, particularly throughout European civilization, could be explained most effectively in terms of economic changes. For it was, according to Marx, above all changes in the economic system, or 'mode of production', of a particular type of society, changes which stem from new productive forces or technology coming into conflict with its existing property relations, that gave rise to major social and political transformations such as the French Revolution of 1789.

These key propositions form, then, the cornerstones of Marx's theory of historical materialism. That theory amounted to his systematic attempt to reinterpret in materialist and economic terms the ideas of the great German philosopher, Georg Hegel (1770–1831), whose work Marx had studied in his twenties. Hegel had developed a distinctive theory of history within the framework of an idealist philosophy which held that reality is more than just a material phenomenon and that ideas, rather than matter, form the essence of ultimate reality in the world. According to Hegel, therefore, human history develops through the conflict, and eventual reconciliation, of opposing ideas towards an ideal end-state, which amounts to an Absolute Idea or ultimate truth emerging out of this process. Marx adopted these ideas which revolved, in particular, around Hegel's principle of the 'dialectic', the notion of change and development resulting from the conflict and reconciliation of opposites. However, Marx gave such ideas a materialist interpretation by arguing that history is the progressive transformation not of ideas, but rather of the material conditions of human existence and, hence, of social relationships, as a result of changes in the methods or forces of production.

The philosophical ideas of Hegel, albeit transformed theoretically, were thus major influences on the development of Marx's economic and political thought. Indeed, Marx was to describe the 'materialist conception of history' that derived from Hegel's influence as the 'guiding thread' of his studies from 1845 onwards. Marx's own theory was first worked out in Part 1 of *The German Ideology*, co-written with Engels in 1846. It is summarized most concisely in the 'Preface' to Marx's *Critique of Political Economy* (1859) and given empirical support in the historical chapters of *Capital*, Vol. 1.

Other intellectual influences, too, shaped Marx's thought, including, in particular, his unorthodox views on social and political equality. Among such influences were the great British classical liberal economists Adam Smith (1732–90), David Ricardo (1772–1823) and Thomas Malthus (1766–1834). From their ideas and theories Marx derived important elements of his economic analysis. It was, however, the influence of the early English and French socialist thinkers that more directly affected his *political* philosophy, including his conception of equality. These thinkers, who included Robert Owen (1771–1858), Henri Saint-Simon (1760–1825) and Charles Fourier (1772–1837), provided Marx with a set of powerful ideas that emanated from their moral and economic critique of capitalism. Among such ideas were their optimistic beliefs that in a socialist society work could be a means to human self-fulfilment rather than a source of drudgery and oppression; that under the right social conditions, human nature could be changed for the better; and that society, the economy and government could be deliberately and rationally organized for the common good rather than left to the vagaries of the capitalist market and for the promotion of minority interests.

Whilst, however, Marx recognized the value of such ideas, he and Engels regarded the early socialist thinkers as essentially 'utopian' in their approach. For they were concerned, in the view of Marx and Engels, mainly with describing and advocating ideal socialist societies of the future founded on ethical values. They were not engaged in the process of elaborating a socialist theory and strategy rooted, as Marx and Engels believed theirs to be, in an economically- and historically-sound analysis. For their own 'scientific' form of socialism could be demonstrated, so they claimed, to be an objectively-valid doctrine. By contrast, the beliefs and hopes of the 'utopian' socialists, including the liberal idea of equality of rights which they had imbibed, lacked the complex 'scientific' analytical basis which Marx and Engels had sought to provide for the revolutionary socialist movement.

Marx's critique of liberal ideas of equality

Marx had rejected the liberal concept of formal equality of civil and political rights in his early work, *On the Jewish Question* (1844).[3] He had adopted this negative stance on the ground that the apparent liberal gains achieved for Jews with regard to civil and political rights in the German Christian state of Prussia were in reality superficial. For they masked, in his view, the continuing oppression of Jews in all areas of Prussian civil society.

The early French socialists, whom Marx and Engels derided as 'utopian' and 'unscientific', had scarcely been more radically egalitarian in their outlook than liberal champions of the 'rights of man' such as Paine and Wollstonecraft in the late eighteenth century. Indeed, Fourier, Saint-Simon and Pierre-Joseph Proudhon (1809–95) had all rejected earlier egalitarian notions, as propounded in the most extreme terms by the early French socialist Gracchus Babeuf, concerning either the common ownership of all possessions or, more broadly, material equality based on physical identity of need. Instead of such radical beliefs, 'utopian' socialists such as Saint-Simon, whilst favouring a collective organization of industrial production, nevertheless accepted the idea of a hierarchical order within a future socialist society, with wide inequalities of wealth and position. Fourier, too, dismissed the notion of an equal distribution of the products of collective labour. Each person should instead, he argued, receive a dividend out of the produce of the community that was commensurate with the capital, labour or talent that he had individually contributed to that community.

The early French socialists thus generally supported the liberal notion of reward according to merit or contribution, which was crystallized in Saint-Simon's famous formula: 'from each according to his capacity, to each according to his works'. Although they wished to transform a capitalist economy by collectivist means, including, in particular, the planned organization of production, they appeared nonetheless to accept a merit-based principle of distribution as advocated by liberal supporters of the market economy such as John Stuart Mill.

It was partly on these grounds that Marx and Engels attacked such early French socialist thinkers as Proudhon and Eugen Dühring (1833–1921) respectively as covert liberals. Marx and Engels also derided the utopian socialists' commitment to the older liberal concept of formal equality of civil and political rights. They did so on two main grounds. In the first place, they argued that the idea of equal rights was one that merely reflected a particular transient phase in the historical development of productive forces and property relations. Engels thus described the 'notion of socialist society as the realm of equality' as:

> a superficial French idea resting upon the old 'liberty, equality and fraternity' – an idea which was justified as a stage of development in its own time and place but which, like all the superficial ideas of the earlier socialist schools, should now be overcome, for they only produce confusion in people's heads and more precise forms of description have been found.[4]

Engels maintained, too, that 'unscientific' socialist thinkers such as Dühring held equality to be an eternally-valid principle when in reality it was merely an intellectual and moral product of the economic stage which society had reached at that particular epoch.[5] The idea of equal rights was thus a historically-specific notion rather than a timeless value or principle.

In addition, both Marx and Engels repudiated this concept of equality on the ground that it was the reflection of bourgeois–liberal ideology. Marx thus claimed in 1877 that German socialists, by advancing such liberal ideas, were thereby ignoring the materialist basis of history and embracing instead 'modern mythology with its goddesses of Justice, Freedom, Equality and Fraternity'.[6] Moreover, Engels argued that the French revolutionaries' celebration of the ideal of equality, from which such 'mythology' in large part derived, was limited in its practical application by the boundaries of bourgeois society. For in practice equality meant, first, equality before the law as determined by the interests of the dominant classes in French society, and second, equality of rights, including in particular the right to private property.[7] In both those respects, therefore, formal equality was an idea that articulated and promoted particular class interests.

Towards communist equality

In response to what he viewed as the non-Marxian socialists' crypto-liberal egalitarianism, Marx sought to develop his alternative, 'scientific' socialist vision. In his view, it was above all the private ownership of the means of production, and the division of labour that it created, that were the root-causes of inequality. For the division of labour resulting from the process of production in capitalist society had generated particular property relations and hence social classes, involving the separation of people into antagonistic groups differentiated by wealth and power.

For Marx, therefore, such inequalities ultimately derived from a particular pattern of ownership of the productive forces of society at a particular historical period. Such a situation would lead in time to an intensification of class antagonisms in the face of the development of new, more advanced productive forces, which would render the existing property relations and division of labour obsolete. The ensuing proletarian revolution would bring about, Marx confidently predicted, the overthrow of capitalism, and with it the elimination of all class differences and hence the eventual disappearance of inequality.

Marx pointed out, however, that the immediate post-revolutionary period, spanning the interval between the fall of capitalism and the emergence of a classless communist society, would be a transitional phase in which a socialist society would be established. The distributive principle governing the allocation of resources in such a society would consist of Saint-Simon's formula: 'from each according to his capacity, to each according to his works'. In other words, the individual worker in a socialist society would be rewarded according to his particular contribution of labour, shaped by his physical or intellectual capacity.

For such reasons the transitional socialist stage would be, as Marx admitted in his *Critique of the Gotha Programme* (1875), 'still stamped with the birth marks of the old society from whose womb it emerges'.[8] It would thus retain, among other things, the liberal principle of distribution according to merit or individual contribution. However, this situation would be transcended, Marx argued, with the attainment of true communism, a state of social advance made possible by the forces of production reaching a higher stage of development, thereby creating unprecedented levels of prosperity and material abundance. Under such conditions not only would inequality vanish, but questions about the distribution of wealth would even become almost irrelevant.

Under communism, moreover, man would no longer be regarded simply as a producer, but rather as an individual person with particular needs, which would replace individual contributions of labour as the new basis for the distribution of goods and resources. The criterion of need would thus become central to the communist principle of justice. A higher form of equality would then be attained, superseding the old liberal notion of formal equality which would 'be fully left behind'. The new communist society would consequently 'inscribe on its banners: from each according to his ability, to each according to his needs!'[9]

Apart from these broad visionary statements, Marx wrote little about the egalitarian character of the future post-revolutionary communist society. There were two principal, related reasons for this omission. First, he considered it unscientific, indeed utopian, to indulge in theoretical speculation of this kind. For according to his own materialist conception of history it was an illegitimate exercise to envisage the form of a future society in the absence of those particular economic conditions that would bring into being new patterns of social organization. Marx thus believed that, in general, theoretical understanding followed practical experience. Ideas and theories were rooted in, and were reflections of, socio-economic conditions.

Second, Marx maintained that the future communist society was inseparable not just from post-revolutionary economic conditions, but also from the actual revolution itself. No-one involved in such turbulent circumstances could therefore jump, as it were, beyond them. Detailed predictions about the future society were thus once again pointless and unscientific. Inevitably, they would tend instead to be vague, sketchy and imprecise.

Marx did nonetheless provide some material for such a sketch of the future communist society – most notably in his 1844 *Economic and Philosophical Manuscripts*, specifically in its section entitled 'Private Property and Communism', as well as in his *Critique of the Gotha Programme*. The *Economic and Philosophical Manuscripts*, in particular, which, while written by Marx in Paris in 1844, were not to be published until 1932, outlined the essential aspects of a communist society.

In the first place, Marx contended that such a society would be a classless one since private property, the division of labour and social classes would all cease to exist. Second, it would be a society with a variety of activities and functions available to each person as means of self-fulfilment. The freedom of each individual in this sense of self-development would also be compatible with the promotion of the common good. A communist society would thus, in the words of *The Communist Manifesto* of 1848, be one 'in which the free development of each is the condition for the free development of all'.[10]

Third, a communist society would involve a transformation of man's relationship both with the material world and with his fellow human beings. This would arise from a major change in the entire mode of production or economic base of society. For common ownership and control of the advanced resources of the new society would ensure that its productive wealth was used for the benefit of the community as a whole.

Fourth, the communist society would be a stateless as well as a classless one. For the superstructure of society – its political, legal, military and bureau-cratic apparatus – would also be transformed. The established and coercive insti-tutions of the state – its police force, standing army, bureaucracy, etc. – which had survived in a modified form in the transitional socialist stage, would thus disap-pear in a communist society. As Engels famously wrote in *Anti-Dühring*:

> The government of persons is replaced by the administration of things ...
> The state is not 'abolished', it withers away.[11]

Finally, even human character and humankind itself would be transformed in a future communist society. For since human consciousness had been liberated from the pressures of the material world through the achievement of material abundance, it could then be directed instead towards a scientific understanding of both the material and social worlds. The result would be the overall improvement and progress of humankind and the realization of man's creative capacities. In Marx's elevated view, the ultimate goal of human existence would thereby be attained, involving nothing less than:

> the positive abolition of private property, and thus of human self-alienation and therefore, the real appropriation of the human essence by and for man. [It is] the complete and conscious return of man as a social, i.e. human being ... It is the genuine solution of the antagonism between man and nature, and between man and man ...[12]

Conclusion

It was, then, within this idealized social vision that the Marxian conception of equality took shape. It was depicted as a condition achieved through the abolition of class differences and the division of labour, and based both on the common ownership of productive forces and on the distribution of resources according to need. This state of 'true' equality amounted, in Marx's view, to the highest form of social relationships at an advanced stage in the evolution of the methods and forces of production. It was thus conceived as a concrete, historical condition to be attained in the future, not some ideological reflection of a particular stage of economic development that had been reached in the past.

Liberal concepts of equality, by contrast, were repudiated by Marx, as we have seen, both because they concealed their true historically-specific character behind an abstract, timeless façade, and because they served, in his view, bour-geois class interests. In the case of the ideal of formal equality of rights – affirmed by liberals from Locke to Paine and Wollstonecraft – Marx considered it superfi-cial or misleading on both those grounds, and in more general terms, too, because it was an abstraction derived from some ahistorical conception of human nature. In the case of the liberal ideal of equality of opportunity, as it was later to be termed, he regarded the notion to which it gave rise – namely, that of reward according to individual merit or contribution – to be one that served to formalize existing natural inequalities within the capitalist labour market. For it was an idea, he argued, that 'tacitly recognizes unequal individual endowment and thus productive capacity as natural privileges'.[13]

The non-Marxian socialists – Proudhon, Saint-Simon, Fourier, Dühring and others – were castigated by both Marx and Engels for covertly incorporating such liberal ideas into their own limited egalitarian vision, and, more, broadly, into their 'unscientific' versions of socialism. Yet the higher form of equality that Marx espoused in his own communist vision, as expressed in the 1844 Paris Manuscripts and elsewhere, was far from devoid of the utopian sentiments and imprecision that he derided in the early ethical socialists. Moreover, the celebration of his own communist egalitarianism rested, in turn, on the materialist conception of history which, through his own analysis, made the description of that future social order so sketchy and imprecise. Objections, therefore, that were later to be levelled at Marx's theory of historical materialism would necessarily raise doubts, too, about the attainability of 'true' equality in the communist society which was that theory's ideal end-state.

Notes

1   L. Kolaskowski, *Main Currents of Marxism*, Vol. 1, Oxford, Clarendon Press, 1978, p. 233.
2   K. Marx and F. Engels, 'The Communist Manifesto' (1848), in K. Marx, *Selected Writings* (ed. D. McLellan), 2nd edn, Oxford, Oxford University Press, 2000, p. 247.
3   See Chapter 4A.
4   F. Engels, letter to August Bebel, in *The Correspondence of Marx and Engels, 1846–1895* (ed. D. Torr), New York, 1937, p. 337.
5   See F. Engels, *Anti-Dühring* (1878) (trans. E. Burns), New York, 1939, pp. 104–5.
6   K. Marx, letter to F.A. Sorge, 19 October 1877, in *The Correspondence of Marx and Engels, 1846–1895*, p. 350.
7   See Engels, *Anti-Dühring*, p. 117.
8   K. Marx, 'Critique of the Gotha Programme' (1875), in Marx, *Selected Writings*, p. 614.
9   ibid. p. 615.
10   Marx and Engels, 'The Communist Manifesto', in Marx, *Selected Writings*, p. 262.
11   F. Engels, *Anti-Dühring*, Progress Publishers, Moscow, 1969, p. 333.
12   Marx, 'Economic and Philosophical Manuscripts' (1844), in Marx, *Selected Writings*, p. 97.
13   Marx, 'Critique of the Gotha Programme', in Marx, *Selected Writings*, p. 615.

SECTION C

Contemporary debates

Since 1945 the history of theoretical reflection on equality may be viewed largely within the context of ideological debate conducted, first, within the boundaries of European democratic socialism, and second, between the forces of the Left and Right throughout the West – particularly in Britain and the United States, in the light of the resurgence since the mid-1970s of market–liberal ideas and policies. Since 1970 the revival, too, in the West of academic political philosophy, together with the dominant influence of market–liberalism upon the policy agenda of Western states during the 1980s, helped to shift the focus of intellectual debate away from arguments over the goal of equality of outcome towards questions about *social justice*. The new area of concern was thus with the validity or desirability of this widely-espoused principle, interwoven in many ways with equality, which holds that the distribution of wealth and resources in society should be shaped by certain identifiable moral principles concerned with the promotion of social well-being.

The debate on the European Left over the place of equality within democratic socialist policy and strategy was powerfully ignited during the 1950s and 1960s in the eloquent and highly-influential writings of the British socialist thinker and Labour Party politician, Anthony Crosland. Repudiating the view that socialism could be adequately identified with the public ownership of the means of production, Crosland attempted, particularly in his major work, *The Future of Socialism* (1956), to reformulate democratic socialist principles through a new analysis of changed economic and social conditions within post-war Britain. From this standpoint he developed an ethical reinterpretation of socialism in terms of distinctive values and ideals such as personal liberty, social welfare and, in particular, social equality. The traditional socialist doctrine of public ownership was, in Crosland's view, merely one important means among several others for realizing those enduring values.

In his interpretation of democratic socialism Crosland was committed to the pursuit of greater equality of wealth and resources by means of high public expenditure and progressive taxation, and upon the basis of sustained economic growth. He was also convinced that the welfarist and egalitarian objectives that he placed at the top of the Labour Party's agenda could be achieved within the context of a market-oriented mixed economy and through the interventions of the British state.

Crosland's revisionist socialism was, however, challenged by those on the Left of the British Labour Party, including the followers of the charismatic Welsh politician Anuerin Bevan who continued to believe that large-scale public ownership of industry, with an economy characterized by a predominant public sector, was a precondition for realizing the kind of egalitarian society that Crosland desired.

By the second half of the 1970s, and particularly during the 1980s, both traditional and revisionist socialist ideas about equality appeared to be under increasing challenge, and later in full retreat, in the face of the revitalization of market–liberal ideas and policies – most notably in the practice of the British governments led by Margaret Thatcher between 1979 and 1990. Free-market conservative thinkers such as Keith Joseph thus developed a trenchant critique of egalitarianism, derived largely from market–liberal thinkers such as Friedrich von Hayek (1899–1992), which stressed the incompatibility between the pursuit of greater equality of outcome, on the one hand, and individual freedom of choice, economic liberty and the smooth workings of a market economy, on the other.[1]

Outside the practical sphere of party politics and government, this ideological debate over equality acquired a sharper intellectual focus following the publication in 1971 of *A Theory of Justice*, the major work by the American political philosopher, John Rawls (1921–). This, 'the most important book on political philosophy since the Second World War',[2] in the view of Norman Barry and many others, sparked a lasting revival in the West of analytical political philosophy and hence of theoretical speculation about politics. It also shifted the philosophical debate away from the merits and shortcomings of social equality, whose advocates were increasingly marginalized politically and ideologically, towards arguments over the meaning, substance and implications of the related concept of social justice.

Rawls's *A Theory of Justice*, which was published, as Barry has observed, against the political background of the culmination of both the American civil rights movement and other forms of radical political dissent, was highly significant, too, since it 'provided, for perhaps the first time in a hundred years, a direct link between a fairly abstract, philosophical theory and particular policy recommendations in both the areas of rights and distribution'.[3] Rawls's conception of 'justice as fairness' was developed in that work upon the basis of a social contract theory that envisaged a hypothetical situation in which individuals, without any prior knowledge either of their own particular talents or abilities, or of their own social position or status, would choose, behind this 'veil of ignorance', to live in a society with a 'fair', and hence broadly egalitarian, distribution of goods and resources.

The two fundamental principles underlying this Rawlsian theory of distributive justice were:

i   'each person is to have an equal right to the most extensive liberty compatible with a similar system of liberty for all;'

ii   'social and economic inequalities are to be arranged so that they are both:
    (a) to the greatest benefit of the least advantaged; and,
    (b) attached to offices and positions open to all under conditions of fair equality of opportunity.'[4]

Rawls's theory thus held that inequalities in the allocation and distribution of goods are acceptable only if they work to the benefit of the least well-off members of society. Inequalities of income, for example, might fall into this justifiable category, if, by providing incentives for the better-off, they help to enlarge the stock of goods available for redistribution to the least advantaged.

By recognizing the existence of such permissible inequalities, Rawls was by no means, therefore, advocating the socialist principle of greater equality of outcome. His theory was nonetheless essentially egalitarian since, by seeking to legitimize inequalities in terms of their beneficial impact on the least well-off, it rested on an underlying presumption in favour of equality and hence of the need to justify departures from equality. Rawls's theory of social justice was also a liberal–egalitarian one since its fundamental principles affirmed the importance both of formal equality in the sense of the equal right to liberty and of equal opportunities to occupy attractive positions or offices in society.

Rawls's theory has generated intense controversy and debate within the field of academic political philosophy and political theory ever since its publication in 1971. Among his critics, Hayek and the American libertarian political philosopher, Robert Nozick (1938–), have emerged since the 1970s as the most influential voices. They have both rejected the very notion of social or distributive justice, arguing instead for a return to the traditional interpretation of justice in terms of certain established legal rules, procedures and rights – all affecting individuals rather than society as a whole.

Hayek, particularly in his *Law, Legislation and Liberty,* Part 2: *The Mirage of Social Justice* (1976), argued that theories of social justice rested on a number of false assumptions concerning the just or unjust distribution of wealth and resources in society. In particular, the notion of social justice presupposed, in his view, the existence of some appropriate agency responsible for determining the distribution of benefits or rewards in society on the basis of an assessment of deserts and needs. In reality, however, Hayek pointed out, rewards in a market economy are distributed through the interplay of unpredictable market forces of supply and demand, and hence through the unplanned activity of countless individual agents. The distribution of material resources is not, therefore, a matter raising moral principles such as justice. Rather, Hayek stressed, it is one concerned with economic considerations such as market value. In addition, the pursuit of the 'mirage', as Hayek regarded it, of social justice involves in practice the replacement of market forces with a centralized state bureaucracy. An agency of this kind will in time, he warned, exercise wide-ranging coercive powers, interfering with the individual's liberty in all kinds of areas.

Another, more philosophically-elaborate attempt to formulate a theory of procedural justice and one, moreover, designed more clearly as a critical response to Rawls's theory, was developed by Robert Nozick in his *Anarchy, State and Utopia* (1974).[5] In advancing an entitlements-based notion of justice, Nozick distinguished between what he termed historical and end-state principles or theories of justice. Historical principles or theories relate, in his view, to free actions of individuals in the past which have created 'differential entitlements' and thereby formed the basis on which resources should be allocated and acquired. End-state principles or theories of justice, by contrast, posit a particular fixed goal, for example social equality or the common good, to which the distribution of resources should conform. Furthermore, Nozick also draws a distinction between two types of historical theory: namely, patterned and unpatterned theories. He defines a patterned theory of social justice as one which holds that resources or wealth in society should be distributed according to a particular predetermined pattern, for example, rewards according to merit or needs.

Nozick rejects both end-state and historical patterned theories on the ground that they involve unacceptable invasions of personal liberty. 'No end-state principle,' he declares, 'or distributional patterned principle of justice can be realised without continuous interference with people's lives.'[6] In their place, he formulates an historical unpatterned theory of justice based on individual entitlement through legitimate procedures. The distribution of resources, he thus maintains, is just if it rests on three procedural rules: first, that a property holding is the consequence of fair acquisition, without having previously been held by another person; or second, that it is the consequence of a fair transfer from one person to another; or third, that the principle of rectification should apply whereby, if wealth or resources have been acquired or transferred unjustly, then such an injustice should be corrected.

Since the 1970s there has been some movement in political philosophy away from the kind of universal principles of justice enunciated by Rawls and, to some extent, by his critics.[7] Instead, there has been some advocacy of a more flexible and realistic theoretical approach to social justice that recognizes diversity both of social goods in different societies and cultures and of principles of justice appropriate for different spheres of social activity. Such an approach is evident, for instance, in communitarian theories of social justice of the kind propounded by Michael Walzer in his work *Spheres of Justice* (1983).

Inherent in all these philosophical debates has been a concern either to elucidate or to repudiate the concept of social justice rather than to formulate in fresh terms the concepts of formal equality, equality of opportunity or equality of outcome developed by earlier liberal and socialist thinkers in the history of modern political thought. However, an affirmation of at least the first two of those principles, together with a general presumption in favour of equality, underlies, as we have seen, Rawls's theory of social justice. In general, too, Rawls and his followers have recognized that justice is interwoven with equality since the former involves the fair treatment of equals, or, in Aristotle's words, treating equals equally. The close theoretical link between the concepts is evident, too, in Aristotle's other fundamental rule, underlined in the contemporary debate by Hayek, Nozick and others, namely, that justice also means treating unequals unequally.

Notes

1   See K. Joseph and J. Sumption, *Equality*, London, John Murray, 1979.

2   N. Barry, *An Introduction to Modern Political Theory*, 4th edn, London, Macmillan, 2000, p. 137.

3   ibid. p. 138.

4   J. Rawls, *A Theory of Justice,* Cambridge, MA, Harvard University Press, 1971, p. 302. For useful introductory accounts of Rawls's theory, see J. Wolff, *An Introduction to Political Philosophy*, Oxford, Oxford University Press, 1996, pp. 168–95; N. Barry, op. cit. pp. 156–67; D.D. Raphael, *Problems of Political Philosophy*, 2nd edn, London, Macmillan, 1990, pp. 145–9. For more detailed studies of Rawls's theory, see N. Daniels (ed.), *Reading Rawls*, Oxford, Blackwell, 1975; C. Kukathas and P. Pettit, *Rawls: 'A Theory of Justice' and its Critics*, Cambridge, Polity Press, 1990.

5   For detailed studies of Nozick's theory, see J. Paul (ed.), *Reading Nozick*, Oxford, Blackwell, 1982; J. Wolff, *Robert Nozick: Property, Justice and the Minimal State*, Cambridge, Polity Press, 1991.

6   R. Nozick, *Anarchy, State and Utopia*, Oxford, Blackwell, 1974, p. 163.

7   Some of Rawls's earlier theoretical positions have been modified in his later work, *Political Liberalism*, New York, Simon and Schuster, 1993. Similarly, some of Nozick's earlier views have been modified in his *The Examined Life*, New York, Simon and Schuster, 1989.

Further reading

J. Barker, *Arguing for Equality*, London, Verso, 1987.

D. Boucher and P. Kelly (eds) *Social Justice: From Hume to Walzer*, London, Routledge, 1998.

T. Campbell, *Justice*, London, Macmillan, 1988.

N. Daniels (ed.), *Reading Rawls*, Oxford, Blackwell, 1975.

A.G.N. Flew, *The Politics of Procrustes*, London, Temple South, 1981.

F.A. Hayek, *Law, Legislation and Liberty*, Vol. 2: *The Mirage of Social Justice*, London, Routledge, 1976.

W. Letwin (ed.), *Against Equality*, London, Macmillan, 1983.

D. Miller, *Social Justice*, Oxford, Oxford University Press, 1976.

R. Nozick, *Anarchy, State and Utopia*, Oxford, Blackwell, 1974.

R. Nozick, *The Examined Life*, New York, Simon and Schuster, 1989.

J. Paul (ed.), *Reading Nozick*, Oxford, Blackwell, 1982.

D. Rae, *Equalities*, Cambridge, MA, Harvard University Press, 1981.

J. Rawls, *A Theory of Justice*, Cambridge, MA, Harvard University Press, 1971.

J. Rawls, *Political Liberalism*, New York, Simon and Schuster, 1993.

M. Walzer, *Spheres of Justice*, New York, Basic Books, 1983.

J. Wolff, *Robert Nozick: Property, Justice and the Minimal State*, Cambridge, Polity Press, 1991.

Select bibliography

METHODOLOGY

Expressions of the contextualist approach

J. Dunn, 'The Identity of the History of Ideas' (1969), in *Political Obligation in its Historical Context*, Cambridge, Cambridge University Press, 1980, pp. 13–28.

J. Dunn, *The History of Political Theory and Other Essays*, Cambridge, Cambridge University Press, 1996.

J.G.A. Pocock, 'The History of Political Thought: A Methodological Enquiry', in P. Laslett and W.G. Runciman (eds), *Philosophy, Politics and Society*, Series II, Oxford, Blackwell, 1962, pp. 183–202.

J.G.A. Pocock, *Politics, Language and Time*, London, Methuen, 1971.

Q.R.D. Skinner, 'Meaning and Understanding in the History of Ideas', *History and Theory*, 8, 1969, pp. 199–215.

Q.R.D. Skinner, *The Foundations of Modern Political Thought*, Vol. 1, Preface, pp. ix–xv, Cambridge, Cambridge University Press, 1978.

R. Tuck, 'The Contribution of History', in R.E. Goodin and P. Pettit (eds), *A Companion to Contemporary Political Philosophy*, Oxford, Blackwell, 1993, pp. 72–89.

J. Tully (ed.), *Meaning and Context: Quentin Skinner and his Critics*, Cambridge, Cambridge University Press, 1990.

Views challenging or questioning the contextualist approach

P. King, 'Historical Contextualism: The New Historicism?', *History of European Ideas*, 21, 2, 1995.

P. King, 'Historical Contextualism Revisited', *Politics*, 16, 3, 1996.

J. Plamenatz, *Man and Society*, Vol. 1, Introduction, London, Longman, 1963, pp. ix–xxii, reprinted in revised 1992 edition.

General discussions

T. Ball, *Reappraising Political Theory: Revisionist Studies in the History of Political Thought*, Oxford, Clarendon Press, 1995, Ch. 1.

R. Berki, *The History of Political Thought: A Short Introduction*, London, Dent, 1977, Ch. 2.

J. Lively and A. Reeve (eds), 'General Introduction', in *Modern Political Theory from Hobbes to Marx*, London, Routledge, 1989.

GENERAL AND INTRODUCTORY WORKS ON THE HISTORY OF POLITICAL THOUGHT

Highly recommended

R. Berki, *The History of Political Thought: A Short Introduction*, London, Dent, 1977.

D. Germino, *Machiavelli to Marx*, Chicago, Chicago University Press, 1972.

I. Hampsher-Monk, *A History of Modern Political Thought*, Oxford, Blackwell, 1992.

D. Miller (ed.), *The Blackwell Encyclopaedia of Political Thought*, Oxford, Blackwell, 1991.

J. Morrow, *History of Political Thought: A Thematic Introduction*, London, Macmillan, 1998.

J. Plamenatz, *Man and Society* Vols 1–3 (revised by M.E. Plamenatz and R. Wokler), London, Longman, 1992; originally published 1963 in 2 volumes. (Not without its critics, but a lucid examination of major political theories and a classic expression of the 'textualist' approach.)

B. Redhead (intro.), *Plato to Nato: Studies in Political Thought*, London, Penguin, 1995. (An excellent collection of concise, historically-grounded introductions to major political thinkers.)

G.H. Sabine, *A History of Political Theory*, 4th edn (revised by T.L. Thorson), Hinsdale, Illinois, Holt-Saunders, 1973 (first published 1937). (A classic, wide-ranging and still very useful history of political thought.)

G. Williams, *Political Theory in Retrospect*, Aldershot, Edward Elgar, 1991. (Succinct and readable introductory accounts of the ideas of major political thinkers.)

Also recommended

T. Ball, *Reappraising Political Theory: Revisionist Studies in the History of Political Thought*, Oxford, Clarendon Press, 1995. (Interesting reinterpretations of major political thinkers from Machiavelli onwards.)

M. Cranston (ed.), *Western Political Philosophers*, London, Bodley Head, 1964.

M. Forsyth and M. Keens-Soper (eds), *The Political Classics: A Guide to the Essential Texts from Plato to Rousseau*, Oxford, Oxford University Press, 1992.

M. Forsyth and M. Keens-Soper (eds), *The Political Classics: Green to Dworkin*, Oxford, Oxford University Press, 1996.

M. Forsyth, M. Keens-Soper and J. Hoffman (eds), *The Political Classics: Hamilton to Mill*, Oxford, Oxford University Press, 1993.

A. Gamble, *An Introduction to Modern Social and Political Thought*, London, Macmillan, 1981.

W.T. Jones, *Masters of Political Thought*, Vol. 2: *Machiavelli to Bentham*, London, Harrap, 1947.

L.W. Lancaster, *Masters of Political Thought*, Vol. 3: *Hegel to Dewey*, London, Harrap, 1959.

A. Little, J. Gingell and C. Winch, *Modern Political Thought: A Reader*, London, Routledge, 2000. (A useful selection of extracts from the classic texts.)

J. Lively and A. Reeve (eds), *Political Theory from Hobbes to Marx: Key Debates*, London, Routledge, 1989. (A selection of influential interpretations of major political thinkers.)

J.S. McClelland, *A History of Western Political Thought*, London, Routledge, 1996.

L.C. McDonald, *Western Political Theory, Part 2: from Machiavelli to Burke*, New York, Harcourt, Brace, Jovanovich, 1968.

L.C. McDonald, *Western Political Theory, Part 3: Nineteenth and Twentieth Centuries*, New York, Harcourt, Brace, Jovanovich, 1968.

L.J. Macfarlane, *Modern Political Theory*, London, Nelson, 1970.

D. Muschamp (ed.), *Political Thinkers*, London, Macmillan, 1986.

B.N. Nelson, *Western Political Thought: from Socrates to the Age of Ideology*, 2nd edn, Englewood Cliffs, NJ, Prentice Hall, 1996.

Q. Skinner, *The Foundations of Modern Political Thought*, Vols 1 and 2, Cambridge, Cambridge University Press, 1978.

P.M.R. Stirk and D. Weigall, *An Introduction to Political Ideas*, London, Pinter, 1995. (An introduction to fundamental political concepts combined with a selection of extracts from the writings of major political thinkers.)

D. Thomson (ed.), *Political Ideas*, Harmondsworth, Penguin, 1966. (A useful collection of introductory essays on major political thinkers.)

S. Wolin, *Politics and Vision: Continuity and Innovation in Western Political Thought*, London, Allen and Unwin, 1961. (A classic historical overview.)

INTRODUCTORY WORKS ON POLITICAL THEORY

These introductory works are either explicitly or broadly philosophical in their approach to political theory. They are therefore concerned, first, with the clarification of the concepts and values used in political analysis and debate, and, second, with critical evaluation of political beliefs and arguments.

Highly recommended

(These are all lucid and accessible introductions to political theory conceived in terms of a philosophical approach.)

N.P. Barry, *An Introduction to Modern Political Theory*, 4th edn, London, Macmillan, 2000.

B. Goodwin, *Using Political Ideas*, 4th edn, Chichester, Wiley, 1997.

A. Heywood, *Political Theory: an Introduction*, London, Macmillan, 1999.

D.D. Raphael, *Problems of Political Philosophy*, 2nd edn, London, Macmillan, 1990.

J. Wolff, *An Introduction to Political Philosophy*, Oxford, Oxford University Press, 1996.

Also recommended

S. Benn and R. Peters, *Social Principles and the Democratic State*, London, Allen and Unwin, 1959.

W. Connolly, *The Terms of Political Discourse*, 3rd edn, Oxford, Blackwell, 1993.

R.E. Goodin, and P. Pettit (eds), *A Companion to Contemporary Political Philosophy*, Oxford, Blackwell, 1993.

J. Hampton, *Political Philosophy*, Boulder, CO, Westview Press, 1997.

D. Held (ed.), *Political Theory Today*, Cambridge, Polity Press, 1991.

W. Kymlicka, *Contemporary Political Philosophy: An Introduction*, Oxford, Clarendon Press, 1990.

R. Plant, *Modern Political Thought*, Oxford, Blackwell, 1991.

A. Quinton (ed.), *Political Philosophy*, Oxford, Oxford University Press, 1967.

WORKS BY OR ABOUT MAJOR OR INFLUENTIAL POLITICAL THINKERS

N.B. The Oxford Past Masters series, consisting of concise and scholarly commentaries (asterisked below) provide, along with the relevant texts, excellent starting-points for studying most of the political thinkers listed here.

Machiavelli

Texts

N. Machiavelli, *The Discourses of Niccolò Machiavelli* (1531), 2 vols (trans. L.J. Walker), London, Routledge, 1975.

N. Machiavelli, *The Prince* (1532) (ed. Q. Skinner and R. Price), Cambridge, Cambridge University Press, 1988.

Commentaries/full-length studies

S. Anglo, *Machiavelli: A Dissection*, London, Victor Gollancz, 1969.

S. Anglo, 'Niccolò Machiavelli: the Anatomy of Political and Military Decadence', in *Plato to Nato*, London, Penguin, 1995.

I. Berlin, 'The Originality of Machiavelli', in I. Berlin, *Against the Current* (ed. H. Hardy), London, Hogarth Press, 1979.

H. Butterfield, *The Statecraft of Machiavelli*, London, Collier Books, 1962 (first published 1940).

J.R. Hale, *Machiavelli and Renaissance Italy*, London, English Universities Press, 1961.

J.G.A. Pocock, *The Machiavellian Moment*, Princeton, NJ, Princeton University Press, 1975.

Q. Skinner, *The Foundations of Modern Political Thought*, Vol. 1, Part 2, Cambridge, Cambridge University Press, 1978.

*Q. Skinner, *Machiavelli*, Oxford, Oxford University Press, 1981.

L. Strauss, *Thoughts on Machiavelli*, Glencoe, The Free Press, 1958.

Hobbes

Texts

T. Hobbes, *Leviathan* (1651) (ed. C.B. Macpherson), Harmondsworth, Penguin, 1968.
T. Hobbes, *Leviathan* (1651) (ed. R. Tuck), Cambridge, Cambridge University Press, 1991.

Commentaries/full-length studies

D. Baumford, *Hobbes's Political Theory*, Cambridge, Cambridge University Press, 1988.
K.C. Brown (ed.), *Hobbes Studies*, Oxford, Blackwell, 1965.
M. Cranston and R.S. Peters (eds), *Hobbes and Rousseau: A Collection of Critical Essays*, New York, Anchor Books, 1972.
J. Hampton, *Hobbes and the Social Contract Tradition*, Cambridge, Cambridge University Press, 1986.
C.B. Macpherson, *The Political Theory of Possessive Individualism*, Oxford, Oxford University Press, 1962.
A.P. Martinich, *Thomas Hobbes*, London, Macmillan, 1997.
M. Oakeshott, *Hobbes on Civil Association*, Oxford, Blackwell, 1975.
R.S. Peters, *Hobbes*, Harmondsworth, Penguin, 1967.
D.D. Raphael, *Hobbes: Morals and Politics*, London, Allen and Unwin, 1977.
T. Sorell, *Hobbes*, London, Routledge, 1991.
*R. Tuck, *Hobbes*, Oxford, Oxford University Press, 1989.
H. Warrender, *The Political Philosophy of Hobbes: His Theory of Obligation*, 2nd edn, Oxford, Clarendon Press, 2000 (first published 1957).
J.W.N. Watkins, *Hobbes's System of Ideas*, 2nd edn, London, Hutchinson University Library, 1973.

Locke

Texts

J. Locke, *Two Treatises of Government* (1689) (ed. P. Laslett) Cambridge, Cambridge University Press, 1988.
J. Locke, *A Letter Concerning Toleration* (1689), (eds. J. Horton and S. Mendus), London, Routledge, 1991.

Commentaries/full-length studies

R. Ashcraft, *Revolutionary Politics and Locke's 'Two Treatises of Government'*, Princeton, NJ, Princeton University Press, 1986.
R. Ashcraft, *Locke's Two Treatises of Government*, London, Unwin Hyman, 1987.
M. Cranston, *John Locke: a Biography*, Oxford, Oxford University Press, 1985 (first published 1957).
J. Dunn, *The Political Thought of John Locke*, Cambridge, Cambridge University Press, 1969.

*J. Dunn, *John Locke*, Oxford, Oxford University Press, 1984.

J.H. Franklin, *John Locke and the Theory of Sovereignty*, Cambridge, Cambridge University Press, 1978.

J.W. Gough, *John Locke's Political Philosophy*, Oxford, Clarendon Press, 1956.

I. Harris, *The Mind of John Locke*, Cambridge, Cambridge University Press, 1994.

D. Lloyd Thomas, *Routledge Philosophy Guidebook to Locke on Government*, London, Routledge, 1995.

C.B. Macpherson, *The Political Theory of Possessive Individualism*, Oxford, Oxford University Press, 1962.

J. Marshall, *John Locke: Resistance, Religion and Responsibility*, Cambridge, Cambridge University Press, 1994.

G. Parry, *John Locke*, London, Allen and Unwin, 1978.

M. Seliger, *The Liberal Politics of John Locke*, London, Allen and Unwin, 1968.

A.J. Simmons, *The Lockean Theory of Rights*, Princeton, NJ, Princeton University Press, 1992.

J. Tully, *An Approach to Political Philosophy: Locke in Contexts*, Cambridge, Cambridge University Press, 1993.

Rousseau

Texts

J.-J. Rousseau, *The Social Contract and Discourses* (ed. G.D.H. Cole, J.H. Brumfitt and J.C. Hall), London, Everyman, 1973.

J.-J. Rousseau, *The Social Contract (1762) and Other Later Writings* (ed. and trans. by V. Gourevitch), Cambridge, Cambridge University Press, 1997.

J.-J. Rousseau, *The Discourses (1751; 1755) and Other Early Political Writings* (ed. and trans. by V. Gourevitch), Cambridge, Cambridge University Press, 1997.

Commentaries/full-length studies

A. Cobban, *Rousseau and the Modern State*, 2nd edn, London, Allen and Unwin, 1970.

M. Cranston, *Jean-Jacques: The Early Life and Work of Jean-Jacques Rousseau, 1712–1754*, London, Allen Lane, 1983.

M. Cranston, *The Noble Savage: Jean-Jacques Rousseau, 1754–1762*, London, Viking/Penguin, 1991.

M. Cranston, *The Solitary Self: Jean-Jacques Rousseau in Exile and Adversity*, London, Allen Lane, 1997.

M. Cranston and R.S. Peters (eds), *Hobbes and Rousseau: A Collection of Critical Essays*, New York, Anchor Books, 1972.

N. Dent, *Rousseau*, Cambridge, Cambridge University Press, 1988.

R. Fralin, *Rousseau and Representation*, New York, Columbia University Press, 1978.

J.C. Hall, *Rousseau: an Introduction to his Political Philosophy*, London, Macmillan, 1973.

J. McDonald, *Rousseau and the French Revolution: 1762–1791*, London, Athlone Press, 1965.

R.D. Masters, *The Political Philosophy of Rousseau*, Princeton, NJ, Princeton University Press, 1968.

A.M. Melzer, *The Natural Goodness of Man*, Chicago, University of Chicago Press, 1990.

J. Miller, *Rousseau: Dreamer of Democracy*, New Haven, Yale University Press, 1984.

J. Shklar, *Men and Citizens*, Cambridge, Cambridge University Press, 1969.

J.L. Talmon, *The Origins of Totalitarian Democracy*, London, Secker and Warburg, 1952.

*R. Wokler, *Rousseau*, Oxford, Oxford University Press, 1995.

R. Wokler, 'Jean-Jacques Rousseau: Moral Decadence and the Pursuit of Liberty', in *Plato to Nato*, London, Penguin, 1995.

Paine

Texts

T. Paine, *The Rights of Man* (1791–2) (ed. H. Collins), Harmondsworth, Penguin, 1969.

T. Paine, *Political Writings* (ed. B. Kuklick), Cambridge, Cambridge University Press, 1989.

Commentaries/full-length studies

A.O. Aldridge, *Man of Reason: The Life of Thomas Paine*, Philadelphia, Lippincott, 1959.

A.O. Aldridge, *Thomas Paine's American Ideology*, London, Associated University Presses, 1984.

A.J. Ayer, *Thomas Paine*, London, Faber, 1988.

G. Claeys, *Thomas Paine: Social and Political Thought*, London, Unwin Hyman, 1989.

R.R. Fennessy, *Burke, Paine and the Rights of Man*, The Hague, M. Nijhoff, 1963.

E. Foner, *Tom Paine and Revolutionary America*, New York, Oxford University Press, 1976.

J. Keane, *Tom Paine: A Political Life*, London, Bloomsbury, 1996.

*M. Philp, *Paine*, Oxford, Oxford University Press, 1989.

Thomas Paine Reader (ed. M. Foot and I. Kramnick), Harmondsworth, Penguin, 1987.

Burke

Texts

E. Burke, *Reflections on the Revolution in France* (1790) (ed. C. Cruise O'Brien), Harmondsworth, Penguin, 1968.

E. Burke, *Pre-Revolutionary Writings* (ed. I. Harris), Cambridge, Cambridge University Press, 1993.

Commentaries/full-length studies

M. Butler, *Burke, Paine, Godwin and the Revolution Controversy*, Cambridge, Cambridge University Press, 1984.

A. Cobban, *Edmund Burke and the Revolt Against the Eighteenth Century*, London, Allen and Unwin, 1960.

C. Cruise O'Brien, *The Great Melody: A Thematic Biography of Edmund Burke*, London, Sinclair-Stevenson, 1992.

R.R. Fennessy, *Burke, Paine and the Rights of Man*, The Hague, M. Nijhoff, 1963.

M. Freeman, *Edmund Burke and the Critique of Political Radicalism*, Oxford, Blackwell, 1980.

I. Hampsher-Monk, *The Political Philosophy of Edmund Burke*, London, Longman, 1987.

*C.B. Macpherson, *Burke*, Oxford, Oxford University Press, 1980.

F. O'Gorman, *Edmund Burke: his Political Philosophy*, London, Allen and Unwin, 1973.

J.G.A. Pocock, 'Introduction', in Burke, *Reflections on the Revolution in France* (ed. Pocock), Indianapolis, Hackett, 1987.

J. Waldron (ed.) *'Nonsense upon Stilts': Bentham, Burke and Paine on the Rights of Man*, London, Methuen, 1987.

Wollstonecraft

Texts

M. Wollstonecraft, *A Vindication of the Rights of Woman* (1792) (ed. M. Kramnick), Harmondsworth, Penguin, 1982.

M. Wollstonecraft, *A Vindication of the Rights of Men* (1790) and *A Vindication of the Rights of Woman* (1792) (ed. S. Tomaselli) Cambridge, Cambridge University Press, 1995.

Commentaries/full-length studies

M. Gatens, ' "The Oppressed State of My Sex": Wollstonecraft on Reason, Feeling and Equality', in M.L. Stanley and C. Pateman (eds), *Feminist Interpretations and Political Theory*, Cambridge, Polity Press, 1991.

G. Kelly, *Revolutionary Feminism: The Mind and Career of Mary Wollstonecraft*, London, Macmillan, 1991.

M. Kramnick, 'Introduction', in Wollstonecraft, *A Vindication of the Rights of Woman* (ed. Kramnick), 1982.

V. Sapiro, *A Vindication of Political Virtue: the Political Theory of Mary Wollstonecraft*, Chicago, University of Chicago Press, 1992.

J. Todd, *Mary Wollstonecraft: A Revolutionary Life*, London, Weidenfeld and Nicolson, 2000.

C. Tomalin, *The Life and Death of Mary Wollstonecraft*, rev. edn, London, Penguin, 1992.

S. Tomaselli, 'Introduction', in M. Wollstonecraft, *A Vindication of the Rights of Men and A Vindication of the Rights of Woman*, 1995.
R.M. Wardle, *Mary Wollstonecraft: A Critical Biography*, London, Richards Press, 1951.

J.S. Mill

Texts

J.S. Mill, *Utilitarianism, On Liberty and Considerations on Representative Government* (ed. H.B. Acton), London, Dent, 1972 (first published 1910).
J.S. Mill, *Three Essays: On Liberty, Representative Government and The Subjection of Women* (intro. by R. Wollheim), Oxford, Oxford University Press, 1975.
J.S. Mill, *On Liberty (1859) and other Writings* (ed. S. Collini), Cambridge, Cambridge University Press, 1989.

Commentaries/full-length studies

M. Cowling, *Mill and Liberalism*, 2nd edn, Cambridge, Cambridge University Press, 1990.
W. Donner, *The Liberal Self: John Stuart Mill's Moral and Political Philosophy*, Ithaca, NY, Cornell University Press, 1991.
J. Gray, *Mill's On Liberty: A Defence*, London, Routledge, 1996.
J. Gray and G.W. Smith (eds), *J.S. Mill: On Liberty in Focus*, London, Routledge, 1991.
R.J. Halliday, *John Stuart Mill*, London, Allen and Unwin, 1976.
J. Hamburger, *Intellectuals in Politics: John Stuart Mill and the Philosophic Radicals*, New Haven, CT, Yale University Press, 1965.
G. Himmelfarb, *On Liberty and Liberalism*, New York, Knopf, 1974.
J.C. Rees, *John Stuart Mill's 'On Liberty'*, Oxford, Clarendon Press, 1985.
A. Ryan, *The Philosophy of John Stuart Mill*, London, Macmillan, 1970.
A. Ryan, *J.S. Mill*, London, Routledge and Kegan Paul, 1975.
J. Skorupski, *John Stuart Mill*, London, Routledge, 1989.
C.L. Ten, *Mill on Liberty*, Oxford, Oxford University Press, 1980.
W. Thomas, *The Philosophic Radicals: Nine Studies in Theory and Practice, 1817–1841*, Oxford, Clarendon Press, 1979.
*W. Thomas, *Mill*, Oxford, Oxford University Press, 1985.

T.H. Green

Texts

T.H. Green, *Lectures on the Principles of Political Obligation (1882) and other Writings* (ed. P. Harris and J. Morrow), Cambridge, Cambridge University Press, 1986.
T.H. Green, *The Philosophy of T.H. Green* (ed. A. Vincent), Aldershot, Gower, 1996.

Commentaries/full-length studies

D. Boucher and A. Vincent, *British Idealism and Political Theory*, Edinburgh, Edinburgh University Press, 2000.

I.M. Greengarten, *T.H. Green and the Development of Liberal–Democratic Thought*, Toronto, University of Toronto Press, 1981.

P. Harris and J. Morrow, 'Introduction', in Green, *Lectures on the Principles of Political Obligation*, 1986.

C. Harvie, *The Lights of Liberalism: University Liberals and the Challenge of Democracy, 1860–86*, London, Allan Lane, 1976.

F. Inglis, *Radical Earnestness: English Social Theory 1880–1980*, Oxford, Martin Robertson, 1982.

A.J.M. Milne, *The Social Philosophy of English Idealism*, London, Allen and Unwin, 1962.

P. Nicholson, *The Political Philosophy of British Idealists: Selected Studies*, Cambridge, Cambridge University Press, 1990.

M. Richter, *The Politics of Conscience: T.H. Green and His Age*, London, Weidenfeld and Nicolson, 1964.

A. Vincent and R. Plant, *Philosophy, Politics and Citizenship: the Life and Thought of the British Idealists*, Oxford, Blackwell, 1984.

Marx

Texts

K. Marx, *Selected Writings in Sociology and Social Philosophy*, (ed. T. Bottomore and M. Rubel), Harmondsworth, Penguin, 1956.

K. Marx, *Selected Writings* (ed. D. McLellan), 2nd edn, Oxford, Oxford University Press, 2000.

Commentaries/full-length studies

General and introductory

S. Avineri, *The Social and Political Thought of Karl Marx*, Cambridge, Cambridge University Press, 1968.

I. Berlin, *Karl Marx: His Life and Environment*, 4th edn, Oxford, Oxford University Press, 1978.

T. Carver, *Marx's Social Theory*, Oxford, Oxford University Press, 1982.

T. Carver (ed.), *The Cambridge Companion to Marx*, Cambridge, Cambridge University Press, 1991.

J. Elster, *An Introduction to Karl Marx*, Cambridge, Cambridge University Press, 1986.

M. Evans, *Karl Marx*, London, Allen and Unwin, 1975.

L. Kolakowski, *Main Currents of Marxism*, Vol. 1, Oxford, Oxford University Press, 1978.

D. McLellan, *The Young Hegelians and Karl Marx*, London, Macmillan, 1969.

D. McLellan, *Marx Before Marxism*, London, Macmillan, 1970.

D. McLellan, *The Thought of Karl Marx*, London, Macmillan, 1971.

D. McLellan, *Karl Marx: His Life and Thought*, London, Macmillan, 1973.

D. McLellan, *Marx*, London, Fontana, 1975.

R. Miliband, *Marxism and Politics*, Oxford, Oxford University Press, 1977.

B. Ollman, *Alienation: Marx's Critique of Man in a Capitalist Society*, Cambridge, Cambridge University Press, 1971.

J. Plamenatz, *Marx's Philosophy of Man*, Oxford, Clarendon Press, 1975.

K.R. Popper, *The Open Society and Its Enemies*, Vol. 2, London, Routledge and Kegan Paul, 1945.

*P. Singer, *Marx*, Oxford, Oxford University Press, 1980.

R. Tucker, *Philosophy and Myth in Karl Marx*, Cambridge, Cambridge University Press, 1961.

F. Wheen, *Karl Marx*, London, Fourth Estate, 1999.

On Marx's theory of historical materialism

H.B. Acton, *The Illusion of the Epoch*, London, Cohen and West, 1955.

G. Cohen, *Karl Marx's Theory of History: A Defence*, Oxford, Oxford University Press, 1978.

Z.A. Jordan, *The Evolution of Dialectical Materialism*, London, Macmillan, 1967.

G. Leff, *The Tyranny of Concepts*, 2nd edn, London, Merlin, 1969.

M. Rader, *Marx's Interpretation of History*, Oxford, Oxford University Press, 1979.

Index